Get the eBooks FREE!

(PDF, ePub, Kindle, and liveBook all included)

We believe that once you buy a book from us, you should be able to read it in any format we have available. To get electronic versions of this book at no additional cost to you, purchase and then register this book at the Manning website.

Go to https://www.manning.com/freebook and follow the instructions to complete your pBook registration.

That's it!
Thanks from Manning!

Learn System Center Configuration Manager
in a Month of Lunches

Learn System Center Configuration Manager in a Month of Lunches

COVERS SCCM 1511 AND WINDOWS 10

JAMES C. BANNAN

MANNING
SHELTER ISLAND

Manning Publications Co.	Development editor: Helen Stergius
20 Baldwin Road	Technical development editor: Deepak Vohra
PO Box 761	Copyeditor: Sharon Wilkey
Shelter Island, NY 11964	Proofreader: Katie Tennant
	Technical proofreader: Richard Siddaway
	Typesetter: Dottie Marsico
	Cover designer: Leslie Haimes

ISBN 9781617291685
Printed in the United States of America
5 6 7 8 9 10 – SP – 21 20 19

brief contents

contents

preface

When I was approached to write this book, I wanted to create a resource that Config-Mgr administrators could use to quickly get up to speed with what is, under the hood, a complicated product. This was driven by many years' experience in consulting, where I saw frustrated ConfigMgr admins struggling with the product due to a simple lack of knowledge about how the product hangs together and where to go to extract critical information about what's happening and what might be going wrong.

In essence, I wanted to write the sort of book on ConfigMgr that I would have liked to have on hand when I installed the product for the first time, with my manager and colleagues looking on saying, "Well? Does it work yet? When can we deploy Windows?"

The book doesn't focus on the underlying architecture of ConfigMgr—at least, no more than is strictly necessary. While it's important for any ConfigMgr administrator to understand what's happening behind the scenes, installing new distribution points or deploying new primary site servers aren't exactly everyday occurrences, whereas patching, software distribution, and reporting definitely are. So this book provides a detailed look at a core set of fundamental tasks that every ConfigMgr administrator will tackle on a regular basis, broken into easily consumed chunks so you can boost your productivity quickly and effectively.

If you're new to ConfigMgr (or relatively inexperienced), this is absolutely the book to get you started. If you already have some ConfigMgr experience, then this book will give you practical examples and in-depth analyses of tasks that you probably already undertake, and will serve to consolidate and strengthen what you already know, while providing some additional knowledge, tips, and tricks to make your everyday job even easier.

Enjoy the book, and happy deploying.

acknowledgments

Writing a book is a massive undertaking, which simply wouldn't be possible without support. My biggest thanks go to my wife Alice for all her love and assistance throughout the writing process, always ensuring that I had space and time to work and encouraging me when a finished product seemed a very long way off. I would also like to thank Richard Siddaway for his excellent technical critique of the content, and the editors and proofreaders at Manning and everyone else who worked behind the scenes—they were unfailingly helpful and encouraging to me as a first-time author.

In addition, I'd like to thank the many reviewers who read drafts of this book in the months leading up to publication, including Terry Rickman, Nasir Naeem, Dave Corun, Jan Vinterberg, Joseph Moody, David Moravec, Nicholas Selpa, Chad McAuley, Alain Couniot, Diana Scheffler, Francis Setash, Mike Taylor, Douglas Duncan, and Allan Miller. Their contributions were invaluable.

about this book

Chapter 1 covers most of what you'll need to know about this book, but there are a few extra points worth covering ahead of time.

While there are a couple of chapters that are theoretical in nature, the majority of content in the book is designed to be hands-on. To this end, chapter 2 covers setting up a fully functional, self-contained lab environment. I strongly recommend that you take the time to get your lab up and running, as the content makes much more sense if you're implementing it in a live environment. If you don't have a system with enough resources to run the lab environment, ask your boss nicely!

The content is designed to be consumed in order, as the labs in each chapter are built on those in the previous chapters. You might be really interested in application deployment, but resist the temptation to jump straight to that chapter (or any other chapter), as the labs are likely not to work if you haven't completed the foundation tasks.

The content has been written for the latest version of Configuration Manager (Build 1511 at the time of writing) and for Windows 10 as the managed client (also Build 1511), but the information and labs will work on previous versions of Configuration Manager 2012, as well as on Windows 7, 8, and 8.1, with little or no modification.

Many of the resources referenced throughout the book, such as the MDT-based lab environment, as well as PowerShell scripts, are available for download on GitHub at https://github.com/jamesbannan/configmgr-month-of-lunches. You can select to download the entire repository as a ZIP file, or clone the repository. (I use Atlassian SourceTree, which is a free utility for Windows and Mac.) All the code has been tested and retested, but if you find something that doesn't work (or something you think could be done better), then please make any changes you see fit and submit a pull request, or let me know via my blog at http://www.jamesbannanit.com.

Author Online

The purchase of *Learn System Center Configuration Manager in a Month of Lunches* includes access to a private forum run by Manning Publications where you can make comments about the book, ask technical questions, and receive help from the author and other users. To access and subscribe to the forum, point your browser to www.manning.com/books/learn-system-center-configuration-manager-in-a-month-of-lunches and click the Author Online link. This page provides information on how to get on the forum once you're registered, what kind of help is available, and the rules of conduct in the forum.

Manning's commitment to our readers is to provide a venue where a meaningful dialogue between individual readers and between readers and the author can take place. It's not a commitment to any specific amount of participation on the part of the author, whose contribution to the book's forum remains voluntary (and unpaid). We suggest you try asking him some challenging questions, lest his interest stray!

The Author Online forum and the archives of previous discussions will be accessible from the publisher's website as long as the book is in print.

about the author

JAMES BANNAN is a multiple-year recipient of Microsoft's Most Valuable Professional (MVP) award in a variety of categories including System Center Configuration Manager and Cloud and Datacenter Management. He has worked in large corporate environments and K–12 education, and now consults across a range of industry spaces, including state and federal governments. He is a regular presenter at Microsoft TechEd/Ignite and lives in Melbourne, Australia.

Before you begin

I still remember vividly my first foray into Microsoft System Center Configuration Manager. I was working as a network and systems administrator, and the IT team that I was a part of had just made an unfortunate discovery. Our fleet of desktops and laptops had increased fourfold in a short space of time, and the deployment techniques we were using, which were just about satisfactory for a small environment, couldn't possibly scale and were now shown to be completely impractical. Even worse, we were facing a hardware refresh of nearly a third of the fleet, with no streamlined way to achieve it.

I jumped online and researched options, and Configuration Manager (ConfigMgr) came up time and time again as the best-of-breed solution for Windows deployment. The next day I spun up a server and spent the next two weeks trawling through TechNet articles and blog posts about how to set it up, configure it, and get Windows deployed.

When I look back at how I set up that first ConfigMgr environment, I'm amazed that it ever worked at all. I didn't know any of the best practices or finer nuances of the product and made some stunning, cringe-worthy errors in the bargain. Despite all of that, ConfigMgr got me and the business where we needed to be, and the whole experience ignited something of a personal zeal to learn as much as I could about the product, and to help educate other administrators who are in the same position as I was.

This book is the result of my experiences with ConfigMgr, the designs, implementations, troubleshooting, and yes, all the mistakes as well. It's the sort of book I wish I had access to when I was first learning to use ConfigMgr to deploy and manage Windows on an enterprise scale. This chapter covers what ConfigMgr is and why you should use it, what you should know before getting started, and how to set up your lab environment.

One word of warning before you get started: setting up ConfigMgr is a lengthy process, and you won't get it all done in an hour. In all probability, if you've never done this before, it'll take about a day's worth of effort. But don't be disheartened; ConfigMgr is a complex product, so it makes perfect sense that the procedure to get it up and running is also complex. It's also absolutely critical that you have an environment of your own to work with, and in the process of setting up the lab, you'll learn a *lot* about how ConfigMgr works, all of which will be incredibly useful as you progress through the book.

1.1   *Why Configuration Manager?*

I'll go out on a limb and state up front that Microsoft System Center Configuration Manager is objectively the best product on the market for deploying and administering Windows in the enterprise. It's designed to deploy and manage desktops, laptops, and servers from the moment they arrive in your environment to the moment they leave, handling operating systems, applications, patching, compliance, antivirus, and reporting, just for starters.

> **There's even more under the hood**
> Configuration Manager has a rich and varied functionality set covering many aspects of system deployment, management, and reporting.
>
> Take a few minutes to read the official list of capabilities online: www.microsoft.com /en-us/server-cloud/system-center/configuration-manager-2012-capabilities.aspx.

ConfigMgr is a mature technology, tracing its roots back to Systems Management Server 1.0, which was released in 1994, as you can see in table 1.1. Given such a history, Microsoft has had a significant amount of time to develop and improve the technology to reflect customer needs based on ever-shifting industry trends: physical to virtual servers, tablets, slates, mobile devices, application management, patching, inventory, and now user-centric computing. It's the product that Microsoft uses to deploy and manage its own global fleet of servers, workstations, and applications, and it has a widespread and dedicated community of administrators and specialists.

Table 1.1   A timeline of Microsoft Systems Management

Year released	Product
1994	Systems Management Server (SMS) 1.0
1995	Systems Management Server (SMS) 1.1
1996	Systems Management Server (SMS) 1.2

Table 1.1   A timeline of Microsoft Systems Management *(continued)*

Year released	Product
1999	Systems Management Server (SMS) 2.0
2003	Systems Management Server (SMS) 2003
2006	Systems Management Server (SMS) 2003 R2
2007	System Center Configuration Manager 2007
2008	System Center Configuration Manager 2007 SP1
2009	System Center Configuration Manager 2007 SP2
2011	System Center 2012 Configuration Manager
2012	System Center 2012 Configuration Manager SP1
2013	System Center 2012 Configuration Manager R2
2015	System Center 2012 Configuration Manager R2 SP1
2015	System Center Configuration Manager (Build 1511)

As good as it is, ConfigMgr also has a dark side. Although it provides a deep and powerful framework, it's also open-ended, providing many ways of arriving at your end goal. Even harder is that one method isn't necessarily superior to another. "It depends" is a phrase you get used to when dealing with ConfigMgr.

This book will give you processes that work, while endeavoring to inform you about the most common administration scenarios that you're likely to encounter. ConfigMgr is a big beast, but tackle it head-on, and the rewards will be substantial.

1.2   Is this book for you?

If you're a systems administrator or a desktop administrator, responsible for deploying and managing Windows in a business environment, then this book is for you. If you're familiar with application deployment or patch management but are tired of doing things manually, this book is for you. If you're looking for a way to gain full, proactive visibility over your entire managed Windows environment, this book is for you.

ConfigMgr is an enterprise-grade infrastructure solution, so getting to grips with it requires a reasonable level of preexisting knowledge. You'll need to know how to set up and configure virtual machines, as well as have a decent working knowledge of both Windows Server and Windows clients. A grasp of networking concepts is essential, especially Internet Protocol version 4 (IPv4) addressing, as well as being comfortable enough with Active Directory (AD) to create and modify users and groups.

If you're unsure whether you meet some of the prerequisites, don't be discouraged—you almost certainly know more than you think you do! My advice is to just get stuck in.

1.3   *How to use this book*

Turn the pages, read the words, marvel at the diagrams, become enlightened.

Hmm, perhaps that's not quite enough detail! The Month of Lunches series is designed so that you can consume one chapter a day while you're consuming lunch. Parallel consumption, if you like. Each chapter should take only about 40 minutes to read, giving you an extra 20 minutes to finish your sandwich or practice what we've covered.

1.3.1   *The main chapters*

Each of the main chapters in this book covers a major section concerning the administration of ConfigMgr. Each chapter is constructed so that by the time you reach the end, you'll be empowered to work with or implement whatever topic was covered.

By the end of the month, you'll have gained a thorough understanding of ConfigMgr, and in the last couple of lunches you'll look at how it can be used in future, advanced scenarios. For example, not many companies are using ConfigMgr for management of Mac OS X or Linux platforms at the moment, whereas others aren't making use of Microsoft Azure or Microsoft Intune. Avoid any temptation to skip these chapters, because centralized cross-platform management and cloud integration are strong industry trends—the way of the future, in fact. These chapters will bring you up to speed on the latest and greatest, so even if you're not using them right now, chances are that you will!

1.3.2   *Try It Now sections*

Throughout each chapter, you'll find Try It Now sections: simple exercises that are included so you can get some practical experience with the technology as you work through each chapter. I've always found that I do my best learning when I get something to work in my own environment, rather than just reading about it, and the Try It Now sections are designed to reinforce what you've just learned.

1.3.3   *Above & Beyond sidebars*

Sidebars are scattered throughout the book, offering nuggets of interesting information about the topic at hand. The material in these sidebars is important, but not necessarily for immediate consumption.

This book isn't written for ConfigMgr architects or solution providers, so there's a deep technical layer that isn't featured here. But I know that you as a systems administrator will still want to know some of that information, so when you encounter an Above & Beyond sidebar in any of the chapters, take a couple of minutes to quickly read it.

1.3.4   *Working with PowerShell*

You can perform many ConfigMgr administrative tasks via either the ConfigMgr console or PowerShell. This book covers both methods, wherever possible. Some PowerShell scripts involve multiple steps and won't be convenient one-liners. Rather than bulk out the book with these scripts, I make them available on a dedicated Git repository (https://github.com/jamesbannan/configmgr-month-of-lunches) and provide the relevant links within the chapters as we go.

1.3.5 Labs

At the end of each chapter, a hands-on lab will get you working with the technology in a more formal, test-based manner. The labs are designed to work within your own testing environment. In chapter 2, you'll set up a fully functional, self-contained ConfigMgr environment to configure and tinker with.

1.3.6 Further exploration

Some of the chapters in this book, such as those on operating system deployment, contain functional tasks that take much longer than a lunchtime to complete.

The content in these chapters is designed to provide as much practical information as possible about the challenging concepts contained within, but implementing outcomes such as creating a master Windows image or deploying a managed system will almost certainly have to be worked through when you have a decent chunk of time available. Having said that, I strongly encourage you to find that time, because conquering difficult concepts within ConfigMgr is the best way to deepen your theoretical and practical knowledge of the product.

1.3.7 Which Log? sections

Log files are absolutely paramount for not only troubleshooting ConfigMgr, but also offering insight into what's happening under the hood. Often the administrative console shields you from what's going on, making the product something of a black box. The real action can be found in the log files.

As you read through each chapter, keep an eye out for the Which Log? sections, which will direct you to the right log file so that you can see exactly what ConfigMgr is up to.

1.4 Setting up your lab environment

You're going to be doing a lot of practicing in ConfigMgr throughout this book, and you'll want to have a lab environment to work in; please don't practice in your company's production environment.

Chapter 2 covers all the details of getting ConfigMgr installed and running for your lab. This chapter will give you a chance to explore some of the key functions at the same time you're having your first run at using ConfigMgr.

1.5 Using online resources

Apart from the MoreLunches.com website, I strongly encourage you to trawl through the ConfigMgr online documentation at Microsoft TechNet. Finding what you're looking for can sometimes be difficult (although I'll give you some tips for searching), but Microsoft has done and continues to do an outstanding job documenting and explaining what is a broad and complex product.

Additionally, you can head over to my blog at www.jamesbannanit.com, where I document features and issues relating to ConfigMgr and operating system and application deployment as I come across them. You can get in touch with me directly via the blog, or through Twitter, where my handle is @jamesbannan.

1.6   *Being immediately effective with ConfigMgr*

Everything you read in this book is designed to get you, as a current or future Config-Mgr administrator, effective straightaway in your production environment. This sometimes means that I don't go into the level of technical depth that sits simmering under the surface of some topics because, frankly, you don't necessarily need to know all the theory right away in order to be effective. Sometimes it's far better to learn enough to be productive, and then come back to the topic later in further depth so that you have context as well as a solid, practical foundation upon which to build a greater understanding.

So with that, let's get stuck into ConfigMgr.

Setting up your
lab environment

Configuration Manager is a hands-on product, so it's important to have a good lab environment for all of your testing and learning. Setting up ConfigMgr from scratch can be daunting; it sits on top of several prerequisite applications, all of which have to be installed and configured correctly before you can install Config-Mgr, such as the following:

- Microsoft Windows Server
- Microsoft Internet Information Services (IIS)
- Microsoft SQL Server
- Windows Assessment and Deployment Kit (ADK)

The versions of each prerequisite application vary from environment to environment.

Figure 2.1 shows how the lab environment hangs together, how and where all of the prerequisite applications are installed, and which version you'll use.

This environment is a bit complicated, but this is the absolute minimum amount of setup required to create your own ConfigMgr lab environment. And you do need a safe, self-contained lab environment, even if you have access to Config-Mgr in your current environment. Getting things wrong in ConfigMgr can lead to some particularly undesirable outcomes (such as wiping production servers), so you definitely want to run your labs isolated away from the wider network.

The good news is that I have some neat tricks on hand to streamline the whole process of building the lab environment. You'll create it using virtual machines and then build them using a *hydration script*: an automated build process developed by

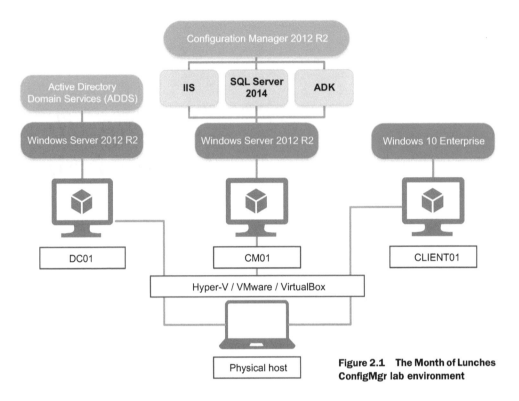

Figure 2.1   The Month of Lunches ConfigMgr lab environment

Johan Arwidmark, a fellow MVP who's based in Sweden. I've taken Johan's process and made some changes that customize the environment with settings more appropriate for this lab. Here's a high-level overview of how the process works:

1 Create the virtual environment.
2 Download the prerequisite software.
3 Install and configure Microsoft Deployment Toolkit (MDT) 2013 Update 2.
4 Populate MDT with all the prerequisite software.
5 Use MDT to generate an automated build DVD (an ISO file).
6 Build the virtual machines with the ISO file.
7 Your lab is created and ready for use.

2.1   Create the virtual environment

The lab consists of two servers—an Active Directory domain controller and the ConfigMgr server, and one workstation. For ease of setup and repeatability, these systems should all be virtual machines.

If you already have a physical machine that hosts virtual machines, that's perfect. You should be able to use that same environment. If you don't run a virtual environment, you'll need to set one up. Here's a list of what you'll need:

- A physical machine with a 64-bit processor that supports Intel or AMD hardware-level virtualization, has at least 10 GB RAM (preferably more), and has enough free hard drive space (approximately 300 GB). The machine should preferably be running a 64-bit operating system.
- A virtualization product to host the virtual machines. This could be any of the following:
  - Microsoft Hyper-V
  - VMware Workstation
  - VirtualBox
  - Parallels

I won't go into the pros and cons of each solution. Suffice it to say that my environment is running Windows 10 x64 Enterprise with Hyper-V enabled, and all my lab systems are Hyper-V virtual machines.

> ### Attention Linux and Mac users
>
> You can set up this environment on a machine running Linux or Mac OS X; it doesn't have to be Windows, because virtualization products are available that run fine on non-Windows platforms.
>
> But you'll need at least one machine running Windows in order to install and configure the Microsoft Deployment Toolkit so that you can create the media that will build and configure the lab environment.
>
> This extra Windows machine could be a different physical system, or even a third virtual machine, but you'll have to build it manually.

If you're fortunate enough to have access to a spare server, that's even better! You can set up the whole environment on Windows Server Hyper-V or VMware ESXi. But unless the host operating system is running a full version of Windows, you'll still need an extra Windows system on which to install and configure MDT, because it can be installed only on Windows.

I won't go into the setup and configuration of each product (that would be a book of its own!), but whichever solution you choose to go with, all have good online documentation to assist you. They're all also straightforward to install.

So after you have a host ready to host virtual machines, you'll need to create three VMs (on Hyper-V, they can be either Generation 1 or Generation 2). Tables 2.1, 2.2, and 2.3 detail how they should be configured, and how the hydration process will configure the networking. Unless you have a lot of hard drive space free on the host, configure the hard drives assigned to each virtual machine as dynamically expanding/thin-provisioned disks. The performance is reduced, but in your lab environment (which is more than likely going to be running on a single physical disk) that's not much of a concern. Better to maximize the hard drive space.

TIP In this lab environment, you'll get the best performance by using fast disks—building systems and running ConfigMgr are disk-intensive processes. If you have access to a solid-state drive (SSD), place the VMs on this disk.

Table 2.1 Lab virtual machine—domain controller

VM setting	Setting value
VM name	DC01
vCPU	1 × CPU
RAM	1 GB (can be dynamic memory on Hyper-V)
Hard disk	1 × 40 GB
Network	1 × NIC
Windows hostname	DC01
IP address	192.168.1.200
Subnet mask	255.255.255.0
Default gateway	192.168.1.1
DNS server	127.0.0.1

Table 2.2 Lab virtual machine—ConfigMgr Server

VM name	CM01
vCPU	2 × CPU
RAM	6 GB (can be dynamic memory on Hyper-V)
Hard disk	1 × 300 GB
Network	1 × NIC
Windows hostname	CM01
IP address	192.168.1.210
Subnet mask	255.255.255.0
Default gateway	192.168.1.1
DNS server	192.168.1.200

WARNING The virtual machines need to be able to talk to the internet as well as to each other. Make sure you configure the virtual networks accordingly; the hydration script will configure the IP information but won't handle physical connectivity.

Table 2.3 Lab virtual machine—Windows client

VM setting	Setting value
VM name	CLIENT01
vCPU	1 × CPU
RAM	2 GB (can be dynamic memory on Hyper-V)
Hard disk	1 × 80 GB
Network	1 × NIC
Windows hostname	CLIENT01
IP address	192.168.1.220
Subnet mask	255.255.255.0
Default gateway	192.168.1.1
DNS server	192.168.1.200

NOTE The IP address settings and/or the hostname may not be appropriate for your lab environment if you have preexisting virtual machines or networks. For example, in my environment, I use different IP addressing, so using addresses on the 192.168.1.*x* range isn't suitable for me. These values can be changed without impacting the build process, and we'll go through that further along in the chapter.

Now that the virtual machines are ready to go, it's time to prepare all the software that will be used to build the lab.

2.2 Download the prerequisite software

The hydration script that you'll use to build the lab uses MDT, the Microsoft Deployment Toolkit, which in turn relies on the availability of prerequisite software. On the Windows system on which MDT will be installed, create a folder called C:\Downloads and download the following software packages to this location.

NOTE For applications such as Windows Server 2012 R2, Windows 10, or SQL Server 2014, I've provided links to download the trial (time-limited) media. If you have access to Volume License or Microsoft Developer Network (MSDN) media, use those instead.

2.2.1 Sysinternals BgInfo

BgInfo is a tool within the Sysinternals suite that gathers information about the local system such as hostname, IP address, and memory, and writes all that information to a bitmap that sits on the desktop. It's incredibly useful for providing visual cues as to which machine you're currently logged on to.

Download location:

http://technet.microsoft.com/en-us/sysinternals/bb897557 .aspx

2.2.2 *Microsoft Deployment Toolkit 2013 Update 2*

MDT 2013 is a deployment solution from Microsoft, enabling you to build automated builds of Windows. MDT will be used to generate the automated image from which the VMs will be built.

Download location: www.microsoft.com/en-us/download/details.aspx?id=50407

2.2.3 *Microsoft Assessment and Deployment Kit for Windows 10 (Version 1511)*

The ADK contains a suite of tools used for system and application compatibility testing as well as enterprise deployment. The latest version of the ADK is required to fully support MDT 2013 Update 2, ConfigMgr, and Windows 10 deployment.

Download location: http://go.microsoft.com/fwlink/p/?LinkId=526740
The ADK file you download is a web installer. It's designed to download and install only the components you need. Another installation option enables you to download the entire ADK for offline installs—choose this option.

> **IMPORTANT**   At the time of writing, the latest build of the ADK (Build 1511) is not recommended as a prerequisite for ConfigMgr; however, this build is needed for the MDT lab, so you'll need to download both the original (RTM) and the latest (1511) builds of the ADK. You can download the RTM build directly from Microsoft via http://download.microsoft.com/download /8/1/9/8197FEB9-FABE-48FD-A537-7D8709586715/adk/adksetup.exe.

2.2.4 *Microsoft SQL Server 2014 SP1*

All the data stored within ConfigMgr resides in a SQL database, and ConfigMgr reporting uses SQL Server Reporting Services (SSRS) to do its job. ConfigMgr requires either the Standard or Datacenter edition of SQL Server, but for the purposes of the lab Standard is fine. SQL Server Express is not supported for a primary site server.

Download location:
http://technet.microsoft.com/en-us/evalcenter/hh225126.aspx

2.2.5 *Windows Server 2012 R2*

Windows Server 2012 R2 is the underlying operating system that supports ConfigMgr. Several server roles and features, such as IIS, must be enabled for ConfigMgr to work properly.

Download location:
www.microsoft.com/en-us/evalcenter/evaluate-windows-server-2012-r2

2.2.6 *Windows 10 Enterprise x64 (Build 1511)*

The first client machine in your lab environment will run the 64-bit version of Windows 10 Enterprise.

Download location:
www.microsoft.com/en-us/evalcenter/evaluate-windows-10-enterprise

2.2.7 *System Center Configuration Manager and Endpoint Protection*

It's going to be a difficult lab to work with without this!
Download location:
http://technet.microsoft.com/en-us/evalcenter/dn205297.aspx

2.2.8 *System Center Configuration Manager Prerequisites*

ConfigMgr checks for prerequisite packages such as .NET Framework 4.0 and Silverlight. These are not necessarily used during the ConfigMgr installation, but are required for future functionality.

To download the prerequisites, you'll need to have downloaded the ConfigMgr installer first. Use a tool such as 7-Zip and run the Setupdl.exe program located in the SMSSETUP\BIN\X64 folder. The application will prompt you for a save location; nominate a temporary folder as in figure 2.2, and the application will download all of the necessary prerequisite packages.

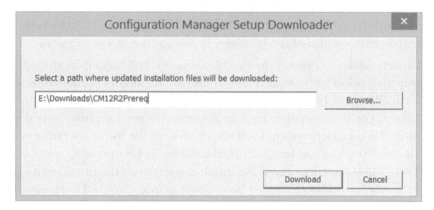

Figure 2.2   Specify a download location for the ConfigMgr prerequisite packages.

TIP   If your operating system can natively mount ISO files (such as Windows 10), this is the easiest way to extract files from within an ISO. Otherwise, a free utility such as 7-Zip will do the job nicely.

2.2.9 *Git repository*

The MDT hydration package, along with all of the PowerShell code used throughout the book (and with a few miscellaneous samples), are all contained in a Git repository that you'll need to download.

Access the repository at https://github.com/jamesbannan/configmgr-month-of-lunches. You can either clone it in your favorite Git client (I use both GitHub for Windows and Atlassian SourceTree) or download the whole thing as a zip file.

After everything has been downloaded, your C:\Downloads folder should look something like figure 2.3. Don't worry if some of the names for Windows, SQL, or ConfigMgr source files are slightly different; they can come from different sources (for example, Volume Licensing, MSDN), and all you're interested in is the content of the images.

Figure 2.3　All of the source content downloaded and ready for use

Now that the content is ready, you can proceed with creating the hydration environment.

2.3　*Install and configure MDT 2013 Update 2*

On the Windows machine that will be used for MDT 2013 Update 2, the first step is to install certain components of the Windows 10 ADK, as this is a prerequisite:

1　Launch adksetup.exe within the Windows 10 ADK folder. In the application launcher, select only Deployment Tools and Windows Preinstallation Environment (Windows PE), and install to the default location.

2　Launch the MDT installer that's appropriate for the operating system architecture: MicrosoftDeploymentToolkit2013_x64.msi for 64-bit operating systems or MicrosoftDeploymentToolkit2013_x32.msi for 32-bit operating systems.

3　There's nothing tricky about the installer—accept all the installation defaults.

4　To be able to run the included PowerShell scripts, you need to change the PowerShell execution policy accordingly, as the scripts are unsigned. Launch an elevated PowerShell window and type `Set-ExecutionPolicy RemoteSigned -Force`.

> **TIP**　The default execution policy for PowerShell is "Restricted": configuration files won't be loaded and scripts won't be run. For more information, refer to this article on TechNet: http://technet.microsoft.com /en-us/library/hh849812.aspx.

5　The next step is to create an MDT deployment share—a local folder that has been shared—and then populated with MDT tools and scripts and referenced via MDT so that the administrator can manipulate the contents. Clients can then connect back to the share to run MDT task sequences and access content, or a deployment share can be used to generate standalone build images in ISO format (like a DVD).

　To create the hydration deployment share, run the following script within the Git repository from an elevated PowerShell session: `.\ HydrationConfigMgr \Source\Create-HydrationDeploymentShare.ps1`. The script is verbose, so

Figure 2.4   The hydration scripts in action, building a deployment share in MDT

you should see output like that in figure 2.4, showing you what's happening behind the scenes.

IMPORTANT   You should change the working folder to .\HydrationConfigMgr \Source in order to run the script.

2.3.1   Populate MDT with required software

Now that the deployment share has been created, it's time to populate it with the content that you previously downloaded. The MDT task sequence will reference this content and incorporate it into the build media.

Table 2.4 shows you where each package needs to be downloaded within the C:\HydrationConfigMgr folder. When referring to packages that come in an ISO format such as Windows Server, you need to extract the contents of the ISO and copy those across, not the ISO itself.

NOTE   The item "ConfigMgr EXTADSCH.EXE" is an application that extends the Active Directory (AD) schema in order to support ConfigMgr in an AD environment. This file is located in the ConfigMgr installation media in the SMSSETUP\BIN\X64 folder.

Table 2.4   Deployment share content locations

Package	Deployment share target (automatically created)
BgInfo	.\DS\Applications\Install - BgInfo\Source
ADK for Windows 10	.\DS\Applications\Install – Windows 10 ADK\Source
SQL Server 2014 SP1	.\DS\Applications\Install - SQL Server 2014\Source
ConfigMgr	.\DS\Applications\Install - ConfigMgr\Source
ConfigMgr Prereqs	.\DS\Applications\Install - ConfigMgr\PreReqs
ConfigMgr EXTADSCH.EXE	.\DS\Applications\Configure - Extend AD for ConfigMgr\Source
Windows 10	.\DS\Operating Systems\W10ENTx64
Windows Server 2012 R2	.\DS\Operating Systems\WS2012R2

Now that the Share is populated, you can create the build image.

2.3.2   *Use MDT to generate an automated build image (ISO)*

You need to trigger the creation of the image within the MDT Deployment Workbench, which is accessible via the Start menu:

1   Open the Workbench and expand the hydration deployment share. Make sure
    that the Applications, Operating Systems, and Task Sequences folders are popu-
    lated with content, as in figure 2.5.

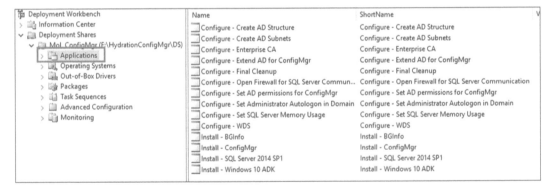

Figure 2.5   **The hydration script has populated the MDT deployment share.**

> **TIP**   Take a look at each task sequence by going into Properties > Task
> Sequence. They use similar logic that you'll use later in the book to deploy
> Windows 10.

2   Expand the Advanced Configuration folder and select "Media."

3 In the main window, right-click the MEDIA001 item, select "Properties," and select the Rules tab. You need to change the TimeZoneName property to whichever is the appropriate time zone for you. The default is "Pacific Standard Time," but, for example, in my case it needs to be "AUS Eastern Standard Time."

4 After you've modified the TimeZoneName property as in figure 2.6, click "OK" to save and close.

TIP To find out which is the correct time zone name for your environment, from a machine running Windows 7/Server 2008 R2 or higher, open a command window, and type `tzutil /l`. This brings up a list of all the available time zones and their correct names (use `tzutil /g` to get the time zone that you're currently in).

Figure 2.6 Set the TimeZoneName property to the right one for your environment.

Customizing server properties

As I mentioned earlier, you might have to change some of the server properties, such as the hostname or IP address, if these would cause problems on your network or with preexisting lab machines.

To change the IP address information for each virtual machine, navigate to C:\HydrationConfigMgr\ISO\Content\Deploy\Control and edit the files called CustomSettings _DC01.ini, CustomSettings_CM01.ini, and CustomSettings_CLIENT01.ini. Change the settings that start with "OSDAdapter0..." to values appropriate to your environment. If you change the OSDAdapter0IPAddressList value for DC01, ensure that this change is reflected in the OSDAdapter0DNSServerList for CM01 and CLIENT01, so that the ConfigMgr server and workstation can join the AD domain hosted on DC01.

To change the hostname for any of the systems, edit the value for HydrationOSDComputerName to whatever is appropriate. If you change the hostname for CM01, you'll also need to reflect this change in the ConfigMgrUnattend.ini file, which is located in C:\HydrationConfigMgr\ISO\Content\Deploy\Applications\Install - ConfigMgr. You need to change the following entries to the new hostname: SDKServer, ManagementPoint, DistributionPoint, and SQLServerName.

(continued)
You also can change the domain that's installed and configured on DC01, but this involves a significant amount of editing, and I suggest that unless this is necessary, you use the default AD configuration.

5 Finally, right-click MEDIA001 again and select "Update Media Content." This triggers a process that will go through all of the source folders that you populated earlier, as shown in figure 2.7, and will create an ISO image containing all of the content as well as a Windows PE boot image and a portable MDT deployment share. The ISO is completely self-contained and doesn't need to download any content from the hydration deployment share.

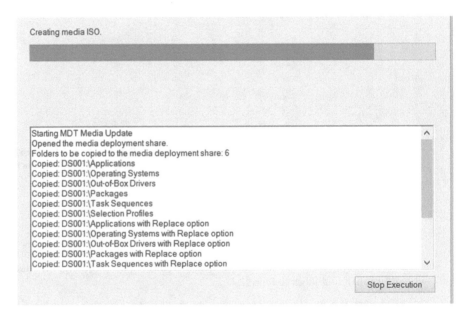

Figure 2.7   Creating the MDT media build that will be used to build the lab environment

The ISO creation process can take a while, depending on the speed of the local hard drive, so this is a good opportunity for a tea break. After it's complete, you'll find the newly created image in C:\ HydrationConfigMgr \ISO\ MoLConfigMgr.iso.

It's worth noting that although this whole process may seem rather time-consuming and convoluted, what you've done is to invest in a process that's automated and therefore repeatable. Chances are that over the course of your experimentation with ConfigMgr, you'll want to rebuild the lab environment a few times over. With the hydration process, you can easily rebuild the entire environment with confidence, and you need to do the preparation work only once.

2.4 Build the virtual machines

Everything is now ready to go, so you can start to build the lab systems.

2.4.1 DC01

The first machine you need to build is the domain controller, which, as you can see in figure 2.8, is responsible for providing AD services to the lab environment.

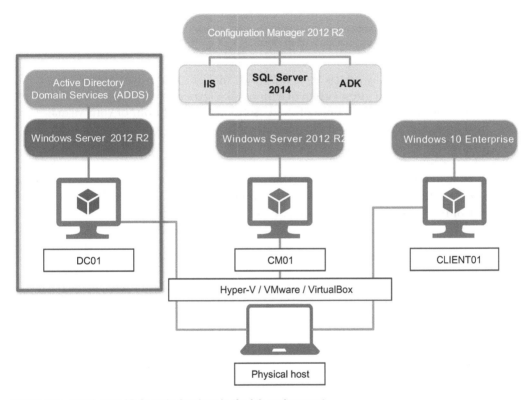

Figure 2.8 DC01 runs AD Domain Services in the lab environment.

1 Attach the hydration ISO to the DC01 virtual machine as a CD/DVD and boot. The machine will boot straight into Windows PE and will load the MDT task sequences.

2 Choose the DC01 task sequence, as shown in figure 2.9, and allow it run all the way through until you see the "Hydration Complete" message. Leave the virtual machine running.

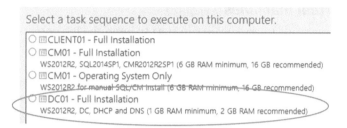

Figure 2.9   **The hydration kit comes with predefined task sequences to build and configure each server.**

TIP   Virtualization products have their own toolset to improve performance and functionality in guest virtual machines, like Hyper-V Integration Services. The build process doesn't install these, so to get the most out of your virtual machines, you should install the relevant tools for your virtualization platform.

2.4.2   CM01

The next step is to build the ConfigMgr primary site server, CM01. As you can see in figure 2.10, CM01 requires building blocks on top of Windows Server in order to support ConfigMgr, so the build process will take longer than DC01.

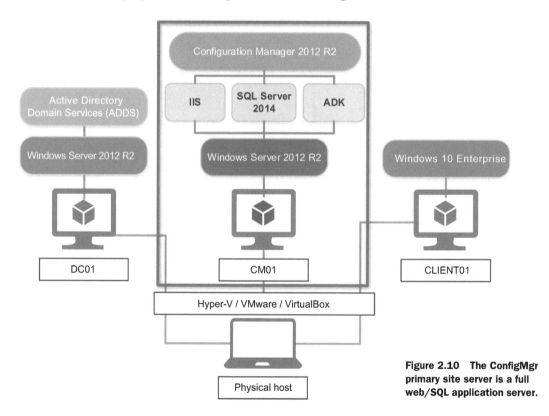

Figure 2.10   **The ConfigMgr primary site server is a full web/SQL application server.**

> **WARNING** ConfigMgr is completely dependent on Active Directory, so the domain controller must be up and running before the ConfigMgr server is powered on, and must remain running the entire time.

1 Attach the hydration ISO to the CM01 virtual machine and boot.
2 This time, choose the CM01 Full Installation task sequence and let it run all the way through to the "Hydration Complete" message.

After CM01 has been built, it's worth leaving it turned on, although it doesn't need to be powered on in order to complete the lab.

2.4.3 CLIENT01

Last but not least, it's time to build CLIENT01, which, as you can see in figure 2.11, is also joined to the lab domain and will communicate with both DC01 and CM01.

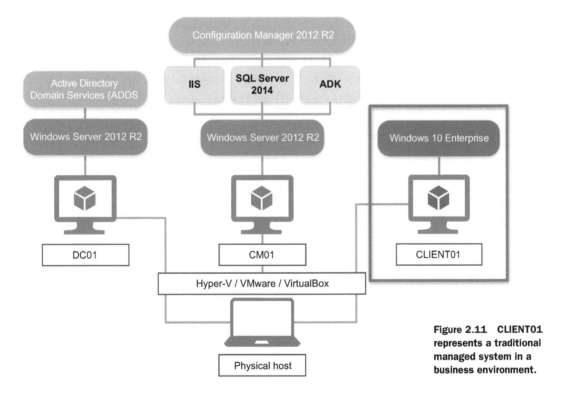

Figure 2.11 CLIENT01 represents a traditional managed system in a business environment.

1 Attach the hydration ISO to the CLIENT01 virtual machine and boot.
2 Choose the CLIENT01 task sequence and let it run all the way through to the end to create the Windows 10 system.

2.5   *Verify the ConfigMgr installation*

You need to verify that the ConfigMgr installation has completed successfully, and the easiest way to do that is to launch the ConfigMgr console. If that launches without error, the supporting server and application framework should all be good.

1 Log on to the CM01 virtual machine with the local administrator account, using the password P@ssw0rd.

> **NOTE** The password for all accounts in this lab environment is "P@ssw0rd." You can change this without impacting functionality; just make sure you make a note of any password changes.

2 Launch the ConfigMgr console from the server Start menu and verify that the console successfully connects to the ConfigMgr site on CM01.

3 Congratulations; your lab environment is up and running!

   The next step is to launch the ConfigMgr PowerShell console. This is an important step, since you'll need to come back to the console many times in order to perform ConfigMgr tasks using PowerShell.

4 In the top-left corner of the ConfigMgr console, select the blue drop-down arrow, and choose "Connect via Windows PowerShell," as shown in figure 2.12.

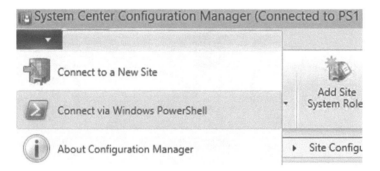

Figure 2.12   **You can launch a ConfigMgr PowerShell session from the console.**

5 A new PowerShell window launches, with the location automatically set to PS1, which is the locally installed ConfigMgr primary site. Type ls and you'll see that you're directly browsing the contents of the site, rather than a traditional Windows file location, as shown in figure 2.13.

   This is one way of interacting with ConfigMgr via PowerShell, but I recommend launching PowerShell Integrated Scripting Environment (ISE) instead; it's a richer PowerShell environment and much more helpful if you're learning the ins and outs of ConfigMgr and PowerShell. You will, however, have to manually import the ConfigMgr PowerShell module, because ISE doesn't automatically load it, unlike the session window that you launched from the ConfigMgr console, which does.

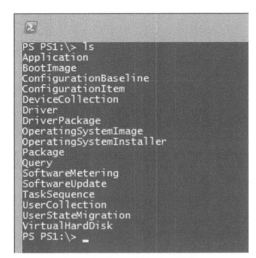

Figure 2.13 The ConfigMgr PowerShell session lets you work directly with the primary site.

6 From the Start menu on CM01, search for `ise,` and you should get two results for Windows PowerShell ISE. One of them is for 32-bit modules (x86), and the other is for 64-bit. The ConfigMgr PowerShell modules are 32-bit, so you want "Windows PowerShell ISE (x86)." Right-click and select "Run as administrator."

7 Accept the UAC prompt, and a new instance of ISE is launched.

8 Type in the following three lines of PowerShell:

```
cd 'D:\ConfigMgr\AdminConsole\bin'
Import-Module .\ConfigurationManager.psd1
Set-Location PS1:
```

Location of the ConfigMgr console

Imports the ConfigMgr PowerShell module

Connects to the ConfigMgr site

9 Type `ls` again and you'll see the same listing as earlier.

TIP Save those lines of PowerShell into ISE's script pane for easy future reference. If you don't see the script pane, go to View > Show Script Pane, or press Ctrl-R. I recommend making heavy use of the script pane, since it saves doing loads of typing and retyping. PowerShell is awesome, so make it as easy as possible!

Now that you have a working lab environment, it's time to get stuck into some ConfigMgr! And remember: now that you're in possession of an automated build process, you can re-create this environment easily using the media build anytime you need to.

Making ConfigMgr
aware of your environment

After it's been installed, the first ConfigMgr primary site server in your environment is a remarkably empty place. Only the most critical ConfigMgr server roles are installed and enabled, so the server is something of a blank slate, waiting for you to tell it what to do.

As you work through the book, you'll add more and more server roles to your ConfigMgr server, making it more flexible and capable, but the first thing to do is to make the server "aware" of the lab environment so that it can start interacting with it.

As shown in figure 3.1, by the end of this chapter you'll be able to configure ConfigMgr to discover machines, users, groups, sites, and subnets in your Active Directory (AD) environment, as well as create management boundaries and boundary groups that are ready to service your ConfigMgr clients. The steps you'll take in this chapter will form a solid foundation for the rest of the book.

You'll deal with Active Directory quite a bit in this chapter. If you're unsure about any of the AD concepts, or if you're comfortable with AD but want to gain even deeper insight, track down *Learn Active Directory in a Month of Lunches* by Richard Siddaway. Given that AD is such a core dependency of ConfigMgr, the more you know about it, the more empowered you'll be as a ConfigMgr administrator!

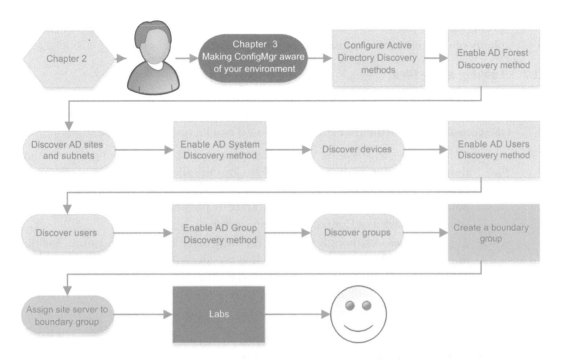

Figure 3.1 By the end of this chapter, you'll be an expert in ConfigMgr discovery methods, among other things!

3.1   *Discovery concepts*

ConfigMgr is an environment-aware and environment-dependent system. It hooks into many aspects of the datacenter, including the network and Active Directory. Picture a spider sitting in the middle of a massive web, where the strands represent all the facets of your datacenter. As shown in figure 3.2, ConfigMgr is that spider, taking in information from all areas, collating it, and allowing you to use that data to effectively manage your environment.

Figure 3.2   ConfigMgr hooks into your entire environment.

By default, however, Config-Mgr doesn't automatically start putting feelers out and trawling your environment for information. Not many customers would be happy with any enterprise server application that behaved like that, so

ConfigMgr will just sit back and wait for you to tell it what to do, which is why there's plenty of post-installation configuration needed. Let's get started.

3.1.1 Looking at log files

ConfigMgr has a *lot* of log files, and pretty much every action gets logged somewhere. This is incredibly useful, because it means that activities that might not be shown in the console are nevertheless exposed to you—if you know where to look.

- *CMTrace.exe*—This is a log viewer that you can find on the ConfigMgr installation media under .\SMSSETUP\TOOLS. Copy this file to somewhere easily accessible, such as the desktop, and launch it. It will ask whether you want it to be the default log viewer; choose "Yes." CMTrace is possibly the most valuable utility you'll ever have as a ConfigMgr administrator.
- *Log file location*—Although this isn't the only place log files are stored, for the moment you'll be looking at log files that are located in D:\ConfigMgr\Logs on CM01. From a remote system, you can access the same logs via \\CM01\SMS_P01 \Logs. If you do look at the log files from a remote computer, make sure you have access to CMTrace.

> **Try It Now—The best log file viewer ever**
> Take a minute to launch CMTrace.exe and open mpcontrol.log, which is located in the log files location described in the preceding paragraph. This particular log file monitors the availability of the Management Point, which is a critical role on the primary site server.
>
> You'll see that every line written to the log file is shown in real time, and that each log entry is timestamped. Using the Tools menu, you can highlight particular text strings within the log file, search for an entry, or filter the log. For example, you could apply a time filter so that only the most recent entries are shown; this is particularly useful for large log files, or for zeroing in on current events.

3.2 Discovery methods

To make ConfigMgr more aware of the environment within which it sits, you'll enable some discovery methods—automated tasks internal to ConfigMgr that allow it to "discover" information about the wider environment, such as details about computers, users, and security groups in AD. In this section, you'll enable and configure the discovery methods that are critical for accurate import of Active Directory–joined systems.

Log in to CM01 as MOL\Administrator and open the ConfigMgr console. If you can't see the console in the Start window (which is likely), start typing in ConfigMgr and the console will fill in the results. Click the tile to launch the console, at which point it's worth right-clicking the console icon in the taskbar and selecting "Pin this program to taskbar" so that it's easily accessible the next time you log in.

After you're in the console, navigate to Administration > Hierarchy Configuration > Discovery Methods. As you can see, six discovery methods are available. Table 3.1 gives you a rundown on the purpose of each one.

Table 3.1 Discovery methods in ConfigMgr

Discovery method	Function
Active Directory Forest Discovery	Discovers sites and subnets in AD forests, and can automatically create boundaries based on discovery
Group Discovery	Discovers security groups in AD, and discovers the membership of both security groups and distribution groups
Active Directory System Discovery	Discovers computer objects within AD
Active Directory User Discovery	Discovers user accounts within AD
Heartbeat Discovery	Communicates with ConfigMgr clients to update their discovery information within the ConfigMgr database
Network Discovery	Discovers devices on the network with an IP address, including noncomputer devices like switches

As you work through the chapters, most of these discovery methods will be addressed, but for the moment you'll focus on two: Active Directory Forest Discovery and Active Directory System Discovery.

3.2.1 *Active Directory Forest Discovery*

The AD Forest Discovery discovers AD sites and IP subnets in AD forests, and it can automatically create ConfigMgr management boundaries based on that discovery. Let's do a bit of digging under the hood in AD to see how the Forest Discovery works:

1 Log in to DC01 as MOL\Administrator, and launch the Active Directory Sites and Services application. You'll see a number of AD sites configured for which DC01 provides the AD Global Catalog.

2 You'll see there are also a number of IPv4 subnets configured. 192.168.21.0/24, 192.168.22.0/24, and 192.168.23.0/24 are dummy subnets—they don't represent logical networks in your lab environment, but are there to show how different physical sites are represented in AD.

3 Right-click "Subnets" and select "New Subnet."

4 In the New Subnet window, type in the IPv4 subnet information that matches your lab environment. If you left everything as the default, the details are 192.168.11.0/24, as shown in figure 3.3.

Figure 3.3   Adding a subnet to the Active Directory Site Lab

5   Click "OK," and now the Sites and Services information should look like that in figure 3.4.

What you've done here is associate an IPv4 subnet to an AD site. Now, when a domain-joined system talks to the domain controller DC01, it will know which AD site it belongs to. This information is of critical importance in ConfigMgr.

Figure 3.4   New subnet added to AD Sites and Services

ConfigMgr can use the information that you've just entered into AD, so let's implement that functionality.

6 Back over on CM01, right-click "Active Directory Forest Discovery" and select "Properties."

7 Click the "Enable Active Directory Forest Discovery" check box and ensure that the check box labeled "Automatically create Active Directory Site Boundaries when they are discovered" is also selected, as shown in figure 3.5.

To perform the same activity with PowerShell, use the following command:

```
Set-CMDiscoveryMethod -ActiveDirectoryForestDiscovery `
-SiteCode PS1 `
-EnableActiveDirectorySiteBoundaryCreation $True `
-Enabled $True
```

Then, to run the discovery method, run the following command:

```
Invoke-CMForestDiscovery -SiteCode PS1
```

8 Click "OK," and you'll be prompted to run a full discovery as soon as possible; select "Yes."

Figure 3.5 Enable Active Directory Forest Discovery in ConfigMgr.

WHICH LOG?   The Active Directory Forest Discovery logs its activity to ADForestDisc.log. Watch this log in CMTrace to see how the discovery method polls AD for sites and subnets.

ConfigMgr is now set up to discover sites and subnets in AD forests. (You'll learn how to automatically create boundaries in section 3.3.2.)

Try It Now—Discover sites and subnets within AD forests

Follow the steps outlined in section 3.3.1 to discover the AD sites and subnets in the lab environment.

Think about the AD configuration in your own environment. How many AD sites do you have defined, and have network subnets been defined and allocated to sites? If you ran this discovery method in your organization, how many boundaries would be automatically created, and how might you go about organizing them logically?

3.2.2 *Active Directory System Discovery*

Next, you'll activate the Active Directory System Discovery. Like the Forest Discovery Method, this method also polls AD, but instead of looking for forest and site information, it scours AD for system objects—the objects that are created when a machine such as CLIENT01 joins an AD domain.

1 Right-click the Active Directory System Discovery method and select "Properties."

2 Select the "Enable Active Directory System Discovery" check box. Under "Active Directory Containers," click the little sunburst icon to create a new container to add to the discovery method.

3 In the AD Container window, select "Browse" next to the "Path" field. This brings up a view of the OU structure in the MoL AD domain.

4 Expand the MoL OU and select Workstations, and then click "OK" and "OK" again. The General tab in the System Discovery window should now look like that in figure 3.6.

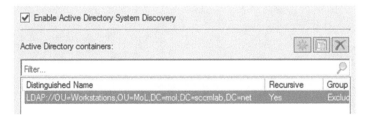

Figure 3.6 Specify an AD search path for System Discovery in ConfigMgr.

What you've done is told the System Discovery to look only in the Workstations container. This is where the computer object of CLIENT01 sits, so when System Discovery runs, it will find that computer object as well as any others in that AD container and import them into ConfigMgr. In such a small AD environment, it would be fine to point the System Discovery method at the top-level container in AD and, as the search is recursive, every computer object in AD would be discovered. In large organizations, you generally need to be a lot more targeted in your searching, because larger searches have a greater resource impact on the server running AD domain services.

5   Next, select the Polling Schedule tab. You'll see that the default polling schedule for this discovery method is 7 days. Click "Schedule" and then "Custom," and change the schedule to every 1 day, leaving the delta discovery interval at 5 minutes. This means that the discovery method performs a full search every 24 hours, ensuring that the discovered data is kept fully refreshed.

> **TIP** In a small environment, it doesn't matter when a discovery method performs a full discovery: the absolute amount of data to be discovered is usually small. But in an organization with many thousands of AD objects, a full discovery can take a long time and should be performed outside business hours to avoid unduly impacting users.

6   Finally, go to the Options tab. Make sure that the two options on this tab are both selected. This allows ConfigMgr to be more discerning when discovering computer objects, minimizing the risk that the ConfigMgr database will be populated by obsolete AD records. Again, it's not necessary in your lab, but is worthwhile in most enterprise environments.

7   Click "OK" and you'll be prompted to run a full discovery. Choose "Yes."

> **WHICH LOG?** The Active Directory System Discovery method logs its activity to adsysdis.log. Watch this log in CMTrace to see how your nominated AD containers are polled for computer objects. This log file also tends to get quite large, so it's regularly saved as an old log file called adsysdis.lo_, which is in the same location as the master log file. You can look at *.lo_ files with CMTrace as well.

ConfigMgr is now set up to discover computer objects within AD. You'll use this information to deploy the ConfigMgr client, and the discovery method will keep running at regular intervals, refreshing the ConfigMgr database with the latest information from AD.

Creating a System Discovery Method using PowerShell is a bit more complex than the Forest Discovery Method. Rather than reproduce all the steps here, the code and comments are available in the .\powershell\Set-CMDiscoveryMethods.ps1 script in the Git repository.

Try It Now—Discover computer objects within AD

Follow the steps outlined in section 3.3.2 to discover the computer objects within the lab AD environment. Make sure they appear in the ConfigMgr console under Assets and Compliance > Devices.

How many systems are there in your organization's AD environment? Would you configure the discovery method to start discovering systems from the root of AD, or would you specify particular OUs so that only a subset of machines would be discovered? Are there any AD systems that you might not want discovered by ConfigMgr?

3.2.3   *Active Directory User Discovery*

Now you'll set ConfigMgr to discover the AD users and group that you set up earlier:

1 In the ConfigMgr console on CM01, navigate to Administration > Hierarchy Configuration > Discovery Methods. Right-click "Active Directory User Discovery," and select "Properties."

2 On the General tab, select the "Enable Active Directory User Discovery" check box, and then select the sunburst icon next to "Active Directory containers" to add an AD location for the discovery method to search.

3 In the Active Directory Container window, select "Browse" next to the "Path" field. In the Select New Container window that opens, navigate to and highlight mol.sccmlab.net/MoL/Users, and then click "OK" and "OK" again, so that the General tab looks like figure 3.7.

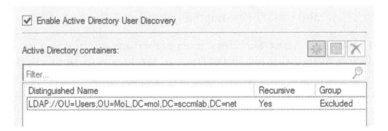

Figure 3.7   Adding the Users OU so that the discovery method can import AD user accounts

4 Click the Polling Schedule tab and change the schedule from every 7 days to every 1 day. This means that the discovery method will perform a full update every 24 hours, ensuring that AD data is kept fully up-to-date. Click "OK" to close the Properties window, and when prompted to run a full discovery, select "Yes."

WHICH LOG?   The AD User Discovery method is logged to adusrdis.log.

The PowerShell code to configure the User Discovery Method is also in the .\power-shell\Set-CMDiscoveryMethods.ps1 script.

> **Try It Now—Discover AD users**
>
> Follow the steps in section 3.2.3 to discover the user accounts that already exist in AD. Have the adusrdis.log open so that you can see the discovery happening in real time.
>
> As you run the discovery, think about your own environment. How many user accounts are there, and how many of them would you want to bring in to ConfigMgr? Are there any accounts that you would never want to have ConfigMgr discover?

3.2.4 *Active Directory Group Discovery*

The last discovery method you'll configure is Group Discovery. This will bring group membership information for both AD users and machines into ConfigMgr. Later, you'll be able to use this information to build ConfigMgr Collections based on group membership, which is a common way of targeting software, settings, and policy in an enterprise environment.

1 Right-click "Active Directory Group Discovery" and select "Properties." On the General tab, click the check box to enable group discovery. Under "Discovery scopes," select "Location" from the "Add" drop-down list. This discovery method lets you nominate specific groups to discover as well as locations in AD.

2 In the "Add Active Directory Location" window, in the "Name" field type `ConfigMgr Lab Groups`. Then, select "Browse" and navigate to mol.sccmlab.net/MoL/Security Groups. The fields should now look like those in figure 3.8.

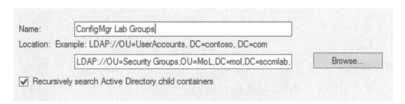

Figure 3.8 Create an AD location to search for groups.

3 Go to the Polling Schedule tab and change the schedule from every 7 days to every 1 day. Finally, go to the Options tab and tick the first two check boxes that relate to computer discovery. This won't impact the discovery of user accounts, but will come into effect if Group Discovery is used to discover computer accounts within a group.

Click "OK" and choose "Yes" to run a full discovery.

WHICH LOG?   The AD Group Discovery method is logged to adsgdis.log.

The PowerShell code to configure the Group Discovery method is available in the .\powershell\Set-CMDiscoveryMethods.ps1 script.

   To verify that the discovery methods worked, navigate to Assets and Compliance > Users, and you should see the five Users and one User group populated into the console, as shown in figure 3.9.

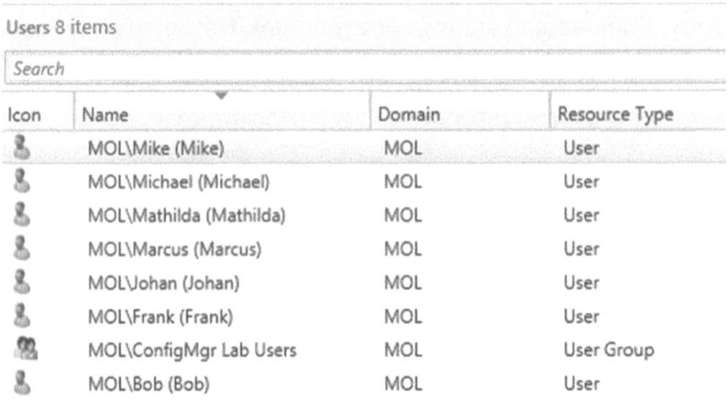

Users 8 items

Icon	Name	Domain	Resource Type
	MOL\Mike (Mike)	MOL	User
	MOL\Michael (Michael)	MOL	User
	MOL\Mathilda (Mathilda)	MOL	User
	MOL\Marcus (Marcus)	MOL	User
	MOL\Johan (Johan)	MOL	User
	MOL\Frank (Frank)	MOL	User
	MOL\ConfigMgr Lab Users	MOL	User Group
	MOL\Bob (Bob)	MOL	User

Figure 3.9   Newly discovered user accounts and a user group

> **Try It Now—Discover AD groups**
>
> Follow the steps in section 3.2.4 to discover the ConfigMgr Lab Users group in the ConfigMgr console.
>
> How many user and system groups are in your production environment? Do you use them to deploy software and settings?

3.3   *Boundaries*

Even after you've configured discovery methods in ConfigMgr, and the server has gone into AD and imported computer objects ready to be managed, ConfigMgr still won't do anything with them until you give ConfigMgr a management framework within which to understand where these newly discovered computers fit. This is where boundaries come into play.

   Boundaries are representations of aspects of your environment that are defined within ConfigMgr: things like AD sites, IP subnets, or IP address ranges. Only systems that fall within those defined boundaries will be managed by ConfigMgr. ConfigMgr uses these boundaries so that when computers start communicating with the Config-Mgr server, it understands whether those computers should be managed, and if so, how to manage them.

As shown in table 3.2, there are four types of ConfigMgr boundary, but the one we'll concentrate on is the AD site boundary.

Table 3.2 Boundary types in ConfigMgr

Boundary type	Description
Active Directory site	Maps a ConfigMgr boundary to a defined site in AD Sites and Services
IP subnet	Maps a boundary to an IPv4 subnet—for example, 192.168.1.0/24
IPv6 prefix	Maps a boundary to a range of IPv6 addresses
IP address range	Maps a boundary to a specific range of IP addresses—for example, 192.168.1.10-192.168.1.20

3.3.1 Creating a boundary

To define a boundary, follow these steps. On CM01 in the ConfigMgr console, navigate to Administration > Hierarchy Configuration > Boundaries. You should see that there's already a boundary in place, called Lab.

This boundary was created by the Active Directory Forest Discovery method. Enabling the option to automatically create AD site boundaries meant that when the discovery agent polled AD Sites and Services and found an existing AD site, it automatically created a boundary based on that site. The work you did earlier in adding an IP subnet to that site means that when a domain-joined computer logs on to AD, both it and the domain controller will know which AD site it belongs to. That information is discovered by ConfigMgr, which can then work out whether the machine object falls within a defined management boundary. If it does, then ConfigMgr can manage the machine after it has the ConfigMgr client installed.

Now that we have a defined boundary, it's time to make it go to work.

The low-down on boundaries

Using each boundary type has pros and cons. AD boundaries have the major advantage that ConfigMgr uses the site and subnet information contained within AD, which means that there's little configuration to do within the ConfigMgr console, and it also means that AD administrators can make changes to sites and services dynamically, which won't require any reconfiguration in ConfigMgr.

On the downside, using AD site boundaries puts the onus on AD to be accurate and up-to-date. Incorrect AD information can have serious consequences for ConfigMgr, such as a computer reporting that it isn't in an AD site, when in fact it is. ConfigMgr can work only with the information that's provided to it, so providing accurate information is paramount.

3.3.2 Creating a boundary group

Without being placed into a boundary group, boundaries on their own don't do much. When you group boundaries together in ConfigMgr, that's when you can start doing meaningful things like assigning ConfigMgr servers to the groups so that managed systems within the member boundaries know which servers to talk to.

Why is this important? Well, ConfigMgr is designed to scale out to manage and support many thousands of systems and users across a wide area. It's quite common to have a ConfigMgr primary site server managing systems in different cities, time zones, and even countries. In complex environments like that, multiple servers are needed to provide quick, local content to nearby systems. For example, if you have an office in Mumbai with 50 machines to which you want to deploy the latest version of Microsoft Office, you don't want those machines to have to talk across your expensive WAN link to the ConfigMgr server in New York. Far better to have a local server that can host the necessary content, as shown in figure 3.10.

Figure 3.10   Configure ConfigMgr to provide content to managed machines from a local source.

To enable this, ConfigMgr boundaries define where your machines are located (for example, New York, Mumbai), and boundary groups define where those boundaries should look for their content.

To create a boundary group:

1   Navigate to Administration > Hierarchy Configuration > Boundary Groups. As you can see, currently no groups are defined.
2   Right-click in the empty space and select "Create Boundary Group."
3   In the window that launches, type `Lab Boundaries` as the group "Name." Then, under "Boundaries" select "Add."
4   Tick the "Lab" check box and click "OK." As shown in figure 3.11, the Lab boundary now appears in the list of boundaries in the group.

3.3.3 Linking the boundary group with ConfigMgr

Next, you'll create a relationship between the newly created boundary group and the ConfigMgr infrastructure. Go to the References tab and select the "Use this boundary group for site assignment" check box. This allows machines within the boundary group to automatically attach to the ConfigMgr site when the agent software is installed. The "Assigned site" should be "PS1-Month of Lunches ConfigMgr Lab." No other sites are available in the drop-down list, but in a more complex environment there might be. Finally, under "Site system servers," click "Add." Put a tick in the check box next to "CM01.mol.sccmlab.net" and select "OK."

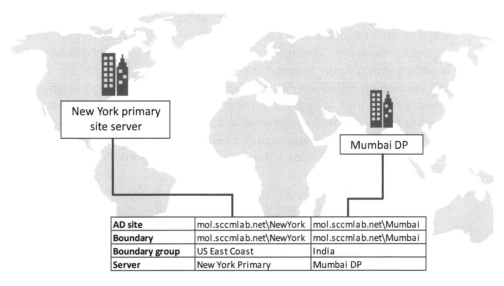

AD site	mol.sccmlab.net\NewYork	mol.sccmlab.net\Mumbai
Boundary	mol.sccmlab.net\NewYork	mol.sccmlab.net\Mumbai
Boundary group	US East Coast	India
Server	New York Primary	Mumbai DP

Figure 3.11 Adding a boundary to a boundary group

The References tab should now look like figure 3.12.

General | References

Site assignment

☑ Use this boundary group for site assignment

The assigned site determines the ConfigMgr site computer resources are assigned to
determines the ConfigMgr site that performs client push installation.

Assigned site: P01-Primary Site 1

Content location

Specify the site system servers that are associated with this boundary group so that client
distribution points and state migration points are valid content location servers.

You can change the connection to identify whether the network connection speed betwe
and connecting clients is fast or slow.

Site system servers:

Filter...

Server Name	Site	Connection
\\LAB-CM01.mol.sccmlab.net	P01	Fast

Figure 3.12 Assigning a site server to a boundary group so clients can access content

The defined connection for this boundary group to CM01 is Fast. In this context, Fast and Slow aren't definitions of particular discrete values for bandwidth. Rather, they're subjective statements about the nature of the connection of machines within the boundary group to the assigned site server. ConfigMgr assumes that machines on a Fast connection will always be able to access content from their assigned site server, whereas those with a Slow connection might have expensive, highly restricted, or intermittent access. Managed systems in a Slow boundary group can be excluded from certain ConfigMgr functions, such as patching or application deployment. This serves to protect sites with limited connectivity from being flooded with high-bandwidth ConfigMgr traffic.

Click "OK," and your boundary group is created. Now let's start working with the ConfigMgr agent and get some more information flowing to the server.

Try It Now—Create a boundary group

Follow the steps in sections 3.3.2 and 3.3.3 to create a boundary group in your lab environment and assign CM01 as the site server for the group.

Think about your own organization. How many boundary groups might you have? Would they be created along geographical lines or business lines? For example, you might have departments that have to maintain separation from others, which includes the data they access.

To create a boundary group, add a boundary member and link the group to a site server. Using PowerShell instead of the ConfigMgr console, check out the code in .\powershell\New-CMBoundaryGroup.ps1.

3.4   Lab

Use PowerShell to add mol.sccmlab.net/MoL/Servers to the Active Directory System Discovery method.

3.5   *Ideas for on your own*

The flexibility of the ConfigMgr framework means that there are often lots of ways of achieving the same outcome, and different people have a variety of preferred approaches to ConfigMgr design, architecture, and administration.

Search as you might, you'll never find best practice guidelines on every aspect of ConfigMgr, because the definition of *best practice* is "What is best for you and your organization?"

As a result, sometimes feelings can run quite high in the ConfigMgr world, as experts attempt to pin down a consistent solution to a given question. Reading community group websites and Microsoft blogs will give you a good idea of what's happening in the wider world of ConfigMgr.

3.5.1 *Controversy over boundaries*

To say that "there are pros and cons to using each boundary type" might be considered the understatement of all time in the world of ConfigMgr boundaries (a narrow world, I grant you).

There are strongly held opinions about which type of boundary is applicable at which time, and because the disagreements are deeply rooted in how ConfigMgr works at a profound technical level, it's worth having a read of some of the latest articles:

- When not to use IP Address Ranges as Boundaries in ConfigMgr (http://blogs .technet.com/b/configmgrteam/archive/2013/03/01/when-not-to-use-ip-address-ranges-as-boundaries-in-configuration-manager.aspx)
- Official Microsoft blog on IP Address Ranges as ConfigMgr Boundaries met with instant rebuttal (http://myitforum.com/myitforumwp/2013/03/02/ official-microsoft-blog-on-ip-address-ranges-as-configmgr-boundaries-met-with-instant-rebuttal/)

Managing ConfigMgr
devices and users

At the heart of ConfigMgr are devices: systems (either physical or virtual) that run an operating system supported by ConfigMgr and that have the ConfigMgr client installed. The client communicates regularly with the hierarchy of ConfigMgr servers, and performs tasks such as downloading and processing policies, reporting on hardware and software inventory, running operating system deployments, installing applications and system updates, and many more. As you can imagine, the health and reliability of your ConfigMgr environment is directly correlated with the overall health of the ConfigMgr agents deployed across your environment, so it's critically important to get this right.

But when you're immersed in the world of managing desktop and laptop systems, deploying applications, scheduling patches, and running inventories, it's remarkably easy to forget that most systems tend to have fleshy attachments called users who are (often surprisingly) the main source of productivity in your business. ConfigMgr can work with users directly, enabling some extremely advanced and intelligent management scenarios.

This raises the question: what's the importance of being able to manage users in ConfigMgr? Isn't that what Active Directory (AD) is for? Yes, but ConfigMgr doesn't seek to become a replacement user-management platform for AD, but rather to bring a much richer and more intuitive user-centric focus to the realm of systems management, using AD as a foundation.

As shown in figure 4.1, in this chapter you'll use the tasks undertaken in chapter 3 to successfully work with the ConfigMgr client and devices, as well as bring the lab users into the mix and establish formal relationships between users and devices via User Device Affinity (UDA). By the end of this chapter, you'll be ready to perform some advanced administration with your lab environment.

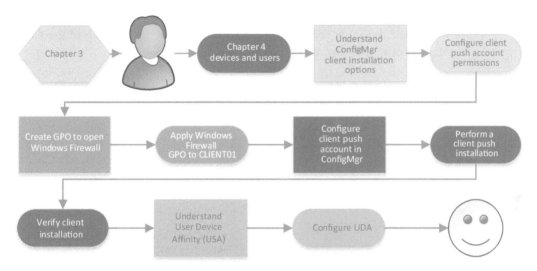

Figure 4.1 By the end of this chapter, the secrets of devices and users will be yours!

4.1 Understanding devices and the ConfigMgr client

In the world of ConfigMgr, a device can be a variety of systems, such as the following (not a definitive list!):

- A Windows 10 tablet
- A virtual Windows server
- A Windows 10 Virtual Desktop Infrastructure (VDI) instance
- A MacBook Pro running OS X
- A physical Ubuntu server
- An Android phone
- An Apple iPad

The platforms and operating systems are vastly different, but the principle is the same with all of them: once a management agent has been deployed to them, you can use ConfigMgr to manage them directly.

4.1.1 Installing the ConfigMgr client on remote systems

As already mentioned, the ConfigMgr client is a software package that needs to be installed on remote systems in order for them to be managed directly within the ConfigMgr environment. The client can be deployed and installed in a variety of ways, which gives you a lot of flexibility about how to get the software out to the systems in your environment.

To install the ConfigMgr client on a remote system, follow these steps:

1 Log in to CLIENT01 as MOL\Administrator (make sure you use the full domain username) and then open File Explorer.
2 In the File Explorer address bar, navigate to \\CM01\SMS_PS1\Client. You should see the same content as in figure 4.2; this is the location of the Config-Mgr client source files and prerequisite files.

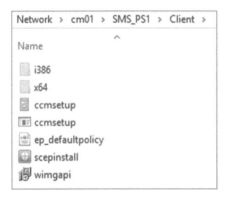

Figure 4.2   The ConfigMgr client software repository on CM01

This share maps to a local folder on the ConfigMgr server and is automatically created and populated when the server is installed. On any ConfigMgr server installation, there should always be a share at \\<SERVERNAME>\SMS_SITECODE\Client. This is one of those consistencies of ConfigMgr, which means that you always know where to find the client software. It's also a good troubleshooting tip: if you can't access that share from a remote machine, something's wrong and needs investigating.

Table 4.1 gives an overview of the most common methods of deploying the Config-Mgr client throughout your environment.

Table 4.1   ConfigMgr client installation methods

Installation method	Description
Client push	The client installer CCMSetup.exe is copied across from the ConfigMgr server to systems that have been discovered.
Group Policy installation	CCMSetup.msi is used to trigger the client installation via a Group Policy Object (GPO). This can be targeted at either systems or users (or both).
Logon script installation	CCMSetup.exe is called from within a logon script to install or reinstall the client.
Manual client installation	CCMSetup.exe is launched with the necessary installation properties from a local machine. All requisite files are automatically copied across.

Table 4.1 ConfigMgr client installation methods *(continued)*

Installation method	Description
Software update-based client installation	Publishes the client to a software update point. Remote clients use the built-in Windows update agent to retrieve or upgrade the client installation files.

Each method has its own pros and cons, and there's no one completely correct way of deploying the client. Most enterprise environments rely on a mixture of multiple methods to ensure that the client is successfully deployed throughout the organization. Time, experience, and familiarity with the processes will allow you to work out which is the best mixture for your organization.

For the purposes of this book, you'll walk through how to do the most common installation method, the client push.

4.2   *Preparing for a client push*

A client push installation requires the ConfigMgr server to be able to authenticate to the remote client in order to copy the software across and then trigger the installation. To enable this, the ConfigMgr server must be able to do the following:

1   Find the target computer on the network
2   Communicate directly to the target computer through the firewall (if any)
3   Authenticate to the target computer

The ability of one server to find, communicate with, and authenticate against a target computer isn't a process specific to ConfigMgr; it's one of the most common scenarios in enterprise computing. In the context of ConfigMgr, you need to specify a client push account that the server will use for the authentication process. The prerequisites in the lab environment are therefore as follows:

1   Set the client push account permissions in Active Directory.
2   Open the Windows firewall on the target system (CLIENT01).
3   Configure the client push account in ConfigMgr.

These prerequisites generally need to be done only once in your organization; they don't need to be repeated every time you want to perform a client push installation.

4.2.1   *Set the client push account permissions*

To assign the client push account the necessary permissions, perform the following steps:

1   On the Domain Controller DC01, open Active Directory Users and Computers, and then navigate to mol.sccmlab.net > MoL > Service Accounts. In this container are specialized user accounts, one of which is called CM_CP. The description given is the ConfigMgr client push account. This is the account you'll configure within the ConfigMgr console.

   2 Right-click the CM_CP account and select "Add to a group."
   3 In the "Enter the object names to select" field, type Domain Admins and then
      click "OK." A dialog box should pop up stating that the operation was success-
      ful.
   4 Double-click the CM_CP account to open the properties and go to the Member
      Of tab. Two groups should be listed: Domain Admins and Domain Users.

Now that the account has sufficient permissions, it's time to configure it in the Config-
Mgr console.

More on client push account permissions

In order to authenticate to remote systems, the CM_CP account needs to have local
administrator access on remote systems. You can do this in various ways, but the
easiest is to make the account a member of the Domain Admins group. On each
domain-joined system, this group is automatically added to the local administrators
group, which is why it's such a powerful AD group, and why access to it must be rigidly
controlled. It's also the reason that many organizations don't like adding the Configuration Manager client push account to the Domain Admins group, preferring instead
to use Group Policy Preferences to add the account to the local administrators group
explicitly. For the sake of your lab environment, however, using the Domain Admins
group is perfectly acceptable.

If you don't want to make the client push account a member of Domain Admins, but
you do want to be able to push the client to Domain Controllers, you'll have to make
the account a member of the BUILTIN\Administrators group in order for the account
to have sufficient permissions, since Domain Controllers don't have local security
groups.

Try It Now—Assign AD permissions

Follow the steps in section 4.2.1 to assign client push rights to MOL\CM_CP, in preparation for using this account for client push.

Consider your own organization. Would making the client push account a member of
the Domain Admins group be acceptable? Is an internal security model in place that
might preclude this? If so, how would you go about giving the push account sufficient
local access to install the ConfigMgr client?

4.2.2 Open the Windows Firewall

Performing a client push requires that the ConfigMgr server can talk directly to the
Windows operating system on the client. By default, the local Windows Firewall settings on the remote system will block the communication attempt, and the client
push will fail.

You can get around this in various ways, but the approach you'll take is to create a Group Policy Object (GPO) in AD that will disable the Windows Firewall for domain-joined systems:

1 Log in to DC01 as MOL\Administrator and open the Group Policy Management utility.

2 Navigate to Forest > Domains > mol.sccmlab.net. Right-click MoL and select "Create a new GPO in this domain, and Link it here." Call the new GPO SEC-Windows Firewall (the *SEC* stands for *Security*, so if you create other security-based GPOs, they'll all appear in the GPO list in order). Click "OK."

3 Expand Group Policy Objects, right-click "SEC-Windows Firewall," and select "Edit."

4 In the Group Policy Management Editor, navigate to Computer Configuration > Policies > Windows Settings > Security Settings > Windows Firewall with Advanced Security.

5 Select "Windows Firewall with Advanced Security" again, and then in the right-hand side of the editor select "Windows Firewall Properties," as shown in figure 4.3.

Figure 4.3   Create a Group Policy Object to change Windows Firewall settings.

6 On the Domain Profile tab, select "Off" from the "Firewall State" drop-down list.

7 Repeat this process on the Private Profile and Public Profile tabs. Click "OK" and then close the GPO Editor.

NOTE Turning off all the firewall profiles is fine in your lab environment but would be unacceptable for most companies, unless they're using a third-party firewall product. Many enterprises disable the domain profile but leave the private and public profiles enabled, in which case you'll be able to deploy the ConfigMgr client via client push without having to worry about firewall configuration or Group Policy.

8 Next, log on to CLIENT01 as MOL\Administrator and open an elevated command prompt.

9 At the command prompt, type `gpupdate /force`. This forces the client to query AD for the latest Group Policy.

10 To verify that the changes have taken effect, navigate to Control Panel > Administrative Tools > Windows Firewall with Advanced Security. The firewall properties should look like those in figure 4.4, with the firewall turned off for all network profiles.

Figure 4.4   Windows Firewall turned off using Group Policy

Now that the environment is ready, you can move on to the ConfigMgr component of the push.

> **Try It Now—Configure Windows Firewall**
>
> Follow the steps in section 4.2.2 to create a GPO that will disable the Windows Firewall, and then apply the GPO to CLIENT01 and verify that the changes were successful.
>
> Think about the approach taken in your own organization. Is the Windows Firewall enabled or disabled? If disabled, are all network profiles turned off or only the Domain profile? How are the firewall settings distributed to managed machines?

4.2.3 *Configure the client push account*

To configure the client push account, in the ConfigMgr console, do the following:

1 Navigate to Administration > Site Configuration > Sites.

2 Right-click the PS1 site and select Client Installation Settings > Client Push Installation.

3 Navigate to the Accounts tab. Click the sunburst icon next to "Client Push Installation accounts," and then choose "New Account."

4 In the Windows User Account window, type in `MOL\CM_CP` for the username, and `P@ssw0rd` for the "Password" and "Confirm Password" fields.

5 Click the "Verify" button to check the details. Leave the "Data Source" field as "Network Share." In the "Network Share" field, type \\mol.sccmlab.net\ SYSVOL (don't click "OK" just yet). This is a default share that's created in an AD environment, and that should be accessible to any authenticated user. The window should look like figure 4.5.

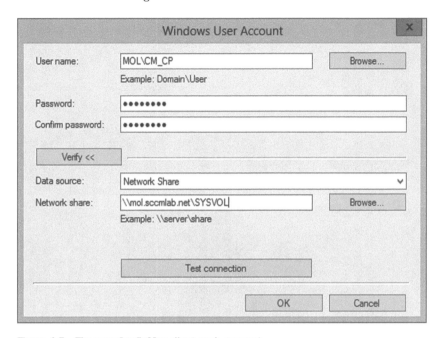

Figure 4.5 The new ConfigMgr client push account

6 Click the "Test connection" button, and a message should pop up stating that the connection was successfully verified.

7 Click "OK" and "OK" again to save the new client push account.

Now that the prerequisites are in place, you can perform the push installation of the ConfigMgr client.

Try It Now—Configure the client push account
On CM01, go through the process of configuring the client push account.

4.3   *Performing a client push*

What happens when you perform a client push? Figure 4.6 details what's happening behind the scenes, and where the process can fail.

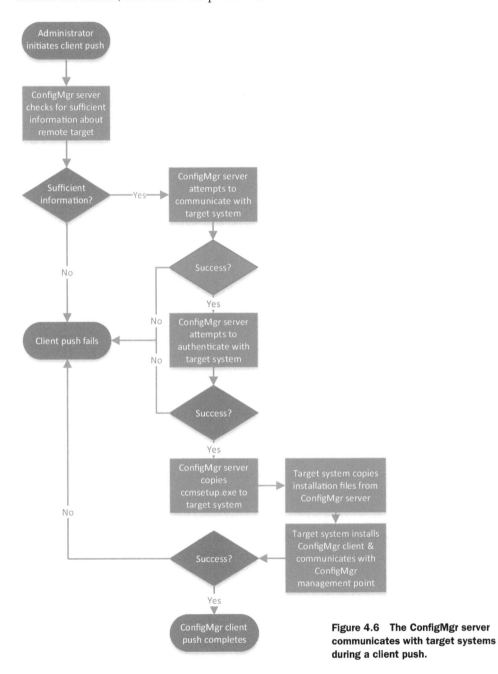

Figure 4.6   The ConfigMgr server communicates with target systems during a client push.

Now for the moment of truth. Because this is an important process, you'll want to have a look at the inner workings to see it in action, so let's quickly set that up:

1 Log on to CLIENT01 as MOL\Administrator. Right-click the taskbar and select "Task Manager."

2 In the Task Manager window, click the down arrow next to "More Details" to expand the view. The default tab is the Processes view; this is the one you're interested in.

3 On CM01, open ccm.log with CMTrace. This is the log file that will be written to during the client push, so you can watch the process happening in real time, as the push process is largely hidden when using the ConfigMgr console.

4 Navigate to Assets and Compliance > Devices. Right-click "CLIENT01" and select "Install Client."

5 The Install ConfigMgr Client window opens. Click "Next." On the following screen, select "Install the client software from a specified site." Click "Next" again.

6 Click "Next" again and then switch to CMTrace. You'll see the ConfigMgr server authenticate to CLIENT01 using the CM_CP client push account. As shown in figure 4.7, the server will copy across the ccmsetup.exe installer and the Mobile-Client.tcf file. This last file contains the installation properties that the ccmsetup.exe file will look for during the installation.

```
Log Text
======>Begin Processing request: "2097152001", machine name: "CLIENT01"
Getting a new request from queue "Incoming" after 100 millisecond delay.
Waiting for change in directory "E:\Program Files\Microsoft Configuration Manager\inboxes\ccr.box" for queue "Incoming".
Execute query exec [sp_IsMPAvailable] N'PS1'
---> Trying each entry in the SMS Client Remote Installation account list
---> Attempting to connect to administrative share '\\CLIENT01\admin$' using account 'MOL\CM_CP'
---> Connected to administrative share on machine CLIENT01 using account 'MOL\CM_CP'
---> Attempting to make IPC connection to share <\\CLIENT01\IPC$>
---> Searching for SMSClientInstall.* under '\\CLIENT01\admin$\'
---> System OS version string "10.0.10240" converted to 10.00
---> Unable to connect to WMI (root\ccm) on remote machine "CLIENT01", error = 0x8004100e.
---> Creating \ VerifyingCopying existence of destination directory \\CLIENT01\admin$\ccmsetup.
---> Copying client files to \\CLIENT01\admin$\ccmsetup.
---> Copying file "E:\Program Files\Microsoft Configuration Manager\bin\I386\MobileClient.tcf" to "MobileClient.tcf"
---> Copying file "E:\Program Files\Microsoft Configuration Manager\bin\I386\ccmsetup.exe" to "ccmsetup.exe"
---> Created service "ccmsetup" on machine "CLIENT01".
---> Started service "ccmsetup" on machine "CLIENT01".
---> Deleting SMS Client Install Lock File '\\CLIENT01\admin$\SMSClientInstall.PS1'
Execute query exec [sp_CP_SetLastErrorCode] 2097152001, 0
---> Completed request "2097152001", machine name "CLIENT01".
Deleted request "2097152001", machine name "CLIENT01"
Execute query exec [sp_CP_SetPushRequestMachineStatus] 2097152001, 4
Execute query exec [sp_CP_SetLatest] 2097152001, N'08/02/2015 00:58:27', 1
<======End request: "2097152001", machine name: "CLIENT01".
```

Figure 4.7 The ConfigMgr server pushing the client installer to a remote machine

7 Now switch back to CLIENT01 and take a look at the Task Manager. You'll see
that under Background Processes is a new entry called ccmsetup.exe (32 bit).
This is the ConfigMgr client installer that has been copied to CLIENT01 and has
been triggered to install silently.

WHICH LOG?   The client installation process will be logged to ccm-
setup.log, which is located in %WINDIR%\ccmsetup\logs on any machine
on which the client is installed.

Depending on the speed of the system, the installation will run for several minutes before the ccmsetup.exe entry disappears from the list of background processes to be replaced by a new one called "Host Process for Microsoft
Configuration Manager," as shown in figure 4.8. Expand the process and you'll
see that the process is underpinned by a Windows Service called SMS Agent Host.

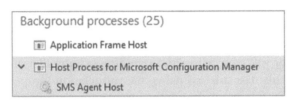

Figure 4.8   The ConfigMgr
client has been successfully
installed and is now running.

8 Navigate to Control Panel and launch the ConfigMgr utility. You should see that
the client is installed, is attached to the PS1 site, and is looking at CM01 as the
assigned Management Point, as shown in figure 4.9.

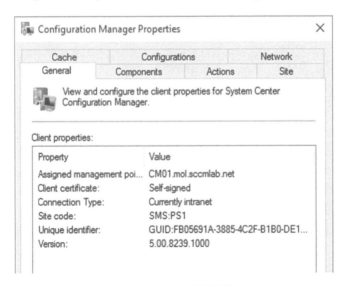

Figure 4.9   The ConfigMgr client on CLIENT01

9 Finally, switch back to CM01 and navigate to Assets and Compliance > Devices. You'll see that ConfigMgr is now reporting that CLIENT01 has a client, is assigned to site PS1, and that the client is active.

Congratulations, you've just performed a successful client push and now have a managed system!

4.4 Working with users in the ConfigMgr world

ConfigMgr 2012 introduced the concept of user and device equivalence. In the world of ConfigMgr, users are now as important as devices when it comes to targeted management. This concept needs to be taken with a grain of salt. The vast majority of your targeted administration will be to devices, because that's where the active agent sits. As tempting as it sometimes might be, you can't deploy an agent on a user—not yet, anyway.

But the concept is sound in principle, and is borne out by the way that users and devices are organized in the ConfigMgr console. Open the console and navigate to Assets and Compliance. As in figure 4.10, you'll see that users and user collections are placed at the same level as devices and device collections. It might seem like a minor thing, but in ConfigMgr 2007, users didn't receive the same level of prominence, and were generally swamped by device collections.

Figure 4.10 Users and devices at the same level in the ConfigMgr console

Let's look at an example of why this equivalence is now so important and powerful. Say that a user has requested access to an application that isn't available by default throughout your organization, such as Microsoft Visio. This application normally isn't installed everywhere because it's licensed separately from the rest of Microsoft Office, so installing it incurs an additional cost.

As the ConfigMgr administrator, you have the Microsoft Visio application ready to be deployed, but which is the best way to target the deployment? Should you target the user or the user's machine? A device-centric management approach introduces some awkward compromises:

- It makes sense to target the user, given that was where the request originated. But the deployment will follow the user around regardless of where that user logs on, which means you could have multiple, unlicensed copies of Microsoft Visio being distributed throughout your environment. Not good.

- You can avoid the preceding situation by targeting the user's system, even though doing so isn't reflective of the business nature of the original request. The downside of this approach is that you have to know which system belongs to the user, and if that system is lost, stolen, or in any other way has to be replaced, you have to keep track of which additional software packages had been deployed to it so that you can replicate them on the user's new machine. This is all feasible, but it adds a level of management and administrative overhead that's time-consuming and, as you'll see, now unnecessary.

A better option is one that reflects the business-centric nature of the request, while eliminating the chance of spreading software beyond where it's needed. You can achieve this in ConfigMgr by focusing on the user and defining the relationships between users and the devices they use. This is called User Device Affinity, or UDA.

4.5   *Creating relationships between users and devices*

UDA allows you to define Primary users for devices, Primary devices for users, or any combination of the two. For example, as shown in figure 4.11, you can assign a primary user to one particular device: the machine that the user always logs on to and that's assigned to that user in your company's asset register. Or you could assign multiple primary devices to a single user, such as a designer who has a desktop, a laptop, and a slate all assigned to them. Alternatively, you could assign multiple primary users to multiple primary devices, such as a team of interns who don't have machines assigned to them, but who rather make use of a pool of systems.

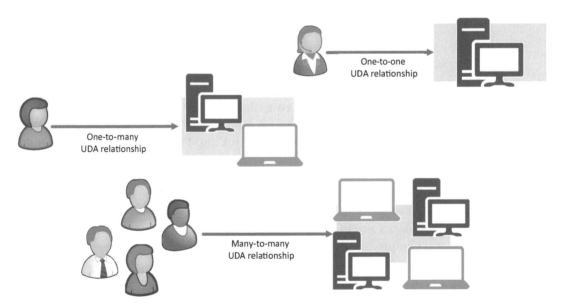

Figure 4.11   You can define a variety of relationships between users and devices.

The importance of UDA is that it allows you to accurately reflect how your managed systems are used by real-life users. Let's go back to the example you looked at earlier concerning Microsoft Visio, except this time let's flesh it out a little.

4.5.1 Understanding a UDA scenario

You receive a request from Alex, a manager in the business. Alex wants access to Microsoft Visio 2016, and has already gone through the necessary processes to purchase a license. As the ConfigMgr administrator, you already have access to Visio 2016 as an application that can be deployed. You want to ensure that Alex gets the software he's asked for in a quick, user-friendly way, so you deploy the Visio application directly to Alex and direct him to open the Application Catalog. Alex now sees Microsoft Visio in his list of available software, and clicks "Install." This triggers an instant policy refresh on the ConfigMgr client, and Visio downloads and is installed.

The following day, Alex forgets his laptop at home, and so logs on to his colleague's system, as his colleague is on training all day. This system doesn't have Visio installed, so Alex goes back to the Application Catalog and installs Visio. This time, Alex is presented with an error, and the software doesn't download or install. What happened?

As the administrator, you assigned Alex's user object in ConfigMgr as the primary user of the laptop that has been allocated to him, and made the primary user/primary device relationship a prerequisite of the software deployment. The ConfigMgr deployment process understands UDA, and because Alex isn't logging on to his primary device, the software installation fails.

Now it's time to look at how to configure UDA.

4.5.2 Creating UDA relationships

ConfigMgr provides various ways to establish a relationship between a user and a device, and all of them have their place for the ongoing maintenance of UDA. Table 4.2 details each of the options.

Table 4.2 Ways to establish User Device Affinity relationships

UDA method	Description
Administrator-defined	The ConfigMgr administrator manually defines the primary user(s) or primary device(s) on a per user/device basis via the console.
Bulk import	The ConfigMgr administrator maintains a CSV file of users and devices, and imports this data into the console.
Client settings	The ConfigMgr client tracks who logs on to the local system, how often, and for how long. When a usage threshold is reached, the client automatically makes the user a primary user of the machine.
OSD variable	During an operating system deployment (OSD) task sequence, the variable SMSTSUdaUsers can be called to create one or more primary users of the machine being deployed.

Table 4.2   Ways to establish User Device Affinity relationships *(continued)*

UDA method	Description
User-defined	If the user has the necessary permissions (which are denied by default), they can nominate themselves to be a primary user of the system that they're currently logged onto.

The method you'll focus on for now is administrator-defined, since this best exposes the inner workings of UDA.

Navigate to Assets and Compliance > Devices, right-click "CLIENT01," and select "Edit Primary Users." The window that opens shows you some of the potential candidates for primary users—users who have logged on to the machine recently, as shown in figure 4.12.

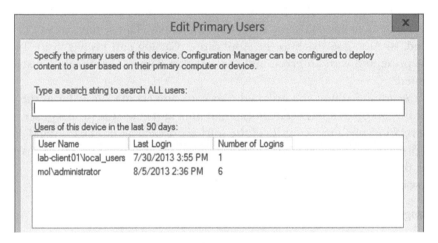

Figure 4.12   Potential primary users of CLIENT01

Rather than select any of the available options, in the field under "Type a search string…" type in MOL\Mike. This will perform a live search against all ConfigMgr users, and the entries in the user list will be replaced with MOL\Mike. Select this user and choose "Add." The user is now added as an Administrator Defined Primary User of CLIENT01, as shown in figure 4.13.

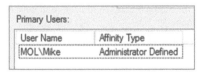

Figure 4.13   An Administrator Defined Primary User of CLIENT01

Creating a primary user relationship for a device is the same as creating a primary device relationship for a user. To verify this, go to users, right-click "MOL\Mike," and select "Edit Primary Devices." As shown in figure 4.14, by defining a primary user for CLIENT01, you've also assigned a primary device to Lab User 01.

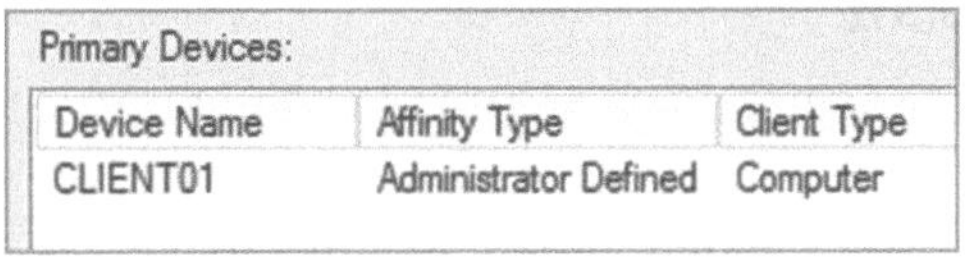

Primary Devices:		
Device Name	Affinity Type	Client Type
CLIENT01	Administrator Defined	Computer

Figure 4.14 Defining a primary user automatically creates a primary device.

You can perform the same administrative tasks with PowerShell. To create a user affinity directly to a device, use the following command:

```
Add-CMUserAffinityToDevice -DeviceName 'CLIENT01' -UserName 'MOL\Mike'
```

Alternatively, to add a device affinity directly to a user, run the following:

```
Add-CMDeviceAffinityToUser -DeviceName 'CLIENT01' -UserName 'MOL\Mike'
```

Congratulations! You've successfully configured user and group discovery as well as established a relationship between a user and a device. You'll be able to use this relationship later in the book for some fancy application deployment.

4.6   Lab

ConfigMgr isn't just used to manage systems running client versions of Microsoft Windows; it's also used to manage servers, particularly in the area of inventory and patch management.

In this lab, you're going to deploy the ConfigMgr client to the Domain Controller DC01 by using a client push. By default, a client push stops if it detects that the remote system is a domain controller, as many customers don't like the idea of having a management agent on a critical piece of AD infrastructure. But in this lab environment, it's perfectly safe, and as the book progresses you'll be making changes and implementing new configurations that will serve to isolate and protect DC01 from incurring any accidental changes or deployments.

To successfully push the ConfigMgr client to DC01, here are the steps you'll need to perform.

4.6.1   Discover DC01

Navigate to Assets and Compliance > Devices, and you'll see that DC01 isn't there. That's because when you configured the Active Directory System Discovery method, the AD container that you specified (mol.sccmlab.net/MoL/Workstations) doesn't contain DC01.

To have the discovery method find and import DC01 into ConfigMgr, you need to add the container that DC01 resides in as a second discovery path. All domain controllers are created by default in the domain controllers container, so in your lab the container is mol.sccmlab.net/Domain Controllers.

Add this path to the Active Directory System Discovery method and ensure that DC01 appears in devices.

4.6.2   *Disable the Windows Firewall on DC01*

Just as with CLIENT01, the Windows Firewall settings on DC01 prevent ConfigMgr from copying across the client installation files, so in this lab you need to disable the firewall.

You can use the same GPO that you created earlier in this chapter. But at the moment, the GPO is linked to the mol.sccmlab.net/MoL container in which DC01 doesn't reside.

So, using the Group Policy Management tool on DC01, you need to link the SEC-Windows Firewall policy to the mol.sccmlab.net/Domain Controllers container as well.

After this is done, run `gpupdate /force` on DC01 and open the control panel to verify that the Windows Firewall has been turned off.

4.6.3   *Push the ConfigMgr client to DC01*

Using the same client push method that you used to deploy the client to CLIENT01, it's time to deploy the client to DC01.

You've already configured the client push account, and because it's a member of Domain Admins, you won't need to do anything there.

The one thing that's different with this client push is that by default, the client won't deploy to a domain controller. The Client Push Wizard includes an option to override this behavior, so look at all the options carefully and choose the right one. Then, push the client out and watch the ccm.log on CM01 and the processes in the task manager on DC01 to ensure that the copy and installation is processed correctly.

Finally, check devices to ensure that the agent on DC01 is talking back happily to CM01.

Organizing
devices and users

Now that your ConfigMgr environment has been populated with users and devices, it's time to start organizing them so that you can start making them work for you.

In a ConfigMgr environment, you don't directly target users and machines on an individual basis mainly because this method of administration becomes difficult to maintain in production when you're dealing with more than a few hundred objects. Therefore, in ConfigMgr you use collections to group users and devices into logical, business-relevant groups, and you target all your administrative actions on those same collections. If devices and users are the bricks of the ConfigMgr environment, collections are the mortar that binds everything together and lets it stand up.

As shown in figure 5.1, in this chapter you'll learn about the built-in collections in ConfigMgr; how to create custom collections; how to populate collections with both static and dynamic members; and how to make the most use of Windows Management Instrumentation Query Language (WQL), which underpins all dynamic collections.

Moving forward, almost all the ConfigMgr administrative work you'll perform will revolve around working with collections, so it's important to be comfortable with the content in this chapter before moving on.

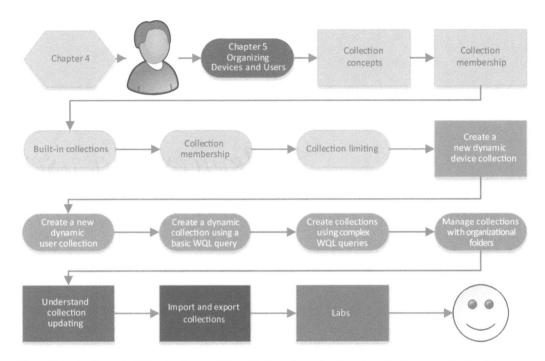

Figure 5.1   By the end of this chapter, you'll be able to make collections to cater to every situation!

5.1   *Understanding collection concepts*

Apart from being critical components of your ConfigMgr environment, collections also enable you to represent your organization's business structure, network, and geography within the ConfigMgr console, giving you a more visual and meaningful way of administering the environment.

Let's delve into this a little deeper. In the ConfigMgr console, navigate to the Assets and Compliance window and select "Device Collections." As shown in figure 5.2, ConfigMgr already has some built-in device collections. These offer a basic way of segregating out the core device types in any ConfigMgr environment, but also act as good building blocks for you to create collection structures that are meaningful to you and your organization.

Device Collections 5 items

Search

Icon	Name	Limiting Collection	Member Count
✔	All Desktop and Server Clients	All Systems	2
✔	All Mobile Devices	All Systems	0
✔	All Systems		5
✔	All Unknown Computers	All Systems	2

Figure 5.2   ConfigMgr comes prepopulated with built-in device collections.

The built-in collections are read-only and can't be modified. Take a look at user collections as well, and you can see that there are some preexisting collections here too. Table 5.1 outlines how each built-in device collection and user collection is defined.

Table 5.1 Built-in device and user collections. Notice that a collection can contain devices or users— but not both.

Collection name	Collection type	Purpose
All desktops and server clients	Device	All systems that have the full ConfigMgr client installed (laptops, desktops, servers, virtual machines, and so forth)
All Mobile devices	Device	All systems that ConfigMgr recognizes as a mobile device, such as Windows Phone handsets or iPads
All systems	Device	Every single discovered device that ConfigMgr knows about, whether physical or virtual, mobile or traditional
All unknown computers	Device	A specialized collection used for operating system deployment, when ConfigMgr needs to be able to respond to systems that it doesn't already know about
All users	User	All users that ConfigMgr knows about
All user groups	User	All user groups that ConfigMgr knows about
All users and user groups	User	All users and user groups that ConfigMgr knows about combined into a single collection

The built-in collections are useful, but they aren't particularly granular—more of a catchall to get you started. The following are examples of collections that would be of more relevance in your organization and that you'll create in section 5.2:

- *All Windows 10 Clients*—All systems running Windows 10 that have the ConfigMgr client installed. Useful for targeting client settings that are specific to those operating systems.
- *All Windows Servers*—All discovered systems running a Windows Server operating system, regardless of whether they have the ConfigMgr client installed or not. Useful as an exclusion; for example, for targeting software updates while excluding All Windows Servers from the software update deployment.
- *All HR Users*—All discovered users in AD that are also members of an HR security group. Useful for distributing software to a specific group of users, while using existing AD group memberships.
- *All Lab Systems*—All discovered systems that reside in an AD Site defined as Lab. Useful for targeting software or a policy to a geographical region, and for running reports that contain geographically specific information.

Collections are where the richness of ConfigMgr's ability to discover information about its environment comes into play. All of the information that ConfigMgr discovers about a device or a user, whether it's from an AD Discovery Method or from the locally installed ConfigMgr client, gets stored in the ConfigMgr database and is used to build complex, meaningful collections.

Let's take a look at how collections are constructed.

5.1.1 Collection membership

At its most basic, a collection is a group with members. Those members are either users or devices—but not both.

> **IMPORTANT NOTE**   With ConfigMgr 2007, it was possible to have a collection with a membership that was a mixture of users and devices. In order to enable strict, reliable targeting, this was removed in ConfigMgr 2012.

The membership of a collection can be defined and populated in four ways: direct, query, include collection, and exclude collection. Let's take a look at all of them.

DIRECT MEMBERSHIP

This is the simplest form of collection membership. As shown in figure 5.3, one or more users or devices are made direct members of a particular collection manually, in exactly the same manner that the membership of a security group in AD is defined.

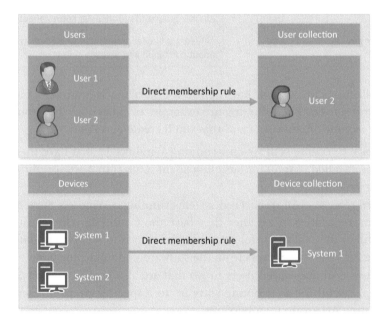

Figure 5.3   Direct membership rules give you what you ask for—useful but inflexible.

Direct membership is useful for testing purposes and lab environments, since statically defined memberships are easy to administer when you're dealing with only a small number of them. But it's recommended that direct memberships not be used in production collections: their static definition makes them inflexible. Collections work best when their memberships change dynamically to reflect the changing nature of a real enterprise environment. A reliance upon static membership means that you'll end up having to update collections manually as the wider environment changes, which introduces too much margin for error.

QUERY

Query-based membership is probably the most common form of collection membership, and is certainly the most flexible, powerful, and useful.

ConfigMgr collection queries use WQL to directly query the ConfigMgr database for specific information. For example, if you had an All Windows 10 Clients collection, it would be built using a query that looked for the following data:

- All systems running Windows 10

or

- All systems running Windows 10, and
- All systems with the ConfigMgr agent installed

All of these are independent queries in their own right, but ConfigMgr can find the common points between them in order to produce a meaningful, dynamic collection, as shown in figure 5.4.

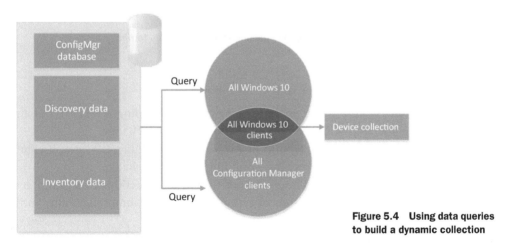

Figure 5.4 Using data queries to build a dynamic collection

INCLUDE COLLECTION

In the include collection membership option, one or more collections are defined as a member of another collection, which is similar to using nested groups in AD. This is useful when you need to be able to target multiple collections at once, but still retain the ability for granular targeting. For example, you might need to be able to update the software across two floors of a building, but need to have the option to target either floor separately or both floors together. In that case, you would create two device collections, each one representing a floor: All Systems—Building A—Level 1, and All Systems—Building A—Level 2. This gives you the ability to target systems on either floor.

To update both floors simultaneously, rather than target both floor-based collections separately, you'd create another collection called All Systems—Building A that will act as a catchall for all systems in that building. Rather than define this collection independently, you can include the previous two collections into All Systems—Building A, as shown in figure 5.5.

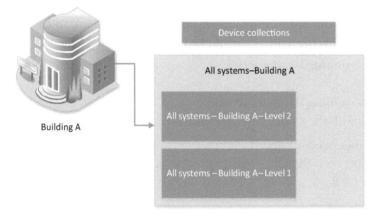

Figure 5.5   Using an include collection membership can give you terrific management granularity.

The advantages of this approach are as follows:

- Whenever the membership of All Systems—Building A—Level 1 changes, the membership of All Systems—Building A will also change.
- Whenever the membership of All Systems—Building A—Level 2 changes, the membership of All Systems—Building A will also change.
- You can continue to target any of the three collections in a granular fashion, while the structure of the collections gives you maximum flexibility and control.

EXCLUDE COLLECTION

An exclude collection membership is the direct opposite of an include collection—a collection is defined as an exclusion, rather than an inclusion.

This membership type is useful when you need to be able to treat a subset of Users or devices as a special case, without impacting the power and flexibility of using catchall collections as already described. Using the include collection example, let's say that in Building A, on Level 2, is a financial trader's office containing a pair of important systems that you want to exclude from any application, policy, or software update tasks that you might otherwise target against the All Systems—Building A Collection. In this case, you could create a collection called Financial Trading—Building A and then exclude this collection from the All Systems—Building A Collection. This way, you can still target all systems in the building while excluding the critical financial trading systems, as shown in figure 5.6.

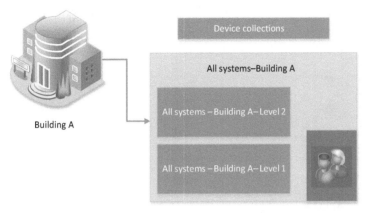

Figure 5.6   An exclude collection membership allows you to protect critical systems.

A collection can incorporate both include and exclude collection membership rules.

> **IMPORTANT NOTE** In the event that there's a conflict between an include and an exclude rule, the principle of least privilege applies, and the exclude rule takes precedence.

5.1.2   Collection limiting

Let's look at a potential management scenario. Say you're going to deploy a newly created 64-bit operating system based on Windows 10 to your environment. Your environment consists of a mix of older machines with less than 4 GB of RAM and without 64-bit processors, so you decide not to deploy the 64-bit operating system to these machines. To do this, you create a device collection with a membership of all systems with at least 4 GB of RAM, called All Systems—4GB RAM Plus. What would happen if you rolled out the new operating system to this collection?

Depending on how your environment is configured, and what devices are present, you potentially just told ConfigMgr to deploy Windows 10 across your managed servers. Why? Because servers are almost guaranteed to have more than 4 GB of RAM, so based on the collection membership query that you constructed, servers are returned as collection members as well as workstations. If you had reimaged your physical servers with Windows 10—well, let's just say that you'd have some serious explaining to do as well as a lot of late nights recovering everything. To prevent this sort of thing from happening, ConfigMgr uses Collection Limiting.

Collection Limiting requires *every* collection in ConfigMgr to take its membership from another collection. In effect, every collection is a subset of another collection. Why is this important? Looking at the preceding example, if you created the All Systems—4GB RAM Plus Collection and *limited* it to another collection that contained only desktop-class systems with the ConfigMgr agent installed, then when the All Systems—4GB RAM Plus Collection passed its query across the ConfigMgr database looking for matching data, it would return *only* desktop-class systems with the ConfigMgr agent installed with at least 4 GB of RAM, as shown in figure 5.7.

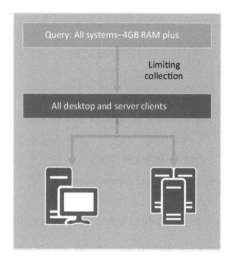
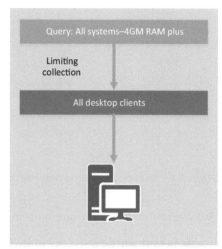

Figure 5.7 Depending on how you configure your limiting collection, the same query can produce different results.

Collection Limiting is an effective way of protecting yourself by restricting the scope of your ConfigMgr queries. It also allows you to use work that you've already undertaken, because when you create a new query, you don't have to reinvent the wheel every single time.

Now that you've had a good look at how collections are constructed, let's get stuck into building some.

5.2   *Creating a new collection*

This section focuses on the manual, wizard-driven process of creating two new collections: one for devices and the other for users. After creating the collections, you'll take a deeper look under the hood at what ConfigMgr does to make those collections happen, and what you need to know for your ongoing administrative tasks.

5.2.1 Creating a new device collection

In this section you'll create a device collection with a query-based membership (remember, this is the most common kind of collection you'll build).

To create a new device collection:

1 Navigate to "Assets and Compliance."
2 Select "Device Collections."
3 Right-click in the right-hand window pane and select "Create Device Collection."

You're presented with the Create Device Collection Wizard. As you can see, the first window has two mandatory fields: "Name" and "Limiting Collection." The collection name should be something unique and descriptive; for this collection, use `All Windows 10 Clients`.

Click the "Browse" button next to the "Limiting Collection" field. This presents you with a browser window showing the current structure of device collections. Select the built-in collection "All Desktop and Server Clients" and click "OK," as shown in figure 5.8.

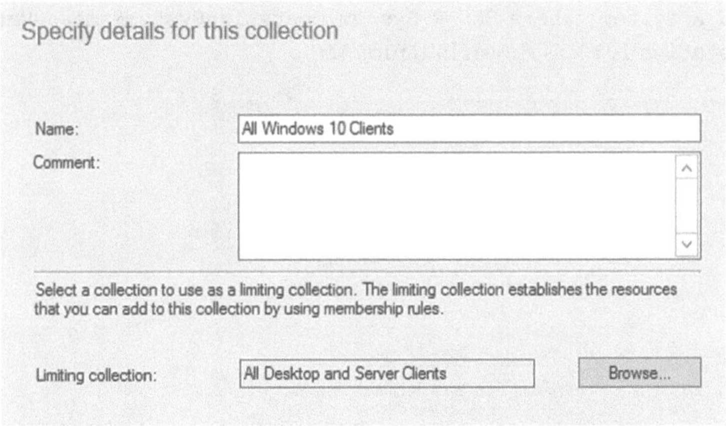

Figure 5.8   Create your new collection and set the limiting collection.

> **TIP** The Select Collection window contains a device collections drop-down option. If you look at this drop-down menu, you'll see that only device collections can be selected at this time. This is because a device collection can't be limited to a user collection, and vice versa. But for other tasks, such as application deployment, you can deploy to either user or device collections, so both options will be available in the drop-down list.

Click "Next" in the wizard, and you'll be taken to the Membership Rules page. This is where you specify how the collection is to be populated. From the "Add Rule" drop-down, select "Query Rule." Construct the query as follows:

1   In the "Name" text box, type `qry-Windows10OperatingSystem`.

2   Click the "Edit Query Statement" button.

3   Click the Criteria tab.

4   Click the sunburst icon to create a new criterion.

5   From the "Criterion Type" drop-down list, select "Simple Value."

6   Click "Select."

7   From the "Attribute Class" drop-down list, select "System Resource" (skip the "Alias" field).

8   From the "Attribute" drop-down list, select "Operating System Name and Version." Then click "OK."

9   From the "Operator" drop-down list, select "Is like."

10   Click the "Value" button.

11   Select the "Microsoft Windows NT Workstation 10" option.

12   Change the "Values" field to `%Workstation 10%` (the % characters are used as wildcards, so that the search returns a wider range of results).

13   Click "OK" multiple times until you get back to the Query Rule Properties window. The text in the query statement field should read `select * fromSMS_R_System where SMS_R_System.OperatingSystemNameandVersion = "%Workstation 10%"`, as shown in figure 5.9.

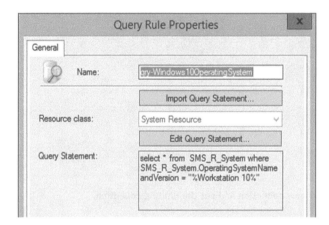

Figure 5.9   Make sure your query rule looks like this.

14   Click "OK."

15   Back in the Membership Rules window, tick the "Use incremental updates for this collection" check box.

16   Click the "Summary" button.

17   Click "Next" and then "Close."

Congratulations, you've just created a query-based device collection!

Creating a device collection populated by a dynamic query is a multistep process in PowerShell (as it is in the console!), so rather than document all the code here, you can find it all in .\powershell\New-CMDeviceCollection.ps1. This script uses a slightly different query to build the collection membership rule, in that it returns a subset of discovered data rather than everything, but the core functionality is exactly the same.

Navigate back to the Device Collections window, and you'll see the newly created collection. Notice that the icon next to the collection is overlaid with a small egg-timer icon. This indicates that the collection is performing a full update. This also explains why the membership count is zero: there's nothing wrong with the collection query, it's just in the process of querying the ConfigMgr database for the first time.

Refresh the console a couple of times until the egg timer disappears and the membership count is incremented. Right-click the collection and select "Show Membership." This opens a new node under Device Collections, where you can see which systems have been populated into the new collection. The same process works for all collections.

WHICH LOG? The colleval.log file shows all collections that are in the active process of evaluating their memberships. If you're seeing collections that should be updating but that don't seem to be reflecting the correct information in the ConfigMgr console, this is an important place to look so that you can ascertain that collection evaluation is taking place properly.

> **Try It Now—Create a new device collection**
> Go through the steps detailed in section 5.2.1 to create a new query-based device collection that will return all Windows 10 clients.

5.2.2 *Creating a new user collection*

The process of creating a new user collection is virtually identical to that for creating a new device collection, but because users and devices have different object properties, the options for creating a user collection aren't the same. In this section you'll create a user collection by copying in the WQL query directly.

To create a new user collection:

1. Navigate to "Assets and Compliance."
2. Select "User Collections."
3. Right-click in the right-hand window pane and select "Create User Collection."
4. For "Name," use `All ConfigMgr Lab Users`.
5. For the "Limiting Collection" field, choose "All Users and User Groups." Note that you can choose only from user collections.
6. In the Membership Rules page, select Add Rule > Query Rule.

In the same way that you created the device collection query, you'll create one for the user collection too. But this time you'll do things a little differently:

1 In the "Name" field, type `ConfigMgr Lab Users`.
2 Click the "Edit Query Statement" button.
3 Click the "Show Query Language" option.
4 Paste in the following WQL code, shown in figure 5.10:

```
select * from SMS_R_User where SMS_R_User.UserGroupName =
"MOL\\ConfigMgr Lab Users"
```

(The double backslash is needed due to its use in WQL as an escape character.)

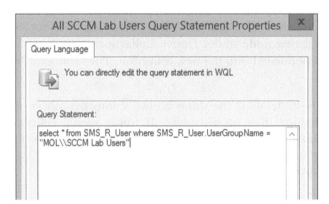

Figure 5.10   Editing the query directly in WQL is a quick and efficient way to create a query.

5 Click the "Show Query Design" button and select the Criteria tab.
6 Verify that a criterion has been created. Click "OK."
7 Click "OK" again to get back to the Membership Rules page. Tick the "Use incremental updates for this collection" check box.
8 Click the "Summary" button.
9 Click "Next" and then "Close."

You've now created a user collection, built on a query that you created by copying in the WQL query directly, rather than needing to select all the query options yourself.

> **Try It Now—Create a new user collection**
> Work through the steps in section 5.2.2 to create a new user collection that will return members of the Active Directory group ConfigMgr Lab Users.
>
> Try creating a new user in AD and adding it to this group. How quickly does the new user appear in the user collection?

5.3 Understanding the WMI Query Language

As you've already seen, the query builder is a useful, graphical way of constructing your ConfigMgr queries, but under the hood, ConfigMgr is translating everything in the GUI into WQL. Therefore, if you know enough about WQL, you can quickly construct complex queries without having to manually click through the query builder every time.

Why is this important? Many queries that you're likely to build during day-to-day administration will be subtle variations of each other. When you're doing a lot of work with collections and queries, it's important to be able to rapidly create accurate queries, and the best way to do that is to take advantage of work that you've already performed in the past. Additionally, after you start working more regularly with queries, you'll be exposed to the wealth of data that ConfigMgr is capable of discovering about systems and users, which in turn will help you in your everyday admin tasks.

> **Build your own query library**
>
> Regardless of how you construct a query in ConfigMgr (via the query builder or using WQL directly), after you've finished the query and it's working the way you want it to, it's good practice to always go back into the query, click "Show Query Language," and copy and paste the WQL code out.
>
> Copy the WQL code from each query into a collaboration tool such as OneNote along with a description of what it does. That way, you'll start to build up a repository of WQL knowledge that you can refer back to when building new queries. It's also incredibly useful for knowledge-sharing among colleagues, for maintaining a sense of change control in your ConfigMgr environment, and for not having to start from scratch each time you build a clean ConfigMgr environment.

Let's take a deeper look at how WQL queries are constructed.

5.3.1 Creating a basic query

Like many query languages, WQL uses a structural syntax that's similar to basic English phrases, so coming to grips with the flow of a WQL statement isn't too onerous. Also, it's not a programming language, so if you don't have a background in programming or coding (like me), that's no barrier to entry.

Let's take a look at this simple query:

```
SELECT * FROM SMS_R_System WHERE OperatingSystemNameAndVersion LIKE '%Server
    6.3'
```

The purpose of this statement is to return all systems that are running Windows Server 2012 R2. The query can be broken down as follows:

1 SELECT * means that the query will return all properties for all instances. In other words, "Select/Return Everything."

2   FROM directs the query to look at a particular Windows Management Instrumentation (WMI) class as the data source for the query.

3   SMS_R_System is the WMI class being used. In your lab environment, this class exists under the root\sms\site_PS1 WMI namespace. SMS_R_System is a dynamic repository of data that's populated with discovery data. So those discovery methods that you enabled earlier in the lab are working behind the scenes to populate this class.

4   WHERE indicates that you're looking for a particular attribute (a subset of data) in the SMS_R_System class; it acts as a filter to restrict the data returned.

5   OperatingSystemNameAndVersion is the particular attribute that the query is filtering on—in this case, the name and version of all discovered operating systems.

6   LIKE is an operator indicating that the query is looking for a particular value in the OperatingSystemNameAndVersion attribute, but that the value provided in the query won't be an exact match. LIKE tells the query to perform a fuzzy search. You have several options for operators, including "greater than," "not equal to," and "uppercase is like."

7   Finally, '%Server 6.3' is the value that the query is searching for. The percentage symbol acts as a wildcard, which in this case means that all operating systems with a name ending with Server 6.3 will be returned in the results.

TIP   When searching for a particular version of a Windows operating system, the version is the Windows kernel version, not the descriptive version. For example, Windows 8.1 is kernel version 6.3, whereas Windows 10 is kernel version 10. To find out which kernel your version of Windows is running, open a command prompt and type ver. Alternatively, open a PowerShell window and type Get-CimInstance -ClassName Win32_OperatingSystem | Select-Object version.

Try It Now—Create a device collection using WQL

Create a new device collection called All Windows Server 2012 R2 Clients Populate the collection by using the preceding WQL query, without using the query-builder GUI. Make sure that you set the limiting collection properly, so that only servers with the ConfigMgr client are returned by the query.

5.3.2   *Using multiple attributes*

You can now take that basic query and turn it into something a little more complex. Let's say you need to build a query based on two criteria: the first is the operating system name and version, and the second is the system name.

In this example, you want the query to return only those matching operating systems whose system names start with *CLIENT*. In this case, the query looks something like this:

```
SELECT * FROM SMS_R_System WHERE SMS_R_System.OperatingSystemNameandVersion
    ➡LIKE "%Workstation 10%" AND SMS_R_System.NetbiosName LIKE "CLIENT%"
```

Note that the class is still `SMS_R_System`, indicating that both attributes in the query exist within this same WMI class. Also, each attribute (`OperatingSystemNameand-Version` and `NetbiosName`) has been appended to `SMS_R_System`. This acts as an explicit path to the WMI attribute. You're telling the query that multiple attributes are going to be referenced, and you're allowing no room for ambiguity as to the location of those attributes. It makes the query more robust.

Finally, the `AND` operator lets you add another attribute and value into the query. Using `AND` means that the values for both attributes must be met in order for the query to return a result. For example, if the `SMS_R_System` class contained discovery data about a system called CLIENT04 but that system was running Windows 8.1 (Windows kernel version 6.3), then the query wouldn't return that system in the results. But if you used the `OR` operator instead of `AND`, CLIENT04 would be returned.

5.3.3 *Querying multiple sources*

Sometimes you need the main query to run against a set of data not contained within the main WMI class. For example, let's say that you want to build a query that will return all systems that don't have Microsoft Outlook installed. Perhaps you're planning to deploy Outlook in your environment and wish to target only those machines that definitely don't have it installed (which is a rational thing to do!).

The trick is that the list of installed applications on each machine isn't discovery data, but rather inventory data. The ConfigMgr agent has run inventory tasks across the system and reported the inventory data back to the ConfigMgr server, which in turn stores it in a different WMI class to the discovery data—in this case, in `SMS_G_System_Add_Remove_Programs`.

In order to cater to these multiple data sources, you'll use what is known as a subselect query—a query within a query. For this example, the entire query looks something like this:

```
SELECT *
  FROM SMS_R_System
    WHERE
        ResourceID NOT IN
        (
            SELECT ResourceID
            FROM SMS_G_System_Add_Remove_Programs
            WHERE DisplayName LIKE '%Outlook%'
        )
```

I've broken the query into multiple lines to make it easier to read. As you can see, the core query is still a basic query, looking for system names (ResourceID) in SMS_R_System. The complexity here is that there's a subselect query that first looks at the inventory data contained within SMS_G_System_Add_Remove_Programs for all systems with Outlook installed. The resulting names are returned to the original query, which then invokes the NOT IN operator to finally return all the system names (ResourceID) that aren't found in the subselect query.

In other words, all systems that don't have Outlook installed. Neat, right?

5.3.4   *Combining data from multiple sources*

The last type of query you're going to look at is one that takes data from two sources, and then presents them both together as a single result. This is called *joining*.

The difference between a join and a subselect is that in a subselect, you use a subquery from a different source to narrow the scope of the main query. A join uses at least two queries, one from each data source, and both are of equal importance. One isn't a subselect of the other.

The example you'll look at is a query that returns all systems with internal batteries. This is a query method used to determine whether a system is a laptop/notebook/tablet or a desktop. At its most basic level, the result you're looking for is something like this:

```
SELECT *
    FROM SMS_R_System
    WHERE
        SMS_G_System_Battery.DeviceID LIKE '%'
```

But this isn't going to work because SMS_R_System and SMS_G_System_Battery are two completely separate WMI classes. The query offers no instruction as to how to bring these two disparate data sources together.

The way to achieve this is to inform the query that there are two data sources and—in order to present the results in a coherent manner—which attributes should be used as a common factor between them. The end result looks something like this:

```
SELECT DISTINCT *
    FROM SMS_R_System
    INNER JOIN SMS_G_System_Battery ON
        SMS_G_System_Battery.ResourceId = SMS_R_System.ResourceId
    WHERE
        SMS_G_System_Battery.DeviceID LIKE '%'
```

This query is informed that the first query against SMS_R_System will also have data brought in from SMS_G_System_Battery, via the INNER JOIN operator. The ON operator informs the query which attributes will be used to match results from one WMI class with the other. In this case, both WMI classes use the ResourceID attribute, so this will be used to line up the results.

The result is a list of systems known to have an internal battery. The use of `SELECT DISTINCT *` rather than the usual `SELECT *` means that only unique results will be returned, and duplicate `ResourceID` entries from `SMS_R_System` will be ignored.

5.4 Managing collections

As a ConfigMgr environment becomes larger and more complex, the number of collections that are created and need to be maintained inevitably increases. This is as it should be, but you need to be aware of a few things so that your collection structure doesn't end up unmanageable and, ultimately, becoming a problem in its own right.

This section explores how your collections can negatively impact the ConfigMgr server as well as your administrative experience, and what you can do to keep a tight rein on your collections.

5.4.1 Use folders

Do you keep all of your files in a completely flat structure? Of course not; it's not logical, and it would make it impossible to find anything. The same holds true for collections. Organizational folders are a convenient way to keep your collections logically structured.

CREATING A NEW FOLDER
To create a new folder:

1 Right-click either "User Collections" or "Device Collections," and select "Folder."
2 Click the "Create Folder" button.
3 Enter a name for the new folder, such as `Application Deployment`, and click "OK."

You now have a new folder underneath the collections root, as shown in figure 5.11.

Figure 5.11   Organizational folders are a great way to keep collection sprawl in check.

EDITING OR DELETING AN EXISTING FOLDER
To change or delete an existing folder:

1 Right-click the folder and select "Folder."
2 Click the "Create," "Move," "Delete," or "Rename" option, as appropriate.

Folders themselves don't have any editable properties; they aren't used for security, and they don't apply any properties or settings to the collections contained within them. They're there solely for your benefit. In general, it's a good idea to avoid creating folder levels that are too deep; two or three levels down is generally fine.

Important notes on organizational folders

If you select a folder and create a new collection, the collection will automatically appear within the folder.

If you select a folder and create a new folder, this will appear as a subfolder.

You can move a folder around after you create it, and any collections contained within that folder will also be moved.

If a folder has any collections within it, you can't delete the folder.

From a PowerShell perspective, folders are a little tricky, as there aren't any cmdlets that let you directly interact with them. You can still use PowerShell, however, and you can find the relevant code in .\powershell\New-CMOrganizationalFolder.ps1.

Try It Now—Organizational folders

Follow the steps in this section to create three new folders at the root of Device Collections: Application Deployment, Operating System Deployment, and Software Update Deployment.

As you create the folders, consider the collection structure in your own production environment. Are organizational folders in use? If so, how have they been created and structured? If not, could the use of folders improve everyday administration?

5.4.2   *Be aware of collection updating*

As you've been working through this lab, you might have noticed that when you create a new collection, there's an option to set a schedule for a full collection update and also one to enable incremental updates, as shown in figure 5.12.

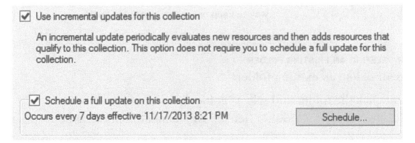

Figure 5.12   Each collection can be updated on a schedule or updated incrementally— or both, or neither.

WORKING WITH FULL-UPDATE SCHEDULES

A full update does what it says on the label; the rules governing membership of the collection are completely reevaluated according to the schedule. The default is every seven days, and you can increase or decrease the aggressiveness of that timing.

When considering full-update schedules, the two most important factors are as follows:

- What is the data source used to determine collection membership?
- What is the update schedule of the limiting collection set to?

In the case of the data source, consider a collection that uses a query looking at data stored in an SMS_G_System WMI class. This data is populated via the hardware and software inventory agents in the ConfigMgr client, which run by default every seven days. There's little point in scheduling a full update on the collection to run more frequently than every seven days, because the source data is unlikely to have been updated.

In the case of the limiting collection, if you create a new collection with a full-update schedule that's more aggressive than that of its limiting collection (and assuming that the limiting collection doesn't have incremental updates enabled), then your collection will show only new memberships after the Limiting collection has also been updated. This is a trap that many administrators fall into: creating a new collection and then updating it aggressively when it doesn't show the membership they were expecting, but then failing to look at any discrepancies of timing between the collection and its Limiting collection as the source of the problem.

WORKING WITH INCREMENTAL UPDATES

When a collection has incremental updates enabled, it will check for any changes since the last full update approximately every 10 minutes. The benefit is that collections built on data sources that are constantly updated (for example, AD group membership) or that need to be refreshed quickly don't have to wait for a full update to be run, and the full-update schedule doesn't need to be set aggressively high.

For example, a collection that looks at the membership of an AD group can be left to perform a full update every seven days, and enabling incremental updates will keep its membership constantly refreshed.

Incremental updates strike the balance between functionality and performance. A full update uses both processing and storage resources, and having too many over-aggressive full-update schedules can result in degraded server performance overall, even leading to the server being in a constant state of updating collections, resulting in potentially significant administrative problems.

5.4.3 *Move collections between hierarchies*

If you have a complex structure of collections, creating a backup repository may be worthwhile in case you ever want to quickly re-create them in another hierarchy—potentially in the event of rebuilding your ConfigMgr environment, or to test a production collection in a lab environment.

Collections can be individually exported and imported. To export a collection:

1 Right-click the collection (you can also select multiple collections, and then right-click) and click the "Export" option.
2 Click "Next."
3 Select the check box next to each collection you want to export and click "Next."
4 Select "The collection data will be saved into a Managed Object Format (MOF) file." Enter a path and filename for the MOF file, as shown in figure 5.13.

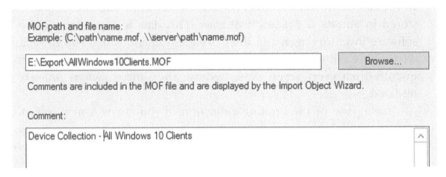

MOF path and file name:
Example: (C:\path\name.mof, \\server\path\name.mof)

E:\Export\AllWindows10Clients.MOF | Browse...

Comments are included in the MOF file and are displayed by the Import Object Wizard.

Comment:

Device Collection - All Windows 10 Clients

Figure 5.13 Export a built collection and then a different ConfigMgr Site or environment.

5 Click the "Summary" button.
6 Click "Next" and then click "Close."

TIP You can open the MOF file in a text editor such as Notepad++ to get a sense of its internal structure.

To export the collection by using PowerShell, use the following command:

```
Export-CMDevicecollection `
-Name 'All Windows 10 Clients' `
-ExportFilePath 'E:\Export\AllWindows10Clients.MOF'
```

To import a collection from a MOF file, do the following:

1 Right-click the root of either user collections or device collections—you can't import a collection directly into a folder—and then select "Import collections."
2 Click "Next."
3 Click the "Browse for the exported MOF file" button. Then click "Next."
4 Review the collection details to be imported.
5 Click the "Summary" button.
6 Click "Next" and then click "Close."

To perform the import with PowerShell, use the following command:

```
Import-CMDevicecollection -ImportFilePath 'E:\Export\AllWindows10Clients.MOF'
```

At this point, right-click the newly imported collection and select "Properties." In the General window, you'll notice that the collection ID has the site code prefix of the site you just imported the collection into. Even though the collection originally had an ID with a different site code prefix, this property isn't exported because this could cause conflict with existing collections.

Additionally, the limiting collection may or may not be populated. If it isn't, a warning icon is shown. The reason it's empty is that the original limiting collection doesn't exist in the destination hierarchy. For example, a collection that's limited to All Desktop and Sever Clients will automatically have its limiting collection populated on import, because its limiting collection is a built-in collection that's present in every ConfigMgr hierarchy. But if the limiting collection is a custom collection that doesn't exist in the destination hierarchy, the property won't be populated.

Without a limiting collection, the newly imported collection won't function. There's no risk to the ConfigMgr hierarchy: the collection will function only after an administrator manually specifies a new limiting collection.

> **Try It Now—Import a collection**
> Follow the steps in this section to import two new device collections into your lab environment.
>
> Import the file from .\mof\ConfigMgrLabcollections.MOF.
>
> Then take a look at the properties of each collection, in particular the WQL statement controlling the membership. Copy the queries out for your own reference.

5.5 Lab

Create a new device collection populated with a query that looks for all systems running Windows Server 2012 R2. Use PowerShell to export the collection after you've created it.

5.6 Ideas for on your own

Using collections and WQL to organize and maintain ConfigMgr data has been around for many years. As a result, plenty of examples of WQL queries are scattered across the internet, which administrators just like yourself have blogged about, documented, and tweaked. So if you're just starting down the path of understanding WQL, remember that a wealth of information is out there.

As a start, look at the example queries contained within this TechNet article, specifically the one that queries for ConfigMgr clients of a specific type (for example, Windows clients or Mac OS X clients): http://technet.microsoft.com/en-us/library/gg712323.aspx#BKMK_Example.

Which of these queries would be useful for your own production environment?

Configuring ConfigMgr clients

The Configuration Manager client—the software package you deployed in chapter 4—is a powerful piece of kit, ready to help you in your daily administrative efforts. Once installed, it will regularly talk back to its assigned ConfigMgr management point, which is a site server role that acts as the main communication point between the ConfigMgr client and the ConfigMgr site server, checking whether there's anything new it needs to be aware of. Welcome to the world of client policy.

Imagine that you want to enable your first-level help-desk operatives to remotely connect to a user's machine in order to assist them with a support call; that's something that you would use a client policy for. Now let's say that a subset of your user base (such as senior managers) doesn't want help-desk operators to be able to remotely connect to their machines. In this scenario, you'd use granular client policies, making sure that only the right policies are applied to the right users and devices, reflecting the needs of your organization.

As shown in figure 6.1, in this chapter you'll look at the default policy options that every ConfigMgr client receives when it's first installed, how that policy is received and updated, how to modify the default policy, and how to create and deploy custom client policies.

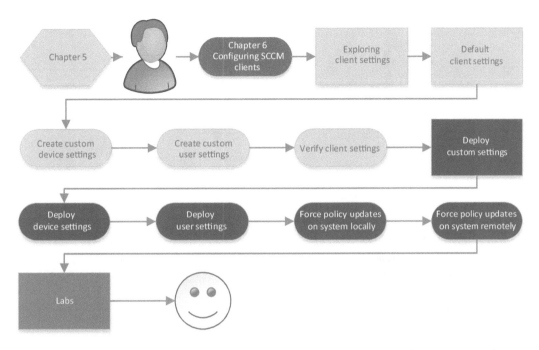

Figure 6.1 This chapter is all about making your deployed ConfigMgr clients do exactly what you want them to.

6.1   *Exploring client settings*

ConfigMgr client settings work in a manner similar to Active Directory Group Policy. Settings, or policies, are centrally defined, and an agent on each system (the Config-Mgr client, in this case) communicates with the ConfigMgr server hierarchy to retrieve its assigned policy set, and then checks back at regular intervals for any new or updated policies, as shown in figure 6.2. Settings define behavior within a ConfigMgr hierarchy—for example, how often a managed device should run inventory scans and which file types those scans should include, whether to manage software updates, and how remote access to managed systems should be configured.

Client settings are divided into two distinct types: device settings and user settings. As the names indicate, device settings are specific to managing the behavior of devices, whereas user settings are relevant for only the logged-on user. Let's take a deeper look at how settings are constructed and deployed.

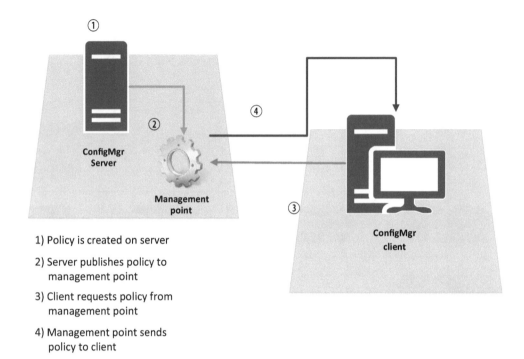

1) Policy is created on server

2) Server publishes policy to management point

3) Client requests policy from management point

4) Management point sends policy to client

Figure 6.2   The workflow by which a ConfigMgr client obtains a policy from the ConfigMgr server

6.1.1   Using Default Client Settings

You'll find client settings in the Administration page of the ConfigMgr console. It's important enough to have its own dedicated, top-level section.

As you can see in figure 6.3, at present only one settings policy is defined: the Default Client Settings policy.

The main page has descriptive columns, which are explained in table 6.1.

Client Settings 1 items

Icon	Name	Type	Priority	Deployments
	Default Client Settings	Default	10000	0

Figure 6.3   Each newly built ConfigMgr always contains the Default Client Settings policy group.

Table 6.1 Client settings columns in the ConfigMgr console

Client settings column	Definition
Icon/Type	Shows whether a settings group is the default set, or whether it applies to users or devices.
Name	The descriptive name of the settings group.
Priority	The importance of the settings group in relation to other custom settings. Settings with high priorities take precedence over settings with lower priorities. The Default Client Settings group has the lowest priority of 10000.
Deployments	Shows how many collections the settings group is applied to. The Default Client Settings group is automatically available to all devices and users, and never needs to be deployed manually.

GET YOUR PRIORITIES STRAIGHT!   Although it has a priority of 10000, the default client policy has the lowest priority, not the highest (confusingly). Custom policies in ConfigMgr have a lower number (for example, 1, 2) but a higher priority. Settings are combined across policies, with settings from higher-priority policies taking precedence. Therefore, the lower the number, the higher the priority. Think of it like winners on an Olympic podium—the athlete with a number 1 on their podium definitely won!

When a ConfigMgr client talks to its assigned management point, in the absence of the existence of any other policies, it'll always receive the default client policy. This is a built-in policy set that defines the default behavior of every ConfigMgr client in the hierarchy, and contains both device and user settings.

The default policy is there so that every ConfigMgr client and user in your environment has a basic understanding of what to do. Without this, a client would be effectively disabled until it receives an admin-defined policy. This way, all clients have a basic, default level of functionality.

Right-click "Default Client Settings" and select "Properties." As you can see in figure 6.4, the left pane contains all the major settings sections, and the right pane shows all the configurable properties for each section.

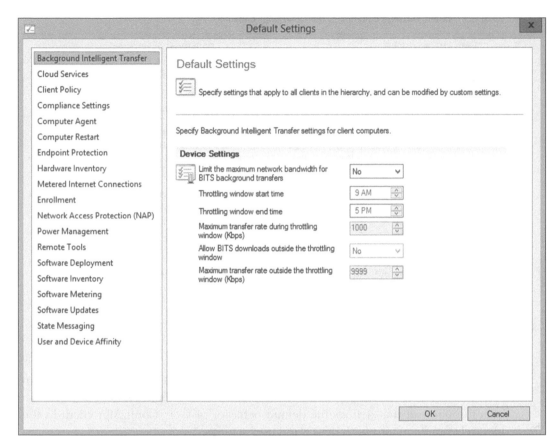

Figure 6.4   All the configurable properties in the Default Client Settings group

As you'll see, ConfigMgr has a *lot* of configurable client settings. At this stage, don't worry if you're not certain what they all do. Table 6.2 gives an overview of the settings that you'll need to work with in order to be immediately effective.

Table 6.2   ConfigMgr client settings

Section	Settings type	Description
Client Policy	Device	Controls how often the ConfigMgr client checks back for policy changes
Computer Agent	Device	Controls communication between the ConfigMgr client and the ConfigMgr server
Hardware Inventory	Device	Enables/disables and configures hardware inventory on ConfigMgr clients
Remote Tools	Device	Enables/disables and configures tools that can remotely connect to the ConfigMgr client

Table 6.2 ConfigMgr client settings *(continued)*

Section	Settings type	Description
Software Inventory	Device	Enables/disables and configures software inventory on ConfigMgr clients
Software Updates	Device	Enables/disables and configures the ConfigMgr client to handle software updates and patching
User and Device Affinity	Device/User	Configures the thresholds for UDA and whether users can nominate their primary device

You can't remove any of the sections from the Default Client Settings group, but you can configure the properties within any of the sections as required.

TIP Microsoft TechNet has some detailed documentation on client settings. It's worth having a read: http://technet.microsoft.com/en-us/library/gg682067.aspx.

6.1.2 Knowing when to change the Default Client Settings

It might be tempting to do all of your settings configuration within the Default Client Settings group, but you can end up painting yourself into a corner. Because settings groups are applied to collections, the settings throughout your ConfigMgr environment can be deployed in a controlled, granular fashion.

Doing all of your work in the Default Client Settings group will lead to an overreliance on a single settings group that will in turn prove to be cumbersome and inflexible. Using custom settings allows the Default Client Settings to stay in a more-or-less pristine state, which is useful if you ever need to roll back changes.

There are two main reasons to edit properties in the Default Client Settings group:

- You need the setting to apply to all systems without exception, such as the organization name in the Computer Agent section.
- You need a policy to apply to a machine as soon as it talks to ConfigMgr for the first time, without having to wait for ConfigMgr to place it in the right collection.

A good example of this is the Endpoint Protection antivirus; if you're going to enable this via ConfigMgr policy, you'll want this enabled as soon as possible.

Apart from those two exceptions, I prefer to configure all my settings by using custom settings, which you'll tackle in section 6.3.

6.1.3 Changing the Default Client Settings

Now you'll make some basic changes to your Default Client Settings group to configure the default behavior of all ConfigMgr devices and users in your lab environment:

1 Right-click the "Default Client Settings" group and select "Properties."
2 Navigate to the Computer Agent section.

3 In the right-hand pane, change "Organization name displayed in Software Center" to MoL ConfigMgr Lab, as shown in figure 6.5.

4 Click "OK" and close the Properties window.

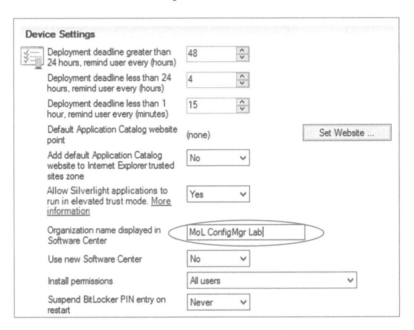

Figure 6.5   Change the default organization name for all ConfigMgr clients.

To make the change using PowerShell, use the following command:

```
Set-CMClientSetting `
-Name 'Default Client Agent Settings' `
-BrandingTitle 'MOL ConfigMgr Lab'
```

The next time your ConfigMgr clients check back with the management point role on CM01 (every 60 minutes, by default), they'll pick up the updated policy and apply the change.

> **WHICH LOG?**   When a policy is updated, you can see the request and the changes in the PolicyAgent.log and PolicyEvaluator.log files.

Now let's move on to creating and deploying custom settings.

Try It Now—Edit Default Client Settings

Follow the steps in this section to change the organization name for all ConfigMgr clients to `MoL ConfigMgr Lab`.

Look through each major settings section to become familiar with what each section is responsible for. Think about your own production organization in terms of whether you want to deploy any settings to all clients (potentially both desktops and servers) and which ones you would want to apply in a more granular, controlled fashion.

6.2 Creating custom settings

Unlike the Default Client Settings group, which can contain both user and device settings, any custom settings that you create must contain *either* user *or* device settings, and can't contain both. Additionally, settings for devices can be deployed only to device collections, and vice versa for user settings. This is to maintain administrative separation between users and devices and to ensure that only the relevant policies are applied.

In this section, you'll create two custom settings: one for devices that will control software inventory, and another one for users that will enable privileged users to nominate their own primary device. As you work throughout the book, you'll keep coming back to custom settings in order to enable more functionality.

6.2.1 Create custom device settings

The first custom setting you'll create is one to enable software inventory so that you can start to get a sense of the software that has been installed throughout the environment. To be more accurate, software inventory is already enabled by default in the ConfigMgr client, but it's not configured to inventory anything in particular, so when the inventory component of the agent runs, it won't return anything back to the ConfigMgr server.

To create the custom settings:

1 Right-click "Client Settings" and select "Create Custom Client Device Settings," as shown in figure 6.6.

2 For the name, enter `Desktop Software Inventory Settings`.

Figure 6.6 Creating new custom settings for devices in the ConfigMgr console

3 Under "Select and configure the custom settings for client devices," select the "Software Inventory" check box.

4 Software Inventory appears as an option in the left pane. Select the "Software Inventory" option.

5 In the right-hand pane, next to "Inventory these file types," select "Set Types."

6 Next to "File types," click the sunburst icon to create a new file type, as shown in figure 6.7.

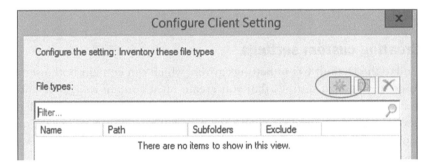

Figure 6.7   Create a new entry to inventory file types on your clients.

7 In the "Name" field, type *.exe and leave all other options unchanged, as shown in figure 6.8; then click "OK."

Figure 6.8   Choose to inventory all application files (.exe).

8 Click "OK" again. The software inventory properties now look like those shown in figure 6.9.

9 Click "OK." Your device settings are ready to be deployed.

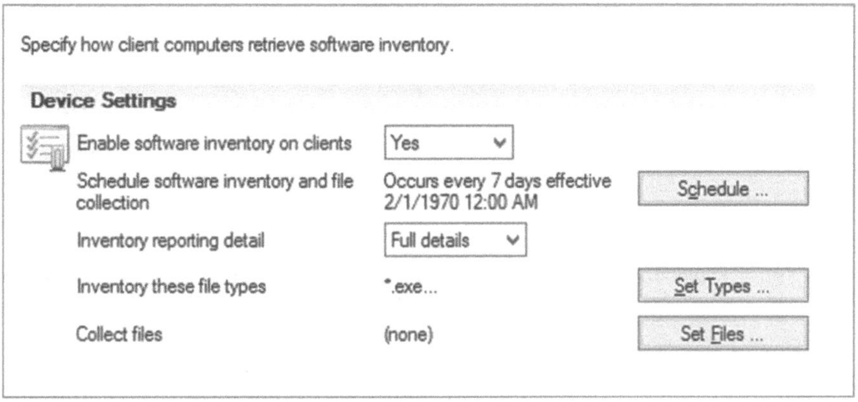

Figure 6.9 Your device inventory settings are ready to go.

You can perform this process with PowerShell, although it takes a couple of lines of code, which you can find in .\powershell\Set-CMClientInventorySettings.ps1.

You'll tackle the deployment shortly, so that you can monitor the deployment process. For the moment, let's create some custom user settings.

> **Try It Now—Create custom device settings**
>
> Follow the instructions in section 6.2.1 to create a new device settings group that will enable software inventory of all application files.

6.2.2 *Create custom user settings*

In this section, you'll configure settings for users, which allow certain users in Config-Mgr to nominate their own primary device in User Device Affinity (remember that you tackled UDA in chapter 4). By default, this functionality is disabled, because if you're using primary user/primary device functionality in UDA, it's not a great plan to automatically allow every user to nominate which machine is theirs. But you might want to give certain privileged users access to do this.

To create custom user settings:

1 Right-click in "Client Settings" and select "Create Custom Client User Settings."
2 For the "Name," enter Admin User UDA Settings.
3 Under "Select and configure the custom settings for client devices," select the "User and Device Affinity" check box.
4 User and Device Affinity appears as an option in the left pane. Select that option.
5 Next to "Allow user to define their primary devices," change the value from "No" to "Yes," as shown in figure 6.10.

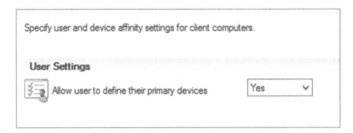

Figure 6.10   Use client settings to give greater UDA functionality to certain users.

6   Click "OK" to close the settings.

To create the policy using PowerShell, enter the following two lines of code:

```
New-CMClientSetting -Name 'Admin User UDA Settings' -Type User
Set-CMClientSetting -Name 'Admin User UDA Settings' -AllowUserAffinity $true
```

You should now have three settings in the Client Settings window: the Default Client Settings and the two custom settings that you just created, as shown in figure 6.11. Click the Priority column to sort the settings by priority, from highest to lowest (remembering that the lower the number, the higher the priority).

Client Settings 3 items

Icon	Name	Type	Priority	Deployments
	Desktop Software Inventory Settings	Device	1	0
	Admin User UDA Settings	User	2	0
	Default Client Settings	Default	10000	0

Figure 6.11   Settings with a high priority take precedence over those with a lower priority of the same type (for example, device or user settings).

Try It Now—Create custom user settings
Follow the steps in section 6.2.2 to create custom user settings that will be used to configure UDA for administrative users.

Now that you've created two custom policies, it's time to deploy them into your Config-Mgr environment. But before you do that, let's take a moment to check your work.

6.3 Deploying custom settings

Like just about everything in ConfigMgr, in order to deploy custom settings, you need to use collections. It's not possible to deploy settings against one particular computer or user object; rather, you must always use collections as the deployment target, even if that collection contains only one device or user.

In your lab environment, you now have two custom settings that need to be deployed. The Desktop Software Inventory Settings policy enables the software inventory component of the ConfigMgr client, but in your environment you want to enable this only on desktop systems rather than on servers.

> **TIP**   In a lab environment it might not matter much, but in a production environment you might want to either exclude servers from software inventory or apply a different type of inventory policy in order to prevent undue performance impact. Therefore, the collection you want to deploy these settings against should reflect this requirement.

6.3.1 Deploying device settings

The Admin User UDA settings will enable UDA functionality for privileged users, but in order to do this, you need a way to define those users by means of a collection.

To deploy Desktop Software Inventory Settings, do the following:

1   Right-click "Desktop Software Inventory Settings" and select "Deploy."
2   In the Select Collection window, choose "All Windows 10 Clients," as shown in figure 6.12, and then click "OK."

Figure 6.12   Device settings must be deployed to device collections, and vice versa for user settings.

3   Back in the Client Settings window, select "Desktop Software Inventory Settings" and then select the Deployments tab (bottom of the window). As shown in figure 6.13, you'll see that the settings are deployed to the All Windows 10 Clients Collection.

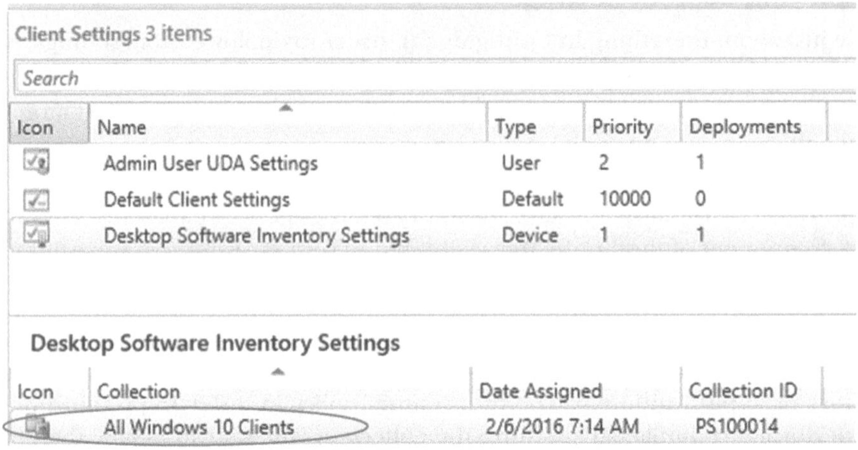

Figure 6.13   The Deployments tab shows you which collections your settings are deployed against.

To deploy the setting using PowerShell, use the following command:

```
Start-CMClientSettingDeployment `
-ClientSettingName 'Desktop Software Inventory Settings' `
-CollectionName 'All Windows 10 Clients'
```

Next you'll create a user collection and deploy user settings against it.

6.3.2   *Deploying user settings*

Before you can deploy the Admin User UDA Settings group, you need a collection to deploy it to. In your lab environment, you don't have a collection set up yet, so let's quickly do that. In a live production environment, you'll likely have collections already set up that you can use.

CREATE A COLLECTION

To create the collection:

1 Go to "Assets and Compliance" and select "Users."
2 Right-click "MOL\Marcus" and select Add Selected Items > Add Selected Items to New User Collection.
3 In the New Collection details, enter ConfigMgr Lab Admin Users as the name, and choose "All ConfigMgr Lab Users" as the limiting collection. Click "Next."
4 On the Membership Rules page, you'll see that Marcus has been added via Direct Membership. Uncheck the "Schedule a full update on this collection" option. (This is a static collection, so it doesn't need to be updated.)
5 Click "Summary," "Next," and then "Close."
6 Click "User Collections," and you'll see the newly created user collection with a membership count of 1.

DEPLOY THE USER SETTINGS

Now that the collection has been created, you can deploy the user settings. To do this:

1 Go to Administration > Client Settings.
2 Right-click "Admin User UDA Settings" and select "Deploy."
3 In the Select Collection window, choose "ConfigMgr Lab Admin Users" and click "OK."
4 Open the Deployments tab to make sure that the settings have been deployed.

To deploy the setting using PowerShell, use the following command:

```
Start-CMClientSettingDeployment `
-ClientSettingName 'Admin User UDA Settings' `
-CollectionName 'ConfigMgr Lab Admin Users'
```

> **Try It Now—Deploy custom settings**
> Work through the steps in section 6.3.2 to deploy the custom device settings and custom user settings to the relevant collections.

6.3.3 *Verify deployed settings*

In a complex production environment, any given device or user could have many settings applied, and working out the results of all these policies can be tricky.

Fortunately, the ConfigMgr console has a useful tool to assist, called Resultant Client Settings. To see it in action, do the following:

1 In the ConfigMgr console, navigate to Assets and Compliance > Devices.
2 Right-click "CLIENT01" and select Client Settings > Resultant Client Settings.
3 You'll see a window that looks similar to the Client Settings window, as shown in figure 6.14.
4 Navigate to "Software Inventory," and you'll see that the value for "Inventory these file types" has been changed to "*.exe."

Resultant Client Settings looks at all the settings policies that have been deployed to either a user or a device, and displays what the end combination of settings will be for each major section. It's a useful way of making sure that the priority and deployment of settings are producing the results you're after.

> **TIP** Resultant Client Settings doesn't show you the active settings on a device or user; it's not communicating with the remote system and retrieving the currently applied set of policies. Rather, it's looking at settings contained within the ConfigMgr database and running a full enumeration and comparison of all the relevant settings.

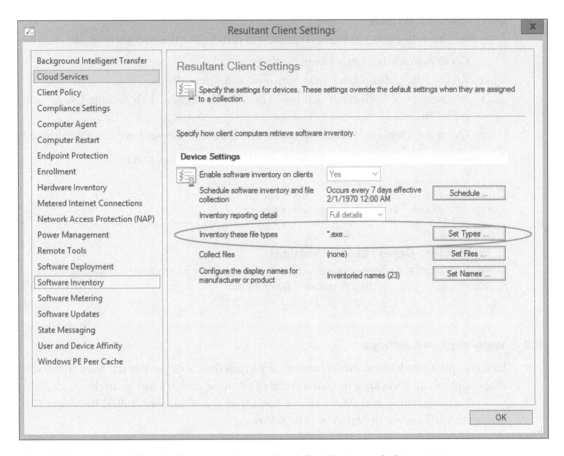

Figure 6.14   **Resultant Client Settings shows the results of all settings on a device or user.**

Try It Now—Resultant Client Settings
Follow the steps in section 6.3.3 to verify that the Resultant Client Settings for both CLIENT01 and Marcus show changes based on the custom settings you created in sections 6.2.1 and 6.2.2.

6.4   *Forcing policy updates*

Now that you've successfully deployed the custom settings, in due course the Config-Mgr client on CLIENT01 will talk back to CM01 and pick up the new deployments; by default this happens approximately every 60 minutes. But at times you might want remote systems to pick up a policy sooner—for example, in test environments.

You can force a policy update in two simple ways: from the local client or remotely via the console. You'll learn about the local approach first, because although it's a little more involved, it's useful for highlighting how the update process works.

6.4.1 Forcing a policy update via a local client

To force a policy update on CLIENT01, do the following:

1 Log in to CLIENT01 as Marcus (MOL\Marcus, P@ssw0rd).
2 Go into the Windows desktop.
3 Right-click the Windows icon in the lower-left corner and select "Control Panel."
4 Change the "View By" value from "Category" to "Small icons."
5 Select Configuration Manager.
6 In the Configuration Manager Properties screen, select the Actions tab.
7 As shown in figure 6.15, select "Machine Policy Retrieval & Evaluation Cycle" and click the "Run Now" button. This forces the client to check for an updated user policy (new or changed user deployments) for the logged-on user.

Figure 6.15   Force a local machine update to retrieve the latest policy.

WHICH LOG?   To monitor the process during a policy update, open the Policy-AgentProvider.log, PolicyAgent.log, and PolicyEvaluator.log files that are part of the ConfigMgr client log files on the local system (not on the ConfigMgr server). Assuming that the Windows operating system has been installed to a remote system's C:\ drive, the client log files are found at C:\Windows\CCM\Logs.

Try It Now—Manual policy updates

Follow the steps in section 6.4.1 to perform a manual update of both Machine and user policies on CLIENT01. Use CMTrace to open the relevant log files and monitor the policy update process.

To check that the settings have taken effect, open the ConfigMgr Software Center application from the Start menu on CLIENT01. As shown in figure 6.16, the Software Center will now have the organization name MoL ConfigMgr Lab.

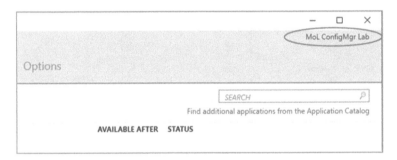

Figure 6.16   The settings changes you made are now represented on remote systems.

6.4.2   *Forcing a policy update remotely via a console*

Another way to force a policy update on a remote system (and a much easier way it is, too) is via the console:

1 In the console, go to Assets and Compliance > Device Collections.
2 Right-click "All Windows 10 Clients" and select Client Notification > Download Computer Policy.
3 Click "OK" in the confirmation window.
4 Perform the same process again, but this time select "Download user Policy."

This method of policy updating sends a remote wake-up to every system in the collection that's online, informing them to initiate the same policy update process that you performed manually on CLIENT01. Because this is done at the collection level, it's a great way to force a policy update on a large number of remote systems. To verify that the settings have taken effect, check the PolicyAgent.log and PolicyEvaluator.log files on a subset of the remote systems.

> **TIP** If any of the systems are offline, the ConfigMgr server will fail to send the request to those particular systems, and the remote systems won't perform a policy refresh ahead of their next scheduled update. Systems that are online will receive the policy update as normal.

Try It Now—Remote policy update
Follow the steps in section 6.4.2 to trigger a remote policy update via the console.

As you do, consider your own production environment: are large numbers of systems reliably offline, so that a remote policy update wouldn't be feasible?

6.5 *Lab*

Use PowerShell to create a new policy for users called `Cloud Distribution Point Access`. Configure the setting "Allow access to cloud distribution point" to be "Yes" and then deploy the policy to "All ConfigMgr Lab users."

Creating and configuring applications with the AppModel

Deploying and managing software is one of the core activities that you'll regularly perform as a ConfigMgr administrator. Things changed radically in ConfigMgr 2012 with the introduction of the AppModel, the new framework for deploying software in ConfigMgr. The AppModel completely redefines what applications are and how they're deployed, so it's critical to get on top of the myriad of changes.

By the end of this chapter, you'll know how to prepare, create, and configure a new AppModel-style application by using these key components: deployment types, requirements, and detection methods (see figure 7.1). And in the next chapter, you'll take this customized application and deploy it.

7.1 Exploring the ConfigMgr AppModel

Before you start creating your first application, it's important to set the scene for the new methods of building and deploying software in ConfigMgr, and understand why they're so important.

7.1.1 ConfigMgr vs. ConfigMgr 2007

Although ConfigMgr 2007 was good at deploying software, it was largely unaware of the environment into which any individual piece of software was deployed. For example, let's say you used ConfigMgr 2007 to deploy an application that relied on .NET Framework 3.5.1 being enabled, but that wouldn't (or couldn't) automatically

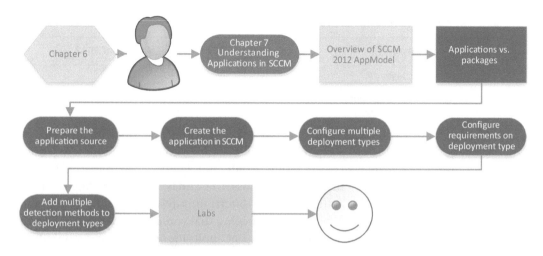

Figure 7.1 **This chapter is all about creating and configuring applications by using the AppModel.**

enable it. ConfigMgr 2007 would rely on you, as the administrator, to make sure that .NET Framework 3.5.1 was enabled before you deployed the software. By default, the application deployment method couldn't help you in this, and if you deployed the software to a system without the necessary prerequisites, it would simply fail. Config-Mgr 2007 provided ways around problematic scenarios like this, but they're definitely workarounds as opposed to elegant solutions.

By comparison, the AppModel in ConfigMgr uses an advanced, highly customiz-able logic engine, which gives the ConfigMgr server full visibility over software deploy-ments, and gives the ConfigMgr client all the necessary information about each application so that the deployment process doesn't become a black box, opaque to both the system and the administrator. Table 7.1 gives you a high-level overview of how much has changed in terms of software deployment from ConfigMgr 2007 to Config-Mgr 2012 and later.

Table 7.1 **Comparison of software deployment functionality**

Feature	ConfigMgr 2007	ConfigMgr 2012
Deployment to computers	✓	✓
Deployment to users	Partial	✓
Verify application presence		✓
Support application dependencies		✓
Self-service deployment		✓
App-V deployment	✓	✓
User-initiated uninstall		✓

Table 7.1   Comparison of software deployment functionality *(continued)*

Feature	ConfigMgr 2007	ConfigMgr 2012
Application revision history		✓
Application lifecycle management		✓

Looking at the earlier example of a .NET Framework–dependent application, in ConfigMgr 2012 and later you can deploy the software into your environment, and if the requisite .NET Framework isn't found, ConfigMgr agent will be able to automatically install it and verify that the installation was successful before proceeding to install the original application. ConfigMgr 2012 offers infinitely greater flexibility and robustness when deploying software, guaranteeing that you get exactly the end result you want. Excited yet? Hope so! Now let's look at applications: the key components in the AppModel.

7.1.2   Applications vs. packages

With ConfigMgr, you now have two distinct types of software for deployment: legacy packages and modern applications, which inhabit their own separate sections of the ConfigMgr console.

   Packages are the equivalent of the software you would deploy with ConfigMgr 2007, such as the ConfigMgr client or the MDT Toolkit. *Applications* are software that fully support the new and advanced installation logic at the heart of the ConfigMgr App-Model—designed to give you, as the administrator, full control and full visibility over each and every software installation, such as MSI-based or App-V–based software.

   Packages still have their uses, and you'll learn more about them in chapter 8, but in terms of software deployment in ConfigMgr, applications are where the action is. This raises the question: is there a particular reason to create an application rather than a package? Well, at times you have no choice but to create a package; for example, you might need to reference a bundle of PowerShell scripts during operating system deployment, and since these have no installers, they can't be created or deployed as AppModel applications. But apart from these isolated cases, in ConfigMgr you should always deploy software as applications so that you can take full advantage of the AppModel's capabilities. It's important to remember that some major features, such as being able to supersede old software or automatically install prerequisites, can be achieved only if *all* the individual components are applications; packages can't handle all the new functionality. So with that, let's create an application.

7.2   Creating a ConfigMgr application

Now you get to the meat in the sandwich: the AppModel comprises several important pieces of functionality working together to produce a coherent outcome. To illustrate this, you'll use Paint.NET (an excellent and free graphics-editing package) to create an application in the ConfigMgr console, using this as the basis to examine the App-Model in depth.

7.2.1 *Preparing the application source*

Before you create the application, it's important to carefully prepare the source files first. When you create an application, ConfigMgr treats the folder in which the installer resides as the top-level folder, and assumes that everything else within that folder (files and other folders) is necessary and important for successful deployment. Therefore, it copies everything within that top-level folder down, so make sure that the only files that exist alongside the installer are those that are needed.

To avoid confusion, I like to have a top folder called Software (or something similar) and then all applications under that folder contained within their own folders, with a separate folder for each version; for example, \Software\Adobe Reader 10.1.3, and \Software\Adobe Reader 10.1.4, as shown in figure 7.2. This keeps everything nicely segregated and avoids the risk of content being included in an application source that isn't meant to be there.

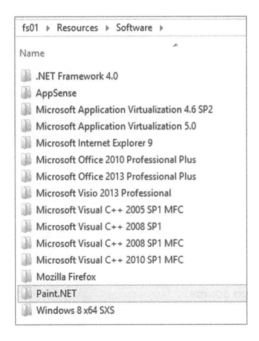

Figure 7.2 Keep software versions separate from each other when creating your master source folders.

When an application has both a 32-bit and a 64-bit version available, I create an x86 folder and an x64 folder, respectively; for example, \Software\App-V 5.0 Client\x86, and Software\App-V 5.0 Client\x64.

Paint.NET has advantages that make it an excellent test application. Apart from being good software (always a plus!), it comes in both 32-bit and 64-bit architectures and can be deployed via MSI, which means it's exactly the type of software that the AppModel is optimized to deploy.

To prepare an application source for deployment, perform the following:

1   Download the Paint.NET installer from www.getpaint.net and extract the compressed file.

2   Open a command window (elevated, if you're running Windows Vista or higher) and then run `paint.net.4.0.9.install.exe /createMsi`. This creates a folder on the Desktop called PaintDotNetMsi that contains the 32-bit and 64-bit MSI installers for Paint.NET.

3   Next, rename the PaintDotNetMsi folder to `Paint.NET`, create a subfolder called `4.0.9`, and create two new subfolders called `x64` and `x86`, respectively.

4   Move each installer into the relevant folder, as in figure 7.3.

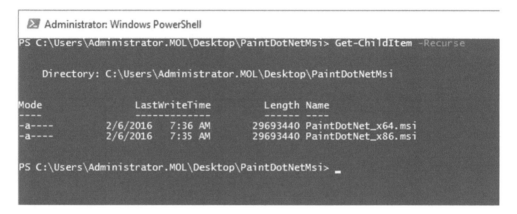

Figure 7.3   Give each application installer its own source and a separate folder for different architectures.

5   Finally, copy the entire folder to a UNC path that's accessible by the ConfigMgr server. Now the application source is ready for you to create the application in ConfigMgr.

Try It Now—Create an application source

Follow the steps in section 7.2.1 to create an application source folder structure to house the 32-bit and 64-bit MSI installers for Paint.NET.

Consider your own production environment, and where application source files are stored: are they stored in a logical structure that would serve as a reliable source for ConfigMgr?

7.2.2   *Creating your application*

Creating an application in ConfigMgr involves pointing the Create Application Wizard at the installer that's used to install your application (such as an MSI). The wizard then automatically extracts the minimum amount of information needed to create an application with a deployment type.

ConfigMgr supports a wide range of installation sources from which it can automatically create an application, such as MSI and App-V 5.0. The advantage of this approach is that it avoids much of the risk from human error during the creation process as well as embeds a lot of installation logic into the application object from the outset.

To create an application from such an application source, perform the following:

1 Open the ConfigMgr console and go to Software Library > Application Management > Applications.

2 Right-click "Applications" and select "Create Application." You're presented with a wizard with the default option "Automatically detect information about this Application from installation files."

3 Navigate to the PaintDotNet.x86.msi in the source folder you created in section 7.2.1, so that the "Location" field looks like "\\UNCPATH\Paint.NET\4.0.9\x86\PaintDotNet.x86.msi," and then click "Next." You may receive a warning that the publisher of the file couldn't be verified; this warning is alerting you that the MSI hasn't been digitally signed by a trusted source. Depending on the circumstances, this may be of concern, but not in this case. Click "Yes" to accept the warning.

4 All of the information contained within the MSI that's necessary to create the ConfigMgr application is imported. Click "Next" to specify any additional information about the application, as in figure 7.4.

5 In the "Specify information about this application" screen, you'll see that the "Name" and "Installation Program" fields have been automatically populated. Because you imported an MSI, ConfigMgr knows to call MSIEXEC as the

Specify information about this application

Name:	Paint.NET 4.0.9
Administrator comments:	
Publisher:	
Software version:	
Optional reference:	
Administrative categories:	

Specify the installation program for this application and the required installation rights.

Installation program:	msiexec /i "PaintDotNet_x86.msi" /q

Figure 7.4 Any additional information about the application such as publisher or software version can be entered manually.

installer, and which installation strings are necessary to perform a silent, unattended installation. At this stage, there's no need to modify any of the application settings, so click "Next," click "Next" again, and then click "Close."

The PowerShell script to create a new ConfigMgr application and MSI-based deployment type can be found in .\powershell\New-CMLabApplication.ps1.

Congratulations; you've created a ConfigMgr application!

Try It Now—Create a ConfigMgr application

Follow the steps detailed in section 7.2.2 to create a new ConfigMgr application: Paint.NET.

Consider the repositories of software in your own production environment: how many of them are based on MSI or App-V, so that ConfigMgr could automatically discover their installation properties?

7.3   *Configuring your application*

Now that you have a basic application, let's flesh it out with some more-advanced functionality using the ConfigMgr AppModel. This section covers the following:

- Deployment types
- Requirements
- Detection methods

Each of these AppModel features provides flexibility and power to ConfigMgr applications. Deployment types give you multiple methods to get each application out to your end users in the most appropriate format (such as locally installed or virtualized). Requirements ensure that only the correct Devices or Users receive a particular deployment type, and detection methods give you all the necessary information to be able to tell whether your application has installed successfully.

Let's start with deployment types.

7.3.1   *Deployment types*

Deployment types sit at the heart of ConfigMgr's flexible software delivery mechanism. The concept is a simple one: one application, many ways to deploy. And no, despite appearances, that's not even Microsoft marketing.

The end goal of multiple deployment types is to allow you, as the administrator, to deploy an application in a variety of ways without having to worry about the mechanics of the deployment after the application has been configured. You focus on deploying the application to the right group of users or machines, and the deployment type ensures that the application is made available using the most appropriate delivery mechanism.

Let's elaborate further. Say you're looking to deploy the latest version of WinRAR (an excellent file archiving and compression tool). WinRAR comes in both 32-bit and 64-bit flavors that are usually deployed to 32-bit and 64-bit operating systems, respectively. In a traditional ConfigMgr 2007 environment, this means creating a separate program (and possibly a separate package) for each architecture, as well as separate deployments and some means of targeting the correct operating system (such as custom collections). In ConfigMgr 2012 and later, the AppModel allows you to create just one application with only one deployment, and then use multiple deployment types to handle the software delivery in the most appropriate fashion. Figure 7.5 shows the deployment types that you'll create for Paint.NET (although you're probably going to be working with a later version of Paint.NET).

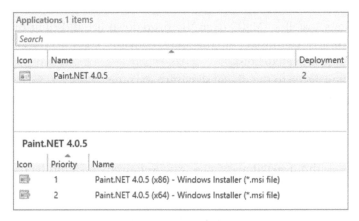

Figure 7.5 ConfigMgr applications handle deployments to different architectures by using a variety of installation methods, such as MSI or App-V.

PRIORITIZING DEPLOYMENT TYPES

When an application has multiple deployment types, the order in which they appear in the console is important. Each deployment type has a priority, and they're processed in order from the highest (priority 1) to the lowest. You can change the run order by right-clicking a deployment type and increasing or decreasing the order.

ADDING ANOTHER DEPLOYMENT TYPE TO AN EXISTING APPLICATION

Your applications can have as many deployment types as you like in order to cater to a variety of deployment scenarios. For example, you might want to deploy Mozilla Firefox in your environment, but want to be able to install it locally on some systems via MSI, whereas others will receive either an App-V 4.6 or an App-V 5.0 package. In ConfigMgr, all these delivery options are handled by deployment types for the same application, with only one deployment needed.

To add another deployment type to an existing application manually (the PowerShell script from earlier will have already done this for you), do the following:

1 In the ConfigMgr console, select the newly created Paint.NET application.

2 In the properties pane at the bottom of the console, select the Deployment Types tab. You should see one MSI-based deployment type, which was created during the wizard process.

3 Right-click the deployment type and select "Properties."

4 In the Properties window, change the "Name" from "Paint.NET 4.0.9" to `Paint.NET 4.0.9 (x86)`. This change reflects the fact that the MSI you initially selected was the 32-bit version, and the name change allows you to create another deployment type for the 64-bit version without encountering a duplicate name conflict (application deployment types must have unique names).

5 In the main Applications window, right-click the Paint.NET application and select "Create Deployment Type."

6 Select "Windows Installer (MSI)" from the drop-down list and then Browse to the 64-bit MSI for Paint.NET, so the field contains \\UNCPATH\Paint.NET \4.0.9\x64\PaintDotNet.x64.msi.

7 Click "Next" and agree to the digital signature warning.

8 When prompted to select the name for the new deployment type, change the automatically detected name of "Paint.NET 4.0.9" to `Paint.NET 4.0.9 (x64)`. Again, don't make any other changes at this stage.

9 Click "Next" through the next two screens, which prompt for requirements and dependencies, without making any changes. Requirements and dependencies are important, but you'll get to them shortly, and you don't need to specify them during the wizard.

10 Click all the way through the rest of the wizard without making changes, and at the end you'll have a second deployment type added to your ConfigMgr application, as shown previously in figure 7.5.

The PowerShell script to add a new deployment type to an existing ConfigMgr application is available in .\powershell\New-CMLabApplication.ps1.

Key tip

When you add another deployment type to an application, you'll be presented with another wizard similar to the one used to initially create the application. Expand the drop-down list. It's worth noting that although this list is nearly identical to the original wizard, there's one extra item: Script Installer. Why wasn't this an option in the original wizard?

The answer is key to how the AppModel works. Legacy installers, like scripts or EXE-based installers, don't contain enough information for ConfigMgr to be able to automatically create a fully functional application, which is why Script Installer isn't an option in the wizard when you create an application for the first time.

But with some manual input, script-based installers *can* be used as deployment types. You'll tackle this in depth in chapter 8.

Deployment types are rather like basic firewall rules: the firewall assesses an incoming or outgoing network packet against the rule with the highest priority first. If there's a match for a particular pattern (for example, FTP traffic), the packet gets processed with the matching rule. If there's no match, the rule with the next-highest priority is assessed, and so on, until a matching rule is found.

Deployment types are the same, in that when an application is deployed, the ConfigMgr agent will look at the deployment type with the highest priority. Whether the deployment type is processed depends upon requirements.

Try It Now—Add a new deployment type

Follow the steps in section 7.3.1 to add a new deployment type to the Paint.NET application that you created earlier.

Consider the applications in your own environment. How many of them need to support both 32-bit and 64-bit versions, which you could combine into a single ConfigMgr application with multiple deployment types?

7.3.2 *Requirements*

Requirements are one or more properties unique to each deployment type that allow the ConfigMgr client to assess which deployment type gets processed. Although requirements are properties of deployment types, they're of equal importance in contributing to the capabilities of the AppModel.

Each requirement specified per deployment type will cause the ConfigMgr agent to run a test to see whether the requirement is true. For example, a requirement could be that the client must have at least 10 GB of hard drive space free, have at least 4 GB RAM installed, and that the machine account must sit within a particular Active Directory Organizational Unit (OU); or whether the user requesting the application is a primary user of the device. Each deployment type supports multiple requirements, and if a predefined requirement doesn't meet your needs, you can define custom requirements.

In the case of your Paint.NET application, you need to configure the deployment types so that they'll install only on the correct client operating system: 32-bit or 64-bit. To do this, perform the following steps:

1 Right-click the 32-bit deployment type and select "Properties," and then go to the Requirements tab, shown in figure 7.6.
2 Click "Add" to create a new requirement.
3 Ensure that the "Category" field is set to "Device."
4 Expand the drop-down menu for the "Condition" field and select "Operating System" from the list. You're presented with a list of all the available Windows operating systems that ConfigMgr supports.
5 Ensure that that the "Operator" field is set to "One of." Expand "Windows 10" and select the "All Windows 10 (32-bit)" check box.

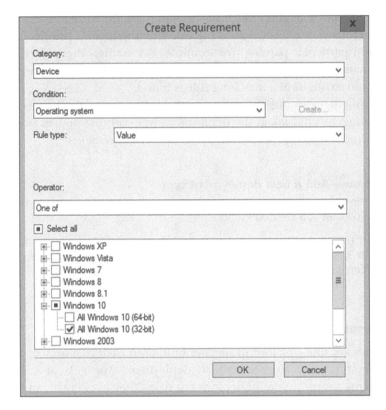

Figure 7.6   Requirements give you granular control over whether a deployment type will be processed on a client system.

6   Click "OK" and then "OK" again to close the Deployment Type Properties window.
7   Now you need to do the same thing for the deployment type for the 64-bit MSI. Create a requirement that checks the operating system for Windows 10 x64.

Try It Now—Add requirements to deployment types

Follow the steps in section 7.3.2 to add operating system requirements to each of the deployment types for the Paint.NET application.

In your own production environment, consider whether other device requirements might be appropriate as deployment type requirements, such as minimum processor speed, amount of available RAM, or hard drive space.

Thanks to the requirements you've specified, when Paint.NET is deployed to a Config-Mgr-managed system, the correct architecture will be installed based on the detected operating system, as shown in figure 7.7.

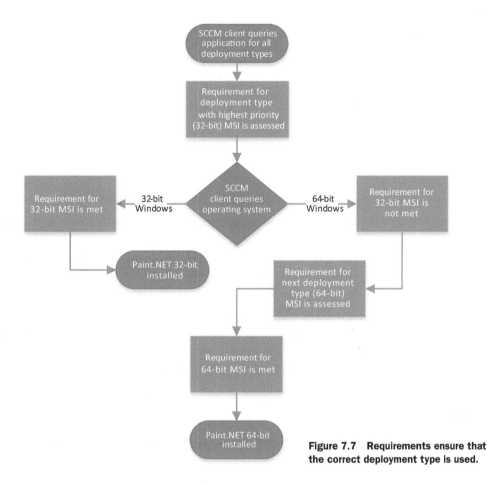

Figure 7.7 Requirements ensure that the correct deployment type is used.

It's all very well to say that a particular deployment type "will be installed," but how does the ConfigMgr agent (and indeed, the ConfigMgr administrator) know which one has been installed?

7.3.3 Detection methods

Detection methods provide underlying resilience to the AppModel, guaranteeing that an application that has been installed via a particular deployment type has indeed been installed. A detection method is a single value or set of values that the ConfigMgr agent will check for after an application installation has returned an expected exit code, in order to ensure that the application is indeed present and correct. Although the installer has reported that everything went well, the ConfigMgr agent isn't going to believe the installer until it goes and checks for itself.

Because the deployment types for your Paint.NET application were automatically created from MSI, each already has a detection rule present, which tests for the presence

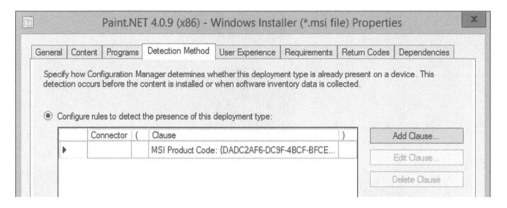

Figure 7.8   Detection methods ensure that an application has been successfully installed or removed.

of the application based on its unique MSI code, as you can see in figure 7.8. For most MSI-based applications, the MSI code is the most reliable detection rule, but you can add in multiple rules for extra resilience or to cater to special circumstances.

ADDING A DETECTION METHOD TO A DEPLOYMENT TYPE

To add another detection method to an existing deployment type, perform the following steps:

1　Open the properties of the Paint.NET 32-bit MSI deployment type. Go to the Detection Methods tab and then select "Add Clause" to create a new detection rule.

2　For the "Setting Type," select "File System." For the "Type," select "File."

3　Set the "Path" to %ProgramFiles%\Paint.NET and the filename to PaintDotNet .exe.

4　Untick the "This file or folder is associated with a 32-bit application on a 64-bit system" check box and ensure that "The file system setting must exist on the target system" is selected.

5　Click "OK." The new detection rule is added beneath the preexisting MSI detection rule. As you can see in figure 7.9, the default connector is set to "And," which indicates that both detection rules must be satisfied before the application is considered to have been installed successfully. You can change this to "Or" so that only one of the rules needs to be satisfied.

6　Click "OK" to close the deployment type. Then perform the same process for the 64-bit MSI deployment type. Because each MSI is architecture-specific, the %ProgramFiles% variable will resolve to the correct installation path on both 32-bit and 64-bit Windows.

TIP　Depending on the deployment type, multiple detection methods are usually unnecessary. For example, the MSI product code is almost always unique, so it makes a resilient detection method. But some applications have updates

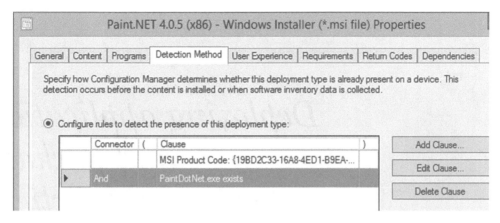

Figure 7.9 Use custom detection methods to give your applications greater resilience—perfect for large-scale enterprise deployments.

or patches that don't modify the MSI code but do modify the filesystem or registry, so in these cases it's necessary to have multiple detection methods. Each application needs to be assessed based on its capabilities and requirements. ConfigMgr gives you the framework for detecting successful installations, but you still need to understand how each particular application works.

Try It Now—Add multiple detection methods

Follow the steps detailed in section 7.3.3 to add another detection method to both the 32-bit and 64-bit deployment types for Paint.NET.

Consider the applications in your own production environment. Think about which detection methods are the most appropriate for your applications, such as registry checks or even custom scripts that check for a particular system value (for example, whether a Windows service is installed and running).

With the addition of another detection method, your deployment types for Paint.NET are more resilient, and will perform additional checks to ensure that the application installed correctly.

Congratulations! Your application is ready to be deployed to clients, which is exactly what you'll do in the next chapter.

7.4 *Lab*

Another good software package to import into ConfigMgr is 7-Zip, because it's freely available and comes as an MSI. Download the 32-bit and 64-bit MSI installers from www.7-zip.org/download.html and create a new ConfigMgr application with two deployment types: one for the 32-bit MSI and another for the 64-bit MSI.

Deploying applications and packages to ConfigMgr clients

Creating and configuring applications in ConfigMgr is all well and good, but ultimately you do this for only one reason: so you can deploy the application out into the big wide world! Deploying software from ConfigMgr requires that you deploy the application against an existing device or user collection, and that the ConfigMgr client can find the software installation files. As you can see in figure 8.1, in this chapter you'll learn how to deploy software against both devices and users, set up and deploy legacy software packages, and turn those legacy packages into shiny new AppModel-type applications.

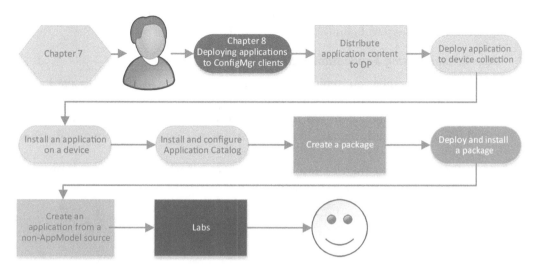

Figure 8.1   This chapter is all about getting applications and packages out to where they're needed.

8.1   Deploying applications

The user-centric approach to deployment that ConfigMgr promotes gives you great flexibility when it comes to deploying software, ensuring that only the people who need a particular application will be able to access it. But at times you still need to deploy software directly to devices.

For example, if company policy mandates that an application should be installed on every single machine in the organization, deploying that software to physical devices rather than to users makes more sense. That way, regardless of who logs on to whichever system, they'll be able to access the required application.

Deploying software to users has two primary purposes:

- To enable you, as the administrator, to target end users who have requested software, rather than the devices that they may or may not be using
- To allow users to request the software they need without having to send the request through you or the help desk

This is a far more targeted and situation-specific method of delivering applications. Let's start off with deploying to devices.

8.2   Deploying applications to devices

The deployment process has three steps:

- *Distribute*—Distribute the content so that clients can access it.
- *Deploy*—Deploy the application to users and/or devices.
- *Install*—The user or the device installs the deployed application.

You already have an application ready for deployment, so let's proceed with step 1, distribution, as you deploy Paint.NET against your lab devices.

8.2.1 Step 1: Distributing application content

Regardless of whether you deploy software against a device or a user, it's the locally installed ConfigMgr agent that will perform the content retrieval and installation. To do this, the ConfigMgr agent has to be able to access the content that it needs to install the software, and you have to make the software content available on a distribution point.

A *distribution point* (or DP) is a ConfigMgr server role that provides content to ConfigMgr clients, as shown in figure 8.2.

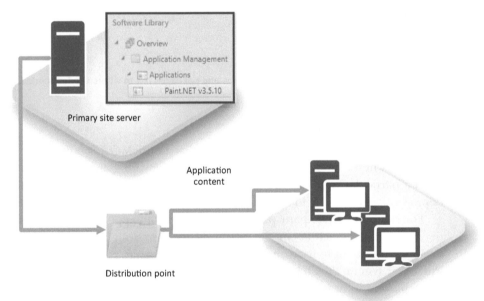

Figure 8.2 A distribution point holds content for ConfigMgr clients to access.

In the case of Paint.NET, the content is the application source files that are needed to perform the installation. But content comes in a variety of flavors, including operating system images, boot images, and software updates. You'll get to these later in the book.

Chapter 9 covers distribution points in much more depth, but suffice it to say for the moment that a distribution point role is already installed on CM01, and this is where CLIENT01 will retrieve the Paint.NET installation files.

To distribute content to the DP, perform the following steps:

1 In the ConfigMgr console, navigate to Software Library > Application Management > Applications and then to the Paint.NET application you created in chapter 7.

2 Right-click the application and select "Distribute Content."

3 The Distribute Content Wizard opens. Click "Next" and "Next" again to bypass the "Dependencies" check box.

4 On the "Specify the content destination" screen, select "Distribution Point" from the "Add" drop-down menu.

5 Only one distribution point should be available in the "Add Distribution Points" screen: CM01.mol.sccmlab.net. Select the check box next to this server and click "OK."

6 Back on the "Specify the content destination" screen, click "Next," "Next," and then "Close." The ConfigMgr server distributes the Paint.NET source files to the DP.

To distribute the application content using PowerShell, use the following command:

```
Start-CMContentDistribution `
-ApplicationName 'Paint.NET 4.0.9' `
-DistributionPointName "CM01.MOL.SCCMLAB.NET"
```

WHICH LOG? Distributing content from the ConfigMgr console doesn't distribute the content in real time. Rather, the console submits the job to the server that handles the request. Depending on the size of the content and the speed of both the disks and the network, distribution could take some time. Open distmgr.log to monitor the progress of all distribution tasks as they take place.

7 To verify that the application has been successfully distributed, navigate to Monitoring > Distribution Status > Content Status.

8 In the "Content Status" list, double-click "Paint.NET." In the Content Status window for Paint.NET, you'll see that the content for the application has been successfully distributed to the DP, as shown in figure 8.3.

Try It Now—Distribute application content

Follow the steps in section 8.2.1 to distribute the content for Paint.NET to the distribution point on CM01, and monitor the distribution process in distmgr.log as well as the distribution status in the Monitoring tab.

In your own production environment, consider the size of the applications you might need to distribute to DPs, and whether those DPs exist at remote sites. Would you have to schedule the distributions for after-hours so as not to negatively impact users by choking WAN links with large content transfers?

Now that the content has been distributed, ConfigMgr clients that can communicate with the DP on CM01 will be able to access the required files for Paint.NET.

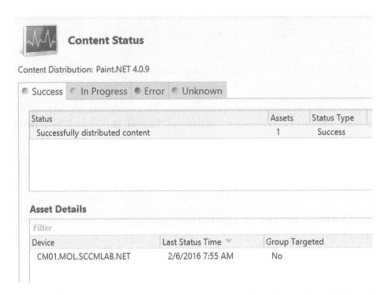

Figure 8.3   ConfigMgr has successfully distributed the files for Paint.NET to the distribution point.

8.2.2 Step 2: Deploying the application to a device collection

The next step is to create a deployment for Paint.NET so that managed devices in your lab environment know that they should receive the application for installation.

To deploy an application, perform the following steps:

1 In the ConfigMgr console, navigate to Software Library > Application Management > Applications.
2 Right-click the Paint.NET application and select "Deploy."
3 In the Deploy Software Wizard, click the "Browse" button next to the "Collection" field.
4 In the Select Collection window, select "Device Collections" from the drop-down menu, and then select "All Windows 10 Clients" from the right-hand pane, as shown in figure 8.4. Click "OK" and then "Next."
5 In the Specify the Content Destination window, you'll see that the wizard detects that the content for the application has already been distributed to the distribution point on CM01. If it hadn't already been distributed, you could have triggered the distribution from this window. Click "Next."
6 In the Specify Settings to Control How This Software is Deployed window, ensure that "Action" is set to "Install" and that "Purpose" is set to "Available." Clients that receive this deployment will see the software as available to install, as opposed to a mandatory install or uninstall (for software packages that you want everyone to receive, no matter what). Click "Next."

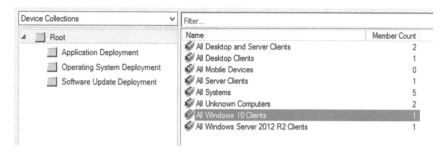

Figure 8.4 Select the appropriate device collection to deploy Paint.NET to.

7 Click through the Scheduling, User Experience, Alerts, and Summary pages (take a moment to read the details on the Summary page), and click "Close" to finish the wizard.

8 Back in the Software Library, select the Paint.NET application, and switch to the Deployments tab at the bottom of the page. You'll see an active deployment for this application, targeted against the All Windows 10 Clients Device collection, as shown in figure 8.5.

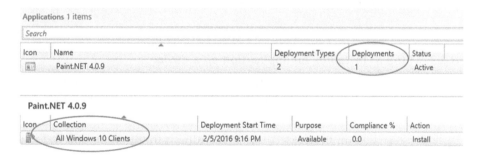

Figure 8.5 Paint.NET is ready to deploy to clients running Windows 10.

9 Navigate to Assets and Compliance > Device Collections.

10 Right-click the All Windows 10 Clients collection and select Client Notification > Download Computer Policy. This prompts CLIENT01 (the only member of this collection) to communicate to CM01 and get the latest computer policy, which will include the new application deployment.

To deploy the application using PowerShell, use the following command:

```
Start-CMApplicationDeployment `
-Name 'Paint.NET 4.0.9' `
-CollectionName "All Windows 10 Clients"
```

Now that Paint.NET has been deployed, you can move on to the final stage: installation!

Important note—Mandatory vs. available

The distinction between a mandatory and an available deployment is an important one. When the ConfigMgr client polls the Management Point for the latest policies and finds a *mandatory* deployment, it will process that deployment—no questions asked. This is the preferred method for distributing business-critical applications, packages, policies, and updates, when you don't want to leave things in the hands of the user.

By contrast, when the ConfigMgr client downloads a policy that contains an *available* deployment, it will make the content of the deployment, such as an application, available for the user to act on. This is useful for applications and packages that users can access as and when they require.

Try It Now—Deploy Paint.NET

Follow the steps detailed in section 8.2.2 to deploy Paint.NET to Windows 10 clients, and then force a computer policy update on those clients.

Does your production environment have applications that you might want to deploy as mandatory rather than available?

8.2.3   Step 3: Installing an application on a device

You've done all the heavy lifting necessary to make Paint.NET available to CLIENT01, so now it's time to experience what an end user might see in a ConfigMgr environment.

To install the application, perform the following steps:

1   Log on to CLIENT01 as MOL\Administrator (note that it doesn't matter which user account you log on with, because the application has been deployed to the device, not to the user).

2   In the Start window, start typing `Software Center` so that Windows will find the ConfigMgr Software Center utility.

3   Click "Software Center" in the search results.

4   As shown in figure 8.6, Paint.NET is listed in the Software Center as an available application. Place a tick in the "Paint.NET" check box and then click "Install Selected."

5   The Software Center automatically changes focus from the Available Software tab to the Installation Status tab. You'll see that Paint.NET will change from "Downloading" to "Installing" and then finally "Installed."

6   Click the Installed Software tab and you'll see Paint.NET listed as being successfully installed. The application also appears as a desktop icon on CLIENT01. Launch the application to verify that it installed correctly, as shown in figure 8.7.

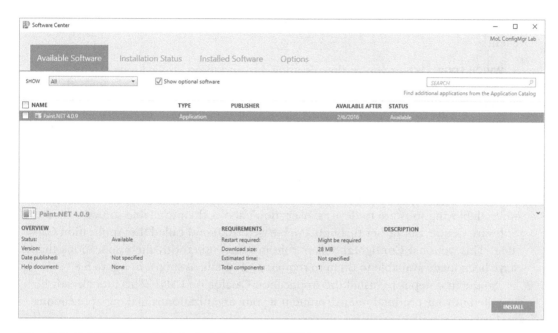

Figure 8.6   Paint.NET is available for installation on CLIENT01.

Figure 8.7   Paint.NET has been successfully installed via ConfigMgr.

Congratulations; you've just successfully deployed Paint.NET to a managed ConfigMgr client!

WHICH LOG?   When you're downloading and installing applications, a number of logs are written to on the ConfigMgr client. Client log files are located in %WINDIR%\CCM\Logs.

Now that you've successfully deployed software to a device, it's time to move on and see how a user-targeted deployment works.

8.3 *Deploying applications to users*

The ConfigMgr experience is a bit different when you deploy software to users. Unlike when deploying software to devices, users don't access their available software via the Software Center, but rather through a web-based front-end called the Application Catalog. This optional ConfigMgr server role presents users with the applications that have been made available to them to request and install, as shown in figure 8.8.

So the first step is to install the Application Catalog on CM01. This may already be installed in your production environment if your organization is making applications and packages available to users to access and install.

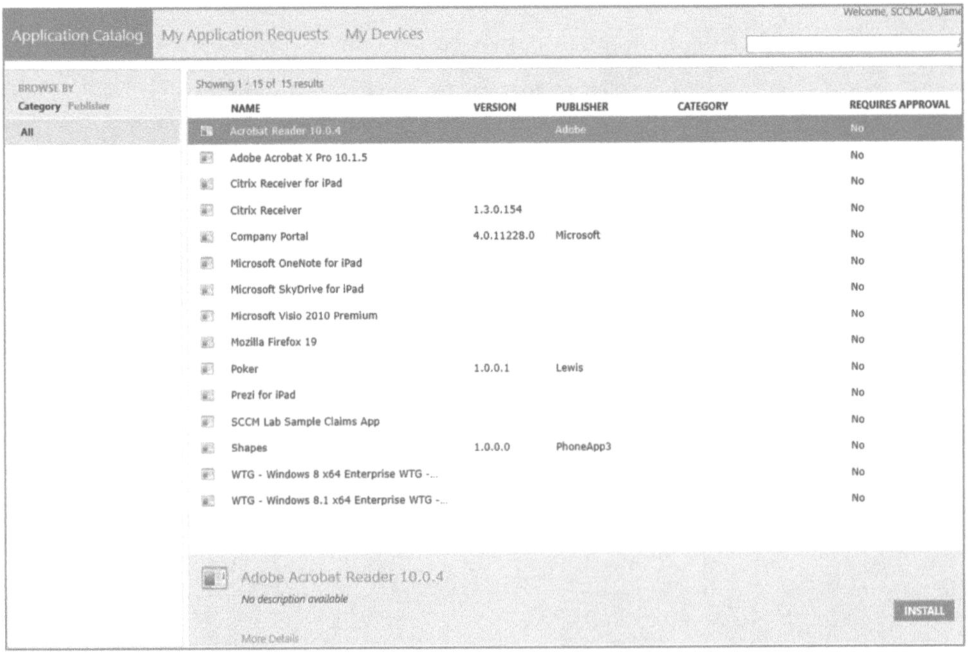

Figure 8.8   The ConfigMgr Application Catalog lets users request and install available software.

8.3.1 Installing the Application Catalog

To install the Application Catalog on CM01, perform the following steps:

1 In the ConfigMgr console, navigate to Administration > Site Configuration > Servers and Site System Roles.
2 Right-click "\\CM01.mol.sccmlab.net" and select "Add Site System Roles."
3 Click "Next" past the General and Proxy pages until you get to the System Role Selection page.
4 Place ticks in the "Application Catalog web service point" and the "Application Catalog website point" check boxes and then click "Next."
5 Click "Next" through the "Application Catalog web service point" and "Application Catalog website point" pages, accepting all the default values.
6 On the Application Catalog Customizations page, enter `MoL ConfigMgr Lab` in the "Organization Name" field. Change the Website Theme to a different color, as shown in figure 8.9.
7 Click "Summary," "Next," and "Close."

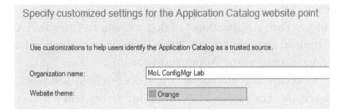

Figure 8.9   You can make basic customizations to the appearance of the Application Catalog website.

To install the Application Catalog roles using PowerShell, use the following commands:

```
Add-CMApplicationCatalogWebServicePoint `
-PortNumber 80 `
-SiteCode 'PS1' `
-SiteSystemServerName 'CM01.mol.sccmlab.net' `
-CommunicationType HTTP `
-IISWebsite 'Default Web Site' `
-WebApplicationName 'CMApplicationCatalogSvc'
Add-CMApplicationCatalogWebsitePoint `
-SiteSystemServerName 'CM01' `
-SiteCode 'PS1' `
-SiteSystemServerNameConfiguredForApplicationCatalogWebServicePoint
'CM01' `
-ConfiguredAsHttpConnection `
-PortForHttpConnection 80 `
-IISWebsite 'Default Web Site' `
-WebApplicationName 'CMApplicationCatalogSvc' `
-OrganizationName 'MoL ConfigMgr Lab' `
-NetbiosName 'CM01'
```

WHICH LOG?   To monitor the installation of the Application Catalog server roles, look at the awebsvcMSI.log file to verify that the installation of the roles went through successfully, and then the awebsctl.log file to verify that the ConfigMgr server is able to communicate with the server role correctly and that no significant errors exist.

8   After installation has completed successfully (as verified by the log files), log on to CLIENT01 as MOL\Administrator.

9   Open Internet Explorer and navigate to http://CM01.mol.sccmlab.net/CMApplicationCatalog.

10   You're prompted for credentials; authenticate as MOL\Administrator.

11   The Application Catalog web page loads, incorporating the customizations you made during the setup wizard. Back on CM01, go to Administration > Client Settings and double-click "Default Client Settings."

12   Go to the Computer Agent page.

13   Next to the Default Application Catalog website point, click "Set Website."

14   Select "CM01.mol.sccmlab.net (use intranet FQDN)" from the drop-down list and then click "OK."

15   For the "Add default Application Catalog website to Internet Explorer trusted sites zone" option, change "No" to "Yes." This removes the need to authenticate again when logging in to the Application Catalog.

16   Click "OK" to accept the change to the default client settings. The next time your managed devices request a ConfigMgr policy, they'll incorporate these changes, or you can trigger a remote policy download from the console.

Congratulations; you've successfully installed and configured the ConfigMgr Application Catalog!

> **Try It Now—Install and configure the Application Catalog**
> Follow the steps detailed in section 8.3.1 to install and configure the ConfigMgr Application Catalog on CM01, and monitor the installation in the relevant log files.

Now that you've created and deployed an application, you're ready to try your hand at something slightly different: packages.

8.4   *Creating and deploying packages*

As we've already discussed, packages are the equivalent of legacy software packages from ConfigMgr 2007. They don't have the built-in smarts of applications: they can't take advantage of the AppModel. But at times you'll still need to use packages in ConfigMgr.

Packages still have their purpose, specifically:

- When you need to use a collection of scripts or batch files that don't run as traditional applications

- When you need to deploy software that can't be treated like a modern App-Model-style application
- When you migrate software packages from ConfigMgr 2007 (except for App-V packages, which are always migrated across to the new ConfigMgr hierarchy as applications)

In this section you'll create and deploy a package in ConfigMgr—specifically, Notepad++. This incredibly useful utility is a great example to use as a package because it's not available as an MSI installer, which means that ConfigMgr can't automatically detect its installation properties in order to set it up as an application. But as you'll see, there are ways and means, and often nothing in ConfigMgr is truly as it seems. Intrigued? Read on!

8.4.1 Creating a package

The first step is to download the Notepad++ installer and create the installation source, just as you did for Paint.NET. Do this:

1 Download the latest version of Notepad++ from http://notepad-plus-plus.org/download/.
2 Make sure that you download the Notepad++ installer, which will have a filename such as npp.6.8.Installer.exe.
3 Copy the installer to a UNC share, just as you did for Paint.NET, as shown in figure 8.10.

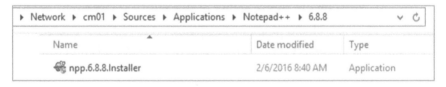

Figure 8.10 Create a network-based location to store the downloaded Notepad++ installer.

4 Next, in the ConfigMgr console, navigate to Software Library > Application Management > Packages.
5 Right-click "Packages" and select "Create Package."
6 In the "Name" field, type `Notepad++ 6.8` (or whichever version you downloaded).
7 Select the "This package contains source files" check box and then click "Browse."
8 In the Set Source Folder window, ensure that "Network path (UNC name)" is selected, and then copy in the network path to the folder that contains the installer (for example, \\CM01\Sources\Software\Notepad++\6.8) and click "OK." The package page should now look like that in figure 8.11.
9 Click "Next." On the Program Type page, ensure that "Standard program" is selected. Click "Next."

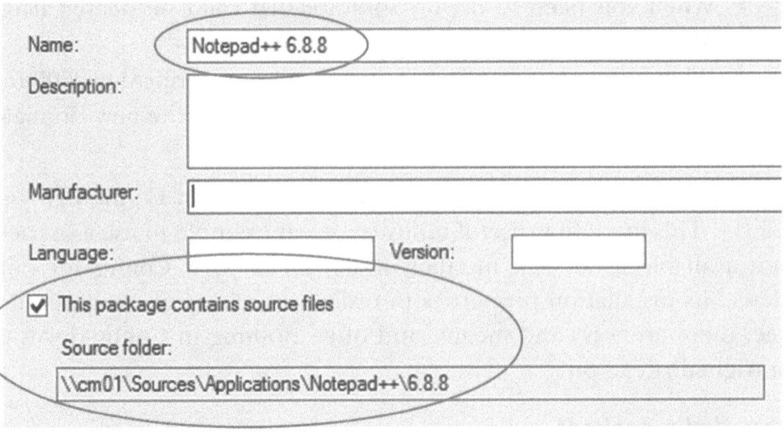

Figure 8.11   Give the new package a unique name (the software version works well) and a path to the installation files.

10 On the "Specify information about this standard program" page, make the following changes:

a Name: `Install — Notepad++ 6.8`

b Command line: `npp.6.5.2.Installer.exe /S` (this is the silent installation switch that allows Notepad++ to be installed without user interaction)

c Run: Hidden

d Program can run: Whether or not a user is logged on

The page should now look like figure 8.12.

11 Click "Summary" and "Close," and the package creation completes.

To create the same package with PowerShell, use the code located in .\powershell\ New-CMLabPackage.ps1.

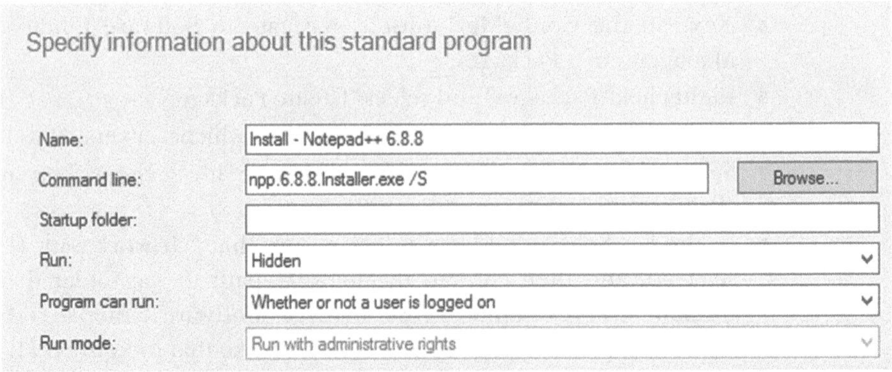

Figure 8.12   Creating a new standard program within a new package

Congratulations; you've successfully created a ConfigMgr package!

You should now have a new entry in the list of packages. Select Notepad++ 6.8 and in the bottom pane select "Programs." You'll see the standard program that you created during the wizard.

It should already be apparent that without the benefit of the AppModel, applications can do plenty that packages can't. Packages have no idea of detection methods or dependencies, and they don't support multiple deployment types. They don't even know how to install or uninstall without direct guidance.

Try It Now—Create a ConfigMgr package

Follow the steps detailed in section 8.4.1 to create a new package for Notepad++.

Consider the software in your own environment: are you responsible for deploying software that would have to be configured and deployed as packages rather than as applications?

8.4.2 *Deploying a package*

Deploying packages is similar to deploying applications, in that the content needs to be available on a distribution point and deployed to a ConfigMgr collection containing either devices or users.

To deploy Notepad++, perform the following steps:

1 Right-click "Notepad++" and select "Deploy."
2 For the "Collection," select the "All Windows 10 Clients device collection" and then click "Next."
3 On the "Specify the content destination" page, select "Distribution Point" from the "Add" drop-down menu.
4 Select the "CM01.mol.sccmlab.net" check box. Click "OK" and then "Next."
5 On the "Specify settings to control how this software is deployed" page, change the "Purpose" from "Required" to "Available" and then click "Next."
6 Click "Summary," "Next," and "Close." The package creation completes.
7 Monitor distmgr.log to ensure that the package content was successfully distributed to the distribution point on CM01.
8 Navigate to Assets and Compliance > Device Collections.
9 Right-click the "All Windows 10 Clients Collection" and select Client Notification > Download Computer Policy. This forces CLIENT01 to pick up the new package deployment.
10 Log on to CLIENT01 as MOL\Administrator and open the ConfigMgr Software Center.
11 In the list of Available Software, select "Notepad++" and click "Install," as shown in figure 8.13.

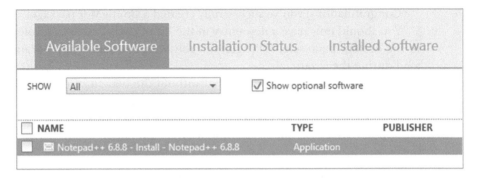

Figure 8.13   Your newly deployed package is ready for installation.

12 The software status changes to "Downloading," then "Installing," and then finally "Installed." Note that the software doesn't appear in the Installed Software tab, because it's a package and therefore doesn't have an associated detection method.

13 Launch Notepad++ to ensure that it opens correctly.

To deploy the package by using PowerShell, use the following command:

```
Start-CMPackageDeployment `
-PackageName 'Notepad++ 6.8' `
-StandardProgramName 'Install - Notepad++ 6.8' `
-CollectionName 'All Windows 10 Clients' `
-DeployPurpose Available
```

That's it—you've successfully deployed a ConfigMgr package! It's worth noting that the end-user experience is virtually identical to that when you installed Paint.NET. This is how it should be; your users shouldn't be aware that the software they're installing is an application, a package, or anything else. As long as they get access to the software they need, why should anything at the back end impact them?

Now you can move on to some ConfigMgr black magic. As you've already seen, Notepad++ can be deployed as a package, but with a little effort, it can also be deployed as an application.

8.5   *Turning packages into applications*

For software such as Notepad++ that has an installer, which in turn supports a silent, unattended installation method, deployment as an application is possible. In this scenario, it's accurate to say that the only thing stopping Notepad++ from being a full AppModel-style application is the lack of a detection method that ConfigMgr can automatically configure. Fortunately, that's something you can provide manually.

AppModel-style applications support a script-based deployment type. This deployment type is a catchall for any type of installer that ConfigMgr can't automatically query for the relevant installation information, such as installation strings and detection methods.

To create an application for Notepad++, perform the following steps:

1 Navigate to Software Library > Application Management > Applications.
2 Right-click "Applications" and select "Create Application."
3 Select "Manually specify the Application information." Click "Next."
4 On the "Specify information about this Application" page, enter `Notepad++ 6.8` into the "Name" field. Click "Next" and then "Next" again.
5 On the Deployment Types page, click "Add" to create a new deployment type.
6 In the "Type" drop-down list, select "Script Installer" and click "Next."
7 In the "Deployment Type Name" field, enter `Notepad ++ 6.8 — (*.exe file)` and click "Next."
8 In the Content page, make the following changes:
   a Location field: UNC path to the Notepad++ installer (for example, `\\CM01\Sources\Software\Notepad++\6.8`)
   b Installation program: npp.6.8.8.Installer.exe /S
   c Uninstall program: %PROGRAMFILES%\Notepad++\uninstall.exe /S
   d Tick: Run installation and uninstall program as 32-bit process on 64-bit clients
   e The page should look like figure 8.14. Click "Next."

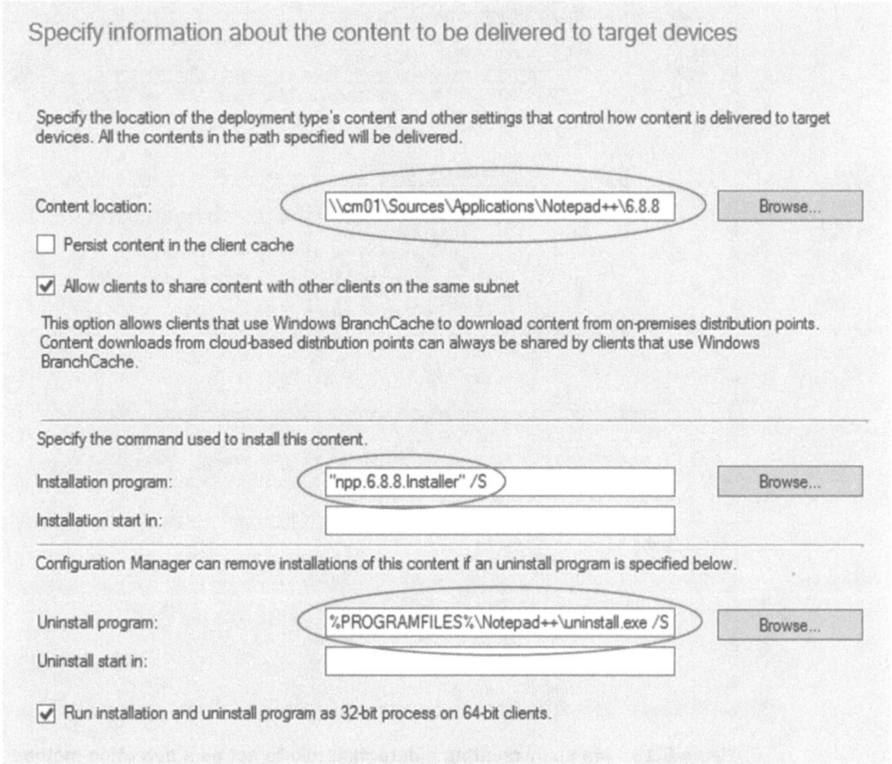

Figure 8.14   Manually creating a new deployment type for a non-AppModel installer

9   On the Detection Method page, click "Add Clause."

10 On the Detection Rule page, make the following changes:

   a   Setting Type: Registry

   b   Hive: HKEY_LOCAL_MACHINE

   c   Key: SOFTWARE\Microsoft\Windows\CurrentVersion\Uninstall\Notepad++

   d   Value: DisplayVersion

   e   Tick: This registry key is associated with a 32-bit application on a 64-bit system

   f   Data Type: String

   g   Select: The registry setting must satisfy the following rule

   h   Operator: Equals

   i   Value: 6.8.8

   j   The page should now look like figure 8.15. Click "OK" and "Next."

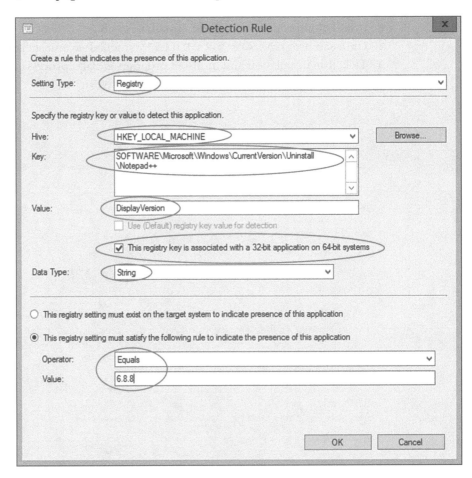

Figure 8.15   Manually creating a detection rule to act as a detection method

11 On the User Experience page, make the following changes:

  a Installation behavior: Install for system if resource is device; otherwise, install for user

  b Logon requirement: Whether or not a user is logged on

  c Installation program visibility: Hidden

12 Click "Summary," "Next," and "Close."

13 Click "Summary," "Next," and "Close" again. The Application Wizard completes.

Phew, you made it! That whole process is a bit convoluted, but to recap what you did, you presented ConfigMgr with an installation file, told it how to install it silently, how to uninstall it silently, and how to accurately detect whether the application installed correctly. That information lies at the core of the AppModel, and you now have a newly created AppModel application with all the embedded smarts you need.

IMPORTANT INFORMATION   The reason you had to tick the check boxes to tell ConfigMgr to handle the installer, uninstaller, and detection method as 32-bit is that Notepad++ is a 32-bit application, which means that it places files in slightly different locations on a 64-bit system than on a 32-bit system. You don't want to create multiple deployment types where one will serve—hence, the extra functionality. For a great explanation of what's happening behind the scenes, read "ConfigMgr 2012 and 32-bit Application Installers," an article written by Configuration Manager MVP Jason Sandys: http://blog.configmgrftw .com/?p=469.

Try It Now—Manually create an application

Follow the steps in section 8.4 to manually create an application for Notepad++.

Consider your own environment: are you able to extract, install, uninstall, and add detection information about your own non-AppModel-type software so as to convert them into applications?

8.6 Labs

WinMerge is a useful free utility for comparing files. Download the latest version from http://winmerge.org/downloads/ and then create an application. You'll have to specify the detection and uninstallation information manually, because the installed is a traditional EXE.

Ensuring that ConfigMgr clients can access content

By now, you may have noticed that ConfigMgr clients interact with the ConfigMgr server hierarchy via a range of dedicated server roles, such as the Management Point role for client communications and policy. The reason for this is that, depending on the environment within which it functions, ConfigMgr can be a highly distributed system, with multiple server roles needed to support a large number of clients located in many places. The ConfigMgr server can support multiple server roles, such as Management Points, in order to cater to such a dispersed environment. Another critical server role that contributes to this modular approach to management is the distribution point (DP). As shown in figure 9.1, this chapter is all about DPs and content—not as sexy as deploying applications with the flair of a Jedi in sunglasses, perhaps, but absolutely vital to the success of any and all ConfigMgr environments.

Chapter 8 briefly touched on distribution points, when you distributed application content to the DP on CM01 so that the ConfigMgr client on CLIENT01 was able to download it. Had the application content not been on the DP, CLIENT01 wouldn't have been able to download and install the application—a situation I've seen many times in enterprise environments.

Therefore, understanding how DPs work is of critical importance in being able to work effectively with ConfigMgr. A wide variety of content, from applications and packages to software updates and operating system images, *must* be distributed to DPs in order for ConfigMgr clients to use them.

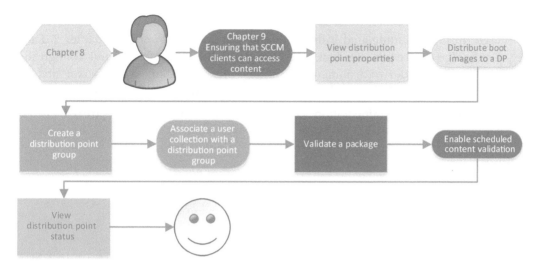

Figure 9.1 Content and distribution points: the foundation of a healthy ConfigMgr environment

So with that, let's jump straight into tackling DPs.

9.1 Understanding distribution points

Conceptually, *distribution points* can be thought of as *content-access points*—where ConfigMgr clients go to access content made available to them by the ConfigMgr server. ConfigMgr's modular approach means that a single ConfigMgr server can support multiple DPs, as shown in figure 9.2.

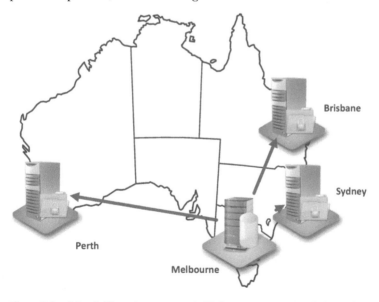

Figure 9.2 A ConfigMgr primary server in Melbourne, supporting dedicated DPs in Sydney, Brisbane, and Perth

In your lab environment, a DP is already installed on CM01; this was set up and configured during the automated hydration build that you performed in chapter 2. Each ConfigMgr site system can have only one active DP, so installing and configuring another DP in your environment will usually mean installing a new server first on which to run it. To see the active DPs in your lab environment, do the following:

1   Navigate to Administration > Distribution Points. As shown in figure 9.3, one DP is available.

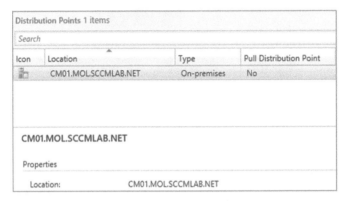

Figure 9.3   The preconfigured DP in your ConfigMgr lab

2   The Summary tab shows you the main properties of the DP, and the Drives tab shows you which drives are visible to ConfigMgr and the priority of each drive for housing content, as shown in figure 9.4. The disk priority is normally based on the amount of available free space on the disk, but you can also manually change the priority if required.

CM01.MOL.SCCMLAB.NET					
Icon	Drive	Total Disk Space (MB)	Free Disk Space (MB)	Content Library Priority	Package Share Priority
	C	60,000.00	34,580.18	2	2
	E	246,072.00	235,729.35	1	1

Figure 9.4   The ConfigMgr console shows you which drives are in use to store the DP.

3   Right-click the distribution point and select "Properties." Here you can view and modify a whole range of properties pertinent to this particular DP. The following properties are important (but please don't change anything!):

   ▪ *General > Enable this distribution point for prestaged content*—This setting allows you to manually copy a compressed content package across to a remote DP in order to avoid distributing the content over a potentially limited or unreliable WAN link.

- *PXE > Enable PXE support for clients*—This setting allows the DP to respond to network boot requests from clients. This is a key feature for operating system deployment.

You can also use PowerShell to return a list of DPs or view the properties of one particular DP:

```
Get-CMDistributionPoint
```

or

```
Get-CMDistributionPoint |
Select-Object SiteCode,NetworkOSPath |
Format-Table
```

or

```
$DP = Get-CMDistributionPoint | `
Where-Object NetworkOSPath -like '*CM01*'
$DP.Props | Select-Object PropertyName,Value1
```

Each of the preceding commands returns information about ConfigMgr DPs. The first bombards you with lots of information (possibly too much), and the second and third commands refine the data and dig a little deeper into each DP.

> ### Try It Now—View DP properties
> Use the ConfigMgr console and the PowerShell commands in this section to view the properties of the DP on CM01. Note how each of the PowerShell commands gives you different levels of detail about each DP.
>
> Follow the same process to gather information about the DPs in your own production environment. See how using PowerShell becomes incredibly useful in environments with lots of DPs, as you can gather and collate large amounts of information into an easy-to-digest format.

9.2 Distributing content

Over the course of the preceding chapters, you've already distributed content to the DP on CM01 as part of various lab exercises. We glossed over the fine details of content distribution at the time, but now it's time to delve deeper.

The best place to start is with an overview of the content distribution status of all the various packages in your ConfigMgr environment. To view the status, navigate to Monitoring > Distribution Status > Content Status. As you can see in figure 9.5, every package type that can be referenced in the ConfigMgr database via a package ID (such as applications and packages) is listed. Table 9.1 explains each column.

Content Status 8 items

Search

Icon	Software	Type	Targeted	Size (MB)	Compliance %	Package ID	Source Version
	Boot image (x64)	Boot Image	0	209.06		PS100005	2
	Boot image (x86)	Boot Image	0	170.97		PS100002	2
	Configuration Manager Client Package	Package	1	183.33	100.0	PS100003	1
	Configuration Manager Client Upgrade Package	Package	1	1.66	100.0	PS100004	1
	Microsoft Corporation User State Migration Tool f...	Package	0	48.69		PS100001	1
	Notepad++ 6.8	Application	0	5.11		PS100008	1
	Notepad++ 6.8	Package	1	5.11	100.0	PS100007	1
	Paint.NET 4.0.5	Application	1	53.43	100.0	PS100006	2

Figure 9.5   The content distribution status of all packages in the ConfigMgr database

Table 9.1   Details of the Content Status dashboard

Column	What it means
Software	The name of the software package in the ConfigMgr database. Packages of different types can have the same name, but packages of the same type can't.
Type	The type of package—for example, boot image, package, or application.
Targeted	The number of targets to which the software has been deployed. A target can be a distribution point, a distribution point group, or a collection. If the value is 0, the package hasn't been distributed to any targets.
Size (MB)	The size of the package in MB.
Compliance %	The number of targets to which the package has been successfully deployed. Useful for determining distribution errors. If the target value is 0, the compliance value will be blank.
Date Created	The date on which the package was created.
Package ID	A unique identifier for the package that's stored in the ConfigMgr database. The package ID consists of the three-character site code (for example, PS1) followed by a five-character hexadecimal number.
Source Version	The version of the source software. For example, when an application or package is first created, it has a version value of 1. If the source is updated in any way (for example, new files are added or the properties in ConfigMgr are changed), the version is incremented by 1.

You'll notice that the built-in boot images haven't been distributed to any targets. That's normal behavior, but when you tackle operating system deployment (OSD), you'll definitely need these packages available to clients, so let's get them distributed. To distribute the boot images to a new target, do the following:

1   Navigate to Software Library > Operating Systems > Boot Images.
2   Right-click "Boot Image (x86)" and select "Distribute Content."

3 Click "Next" to go to the Content Distribution page.

4 Select Add > Distribution Point > CM01.mol.sccmlab.net. Click "OK."

5 Click "Summary," "Next," and "Close."

Navigate back to Monitoring > Distribution Status > Content Status, and you'll see that the boot image (x86) package now has a targeted value of 1. Depending on the disk speed of your system, the compliance % value may already be at 100%.

> **TIP** Double-click the package to drill down into the content distribution status, which should look like figure 9.6. If anything goes wrong with content distribution, this is a great place to start the troubleshooting process.

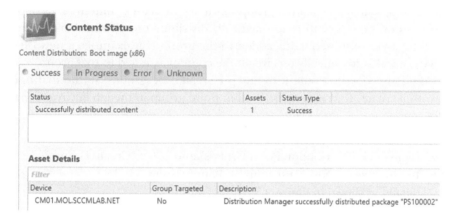

Figure 9.6   The detailed content status for boot image (x86)

You also need to distribute the content for boot image (x64), but rather than use the console, let's use PowerShell:

```
Start-CMContentDistribution `
-BootImageName 'Boot Image (x64)' `
-DistributionPointName 'CM01.MOL.SCCMLAB.NET'
```

Again, check the Content Status page to make sure that the content distributed correctly.

> **WHICH LOG?** For every content distribution action you perform, distmgr.log is where you want to be looking. Everything to do with content distribution is logged right there.

> ## Try It Now—Distribute content
> Follow the steps in this section to distribute the content for the x86 and x64 boot images to the DP on CM01, using both the console and PowerShell.

9.3   *Working with distribution point groups*

As an administrator in a small ConfigMgr environment with only one or two DPs, the task of choosing where to distribute content is an easy one. But what about a complex environment with 10, 50, or 100 DPs?

The challenge is that in a large environment, DPs are more likely to have different purposes: some will need to provide PXE services for operating system deployment, whereas others may be secured with HTTPS. Keeping track of which content is deployed to which DP can quickly become burdensome and inaccurate if you try to handle distribution manually.

ConfigMgr caters to this by enabling you to group DPs together into distribution point groups. Similar to security groups in Active Directory, content that's deployed to a distribution point group is automatically distributed to all members of the group, and if any DPs are subsequently added to the group (for example, a new DP is provisioned), it will automatically receive all the content assigned to that group.

ConfigMgr doesn't come with any pre-created DP groups, so the first one is one that you'll create. To create a distribution point group in the lab environment, do the following:

1 Navigate to Administration > Distribution Point Groups.
2 Right-click "Distribution Point Groups" and select "Create Group."
3 In the Create New Distribution Point Group window, enter the following details, as shown in figure 9.7:

   a Name: MoL Lab DPs
   b Description: All DPs in the MoL ConfigMgr Lab
   c Members: CM01.mol.sccmlab.net (click Add to add this DP)

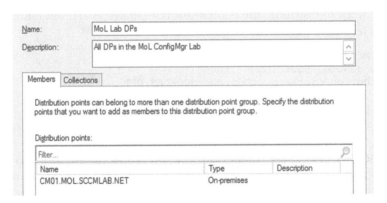

Figure 9.7   Adding the DP to a new distribution point group

4 Click "OK." You now have a distribution point group, with the local DP as a member.

To create the distribution point group in PowerShell, run the following:

```
New-CMDistributionPointGroup `
-Name 'MoL Lab DPs' `
-Description 'All DPs in the MoL ConfigMgr Lab'
Add-CMDistributionPointToGroup `
-DistributionPointName 'CM01.mol.sccmlab.net' `
-DistributionPointGroupName 'MoL Lab DPs'
```

You can also associate a collection with a distribution point group. Why would you want to do this? Let's say you create a new application that's going to be deployed to a specific user collection. By deploying the application content to the user collection, the collection association with the distribution point group will then automatically distribute the content to all DPs in the group, as shown in figure 9.8.

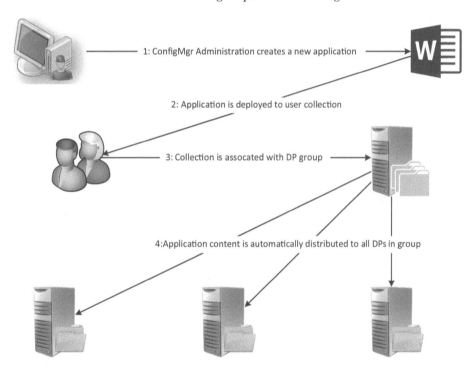

Figure 9.8 Deploying content to a user collection that's associated with a DP group

To associate a collection with a distribution point group (although this bit isn't needed for your lab environment), do the following:

1 Navigate to Administration > Distribution Point Groups.
2 Right-click the group that you want to associate with a collection and select "Properties."
3 Go to the Collections tab and click "Add."

4   Select the collection that you want to associate. Click "OK" and then "OK" again.

5   The Collections tab should look like figure 9.9.

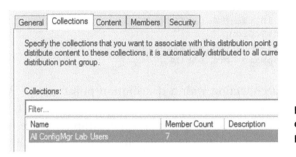

Figure 9.9   Associating a user collection with a distribution point group

To associate a collection using PowerShell, run the following:

```
Add-CMUserCollectionToDistributionPointGroup `
-UserCollectionName 'All ConfigMgr Lab Users' `
-DistributionPointGroupName 'MoL Lab DPs'
```

Your lab environment may never be big enough to take full advantage of distribution point groups, but they're of particular benefit in any production environment. Look for opportunities to group DPs in a way that makes sense in your environment, such as by geographical location or specific function.

Try it Now—Create a DP group

Use the steps in this section to create a new DP group and then associate the DP group with a user collection.

Think about your own production environment: do you have enough DPs to warrant using groups, and if so what's the logical structure that makes the most sense for your business?

9.4   *Keeping content healthy*

Given that the whole reason you distribute content to distribution points is so that your managed clients can access it, it's clearly important to ensure that the distributed content is always correct. The last thing you want is to be enjoying your (fifth) morning coffee in peace, only to discover that half the content on your remote DPs has been quietly corrupting over the last couple of weeks. Farewell serenity.

For example, say you distribute a package to a number of remote DPs and the process appears to go through without error. But unbeknownst to you, there was a subsequent issue on one of the DPs; maybe the antivirus on that server was out-of-date and aggressively scanned the content location, or the server was compromised in some other way. Whatever the issue, the hash value on the package has changed. When a ConfigMgr client goes to access that package from the DP, the process will fail.

ConfigMgr comes to the rescue with a feature called *content validation*. This is designed to allow you to ensure that content that has already been distributed out to DPs is in a healthy state. In this content, ConfigMgr determines that distributed content is healthy if the hash for a particular package (which is the unique value assigned to the package when it gets compressed and distributed) is what the ConfigMgr site server expects it to be.

You can validate content in a few ways: validating individual packages manually, validating all content on a particular DP, and automatically validating DP content on a schedule.

9.4.1 Validating an individual package

You can validate a particular package on a particular DP, either from the DP itself or from the package:

1 Navigate to Administration > Distribution Points.
2 Double-click a DP and go to the Content tab.
3 Select a deployment package in the list and click "Validate," as shown in figure 9.10.

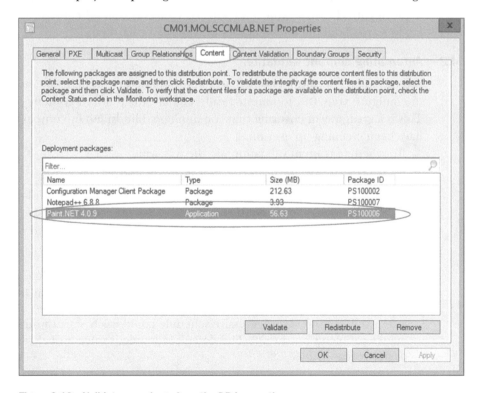

Figure 9.10 Validate a package from the DP in question.

Alternatively:

1 Navigate to the Software Library.

2 Double-click the software package that you want to validate (for example, boot image or application) and go to the Content Locations tab.

3 Select the DP that you want to validate the content on, and click "Validate."

Rather than use the console, you can achieve the same outcome with PowerShell; for example:

```
Invoke-CMContentValidation `
-BootImageName 'Boot Image (x64)' `
-DistributionPointName 'CM01.mol.sccmlab.net'
```

> **WHICH LOG?**   It should come as no surprise to learn that, once again, everything you need to know about content validation sits in distmgr.log. If you haven't realized it yet, you'll be spending a *lot* of time in distmgr.log.

Regardless of the validation method you use, it's important to note that content validation is a disk-intensive operation that takes time to complete. Triggering manual content validation during business hours can be risky, because you can impact other operations on the site system, such as operating system deployment or application deployment. The more you work with DPs and distributed content, the more you'll get to learn about the idiosyncrasies of your server hardware!

9.4.2   *Automating content validation*

You can always perform a one-off validation whenever you like, but another option is to configure your DPs to automatically validate their stored content on a schedule. This is a great way of ensuring that you don't get blindsided by content problems that have been creeping up over time.

To schedule content validation, do the following:

1 Navigate to Administration > Distribution Points.

2 Double-click the DP for which you want to enable content validation and go to the Content Validation tab.

3 Click "Validate content on a schedule" and set the schedule to something that suits your organization.

> **TIP**   Although it might be tempting to set the validation schedule to something aggressive, try to resist temptation. Content validation can be a CPU- and disk-intensive process, and the more content you have stored, the more intensive it is. An overly aggressive schedule could easily start causing performance problems on the DP. The default schedule is once a week, and that's perfectly reasonable.

9.4.3   *Spotting validation errors*

If your exercises in content validation are determining that yes, content errors are occurring, where would you expect to see those errors reported?

Head over to Monitoring > Distribution Status > Distribution Point Configuration Status. Here you'll see the status of all your DPs, and if any of the DPs have reported content validation errors, this is where you'll see them.

Content validation doesn't automatically fix the error—mainly because there could be numerous reasons why a DP has problematic content, so there isn't an auto-magical-twinkly-fairy fix that ConfigMgr can apply. Normally, updating the content or (at worst) removing and then re-adding the content fixes the issue.

> **Try It Now—Validate content**
> Use the steps in section 9.4 to manually validate an individual deployment package as well as all the content on the DP on CM01.

Now that you have a solid grounding in the types of content that ConfigMgr can handle, you're going to extend what you've covered so far into something near and dear to us all: patching! Ah, I can almost feel your sighs of delight at the prospect.

Stick with me—no one likes patching—but ConfigMgr can turn a mind-numbing monthly chore into a slick, automated task. Read on!

9.5   *Lab*

Let's assume for a moment that the lab environment is your production environment. The backup window closes at 2:00 a.m., so you're confident that no disk-intensive operations are happening at that time.

You've been instructed to ensure that all content held within the DP on the primary site server is automatically validated regularly.

Set up a custom schedule on the DP on CM01 that validates the content once per week, starting at 2:30 a.m. on Saturdays, and that runs with a medium priority.

9.6   *Ideas for on your own*

Distribution points are an absolutely critical part of your ConfigMgr environment. You might have the best applications and the most well-defined, sculpted, and glistening Boundaries in the business, but if your DPs are unhealthy—well, bad times, people. Bad times.

It's worth spending a bit of time learning how content is stored on a DP, and how each DP can handle content.

Yvette O'Meally from the Configuration Manager product team in Redmond wrote a great article in late 2013 entitled "Understanding the Configuration Manager Content Library." I strongly urge you to take some time out to have a read and add it to your bookmarks: http://blogs.technet.com/b/configmgrteam/archive/2013/10/29/understanding-the-configuration-manager-content-library.aspx.

O'Meally also posted another article called "Troubleshooting Content Mismatch Warnings on a Distribution Point in System Center 2012 Configuration Manager" (yes, everything to do with ConfigMgr is wordy—even the titles). It's a great article that goes into technical depth about why these issues arise and what you can best do to fix them. Head on over to the blog and have a read: http://blogs.technet.com/b/configmgrteam/archive/2012/05/07/troubleshooting-content-mismatch-warnings-on-a-distribution-point-in-system-center-2012-configuration-manager.aspx.

Keeping ConfigMgr
clients patched

10

In 1789, Benjamin Franklin wrote (among many other things) that "in this world nothing can be said to be certain, except death and taxes." It's been well over 200 years since that statement, so I think it could do with a little update. Let's change that list to read "death, taxes, and patching." True, it's not as statesman-like as the original, but it stands up to scrutiny, I feel.

Who likes patching so much that they're more than happy to sort it out manually? Every month. Any takers? No, I didn't think so.

As administrators, patching—that's downloading, deploying, and managing software updates, for the uninitiated—is just one of those things we do. All the time. And just when you're up-to-date on all the latest patches, you know that it's only a matter of time before the next round. So why not let ConfigMgr do the heavy lifting for you? Patching is a core component of ConfigMgr, and as you can see in figure 10.1, that's what this chapter is all about.

Software updates in ConfigMgr are managed by a software update point (SUP), which in turn uses traditional Windows Server Update Services (WSUS), which you may already use in your production environment. In this chapter, you'll install and configure the SUP, download updates, and deploy updates to your managed client.

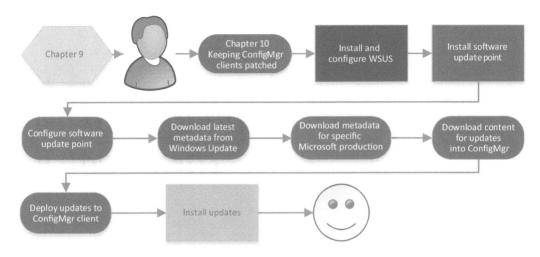

Figure 10.1   Patching: Fun? No. Much easier with ConfigMgr? Yes!

10.1   Install the software update point

The SUP is the heart and soul of managing updates in the ConfigMgr environment. Depending on the size and complexity of your production environment, you may even have multiple SUPs distributed around the place.

Many companies use WSUS, which is a function of Windows Server. It enables you to distribute updates for Microsoft products from an internal location, rather than have every machine in your environment download their updates directly from Microsoft.

10.1.1   Install WSUS prerequisites

The latest build of ConfigMgr is designed to give you full manageability of Windows 10, including the feature upgrades. By default, ConfigMgr will show you this new update classification in the SUP, but unless you install a number of WSUS prerequisites first, then WSUS, and then finally a WSUS hotfix, this functionality won't work.

Starting off with the pre-WSUS updates, you'll need to download and install Windows Server 2012 R2 updates from Microsoft. The installation order is important, and you should reboot when prompted to. Install all of these updates on CM01. If you've already patched CM01 using Windows Update, some of these updates may not be relevant. Download the following updates:

- KB2919442—https://support.microsoft.com/en-us/kb/2919442
- KB2919355—https://support.microsoft.com/en-us/kb/2919355

Then, install the updates in the following order:

1 KB2919442
2 KB2919355
3 clearcompressionflag.exe

  4 KB2932046

  5 KB2959977

  6 KB2937592

  7 KB2938439

  8 KB2934018

After they're installed and CM01 has been restarted for the last time, you can move on to installing and configuring WSUS.

10.1.2 *Install and configure WSUS*

The first thing you need to do in order to install the SUP is to install and configure WSUS on the CM01 server. The SUP uses the WSUS binaries and database to function, but then extends the management experience into ConfigMgr. So even though you'll be installing WSUS, you won't be managing software updates via WSUS, but rather via ConfigMgr. Beyond installing WSUS, you won't need to interact with it at all.

  To install WSUS, log on to CM01 and launch a PowerShell console as administrator. Then type in the following:

```
Install-WindowsFeature `
-Name UpdateServices-Services,UpdateServices-DB `
—IncludeManagementTools
```

This installs WSUS without also installing the Windows Internal Database (WID), as shown in figure 10.2. You don't need WID because you already have SQL Server running on CM01, and this can be used to host the WSUS database.

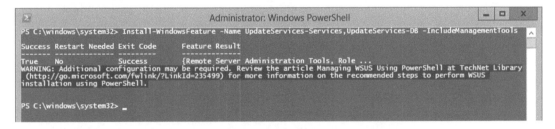

Figure 10.2 Use PowerShell to install Windows Server Update Services on CM01.

Next, create a new folder for the WSUS content:

```
New-Item -Path E: -Name WSUS -ItemType Directory
```

Then, navigate to C:\Program Files\Update Services\Tools and type this:

```
.\WsusUtil.exe postinstall SQL_INSTANCE_NAME='CM01' CONTENT_DIR=E:\WSUS
```

This performs the post-installation configuration of WSUS. To verify that it succeeded, open SQL Server Management Studio and check that there's a new database called SUSDB (the default database created by WSUS), as shown in figure 10.3.

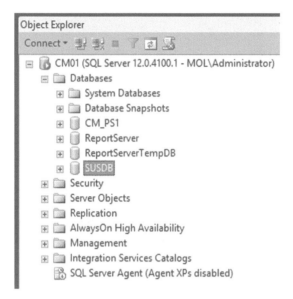

Figure 10.3   Use WsusUtil.exe to create and configure a new WSUS database on CM01.

You can also type in `netstat –an –p tcp` to verify that CM01 is now listening on TCP ports 8530 and 8531. These are the TCP ports that WSUS/SUP uses for client connectivity, as shown in figure 10.4.

```
                           Administrator: Windows PowerShell
PS C:\Program Files\Update Services\Tools> netstat -an -p tcp
Active Connections
   Proto  Local Address          Foreign Address        State
   TCP    0.0.0.0:80             0.0.0.0:0              LISTENING
   TCP    0.0.0.0:135            0.0.0.0:0              LISTENING
   TCP    0.0.0.0:443            0.0.0.0:0              LISTENING
   TCP    0.0.0.0:445            0.0.0.0:0              LISTENING
   TCP    0.0.0.0:1433           0.0.0.0:0              LISTENING
   TCP    0.0.0.0:4022           0.0.0.0:0              LISTENING
   TCP    0.0.0.0:5040           0.0.0.0:0              LISTENING
   TCP    0.0.0.0:5985           0.0.0.0:0              LISTENING
   TCP    0.0.0.0:8530           0.0.0.0:0              LISTENING
   TCP    0.0.0.0:8531           0.0.0.0:0              LISTENING
   TCP    0.0.0.0:10123          0.0.0.0:0              LISTENING
   TCP    0.0.0.0:47001          0.0.0.0:0              LISTENING
   TCP    0.0.0.0:49152          0.0.0.0:0              LISTENING
   TCP    0.0.0.0:49153          0.0.0.0:0              LISTENING
   TCP    0.0.0.0:49154          0.0.0.0:0              LISTENING
   TCP    0.0.0.0:49155          0.0.0.0:0              LISTENING
   TCP    0.0.0.0:49156          0.0.0.0:0              LISTENING
   TCP    0.0.0.0:49169          0.0.0.0:0              LISTENING
   TCP    0.0.0.0:49239          0.0.0.0:0              LISTENING
   TCP    127.0.0.1:1434         0.0.0.0:0              LISTENING
   TCP    172.16.100.210:80      172.16.100.220:50461   ESTABLISHED
   TCP    172.16.100.210:139     0.0.0.0:0              LISTENING
   TCP    172.16.100.210:49222   172.16.100.200:3268    ESTABLISHED
   TCP    172.16.100.210:49224   172.16.100.200:49157   ESTABLISHED
   TCP    172.16.100.210:49236   172.16.100.200:389     ESTABLISHED
   TCP    172.16.100.210:49238   172.16.100.200:49157   ESTABLISHED
   TCP    172.16.100.210:49248   172.16.100.200:389     ESTABLISHED
   TCP    172.16.100.210:49286   172.16.100.210:1433    TIME_WAIT
   TCP    172.16.100.210:49297   172.16.100.200:135     TIME_WAIT
   TCP    172.16.100.210:49321   172.16.100.210:1433    TIME_WAIT
PS C:\Program Files\Update Services\Tools> _
```

Figure 10.4   CM01 is listening on the correct WSUS TCP ports.

Now that WSUS is correctly installed and configured, you can move on to configuring ConfigMgr to use it for software updates. Note that you don't have to launch the WSUS administration console at any point in this process; everything is handled via ConfigMgr.

Try It Now—Install and configure WSUS

Follow the steps in this section to enable WSUS and create the SUSDB database on CM01.

Consider your own environment: do you currently use WSUS to deploy Microsoft updates?

10.1.3 *Install post-WSUS hotfix*

The final task before you can install the SUP is to download and install KB3095113, which you can request from Microsoft here: https://support.microsoft.com/en-us/kb/3095113.

This hotfix is required for WSUS (which you've just installed) to support Windows 10 feature upgrades so that you can make use of this functionality in ConfigMgr. Unlike the previous updates, KB3095113 is an optional hotfix, which means that you have to enter a valid email address so that Microsoft can send you the download link. Installing the update also requires you to reboot the ConfigMgr server.

10.1.4 *Install the software update point*

WSUS is a prerequisite of the SUP, so now you're ready to proceed.

To install the SUP, do the following:

1. In the ConfigMgr console, navigate to Administration > Site Configuration > Servers and Site System Roles.
2. Right-click "CM01.mol.sccmlab.net" and select "Add Site System Roles."
3. Click "Next" until you get to System Role Selection. Select the "Software Update Point" check box and click "Next."
4. Configure the remaining options according to table 10.1.
5. Click "Summary" and then click "Next" to finish.

Table 10.1　Configuration settings for the SUP installation

Section	Setting(s)
Software Update Point	WSUS is configured to use ports 8530 and 8531 Allow intranet-only client connections
Proxy and Account Settings	Default
Synchronization Source	Default

Table 10.1   Configuration settings for the SUP installation *(continued)*

Section	Setting(s)
Synchronization Schedule	Enable synchronization on a schedule
Simple Schedule	Run every seven days
Supercedence Rules	Default
Classifications	Uncheck all options
Products	Uncheck all options
Languages	Software update file: English (plus any additional needed) Summary details: English (plus any additional needed)

WHICH LOG?   After you finish the installation wizard, CM01 starts installing the SUP in the background. A new log file called SUPSetup.log is created in the default log directory on CM01. Monitor the installation from there, and then open WSUSCtrl.log to ensure that ConfigMgr is communicating with WSUS correctly.

No classifications or products? What gives?

It may seem somewhat confusing that in table 10.1 you unchecked all the classifications and products. This means that after the SUP is installed, it's not configured to look at any updates.

The reason you do this during installation is that at the time of installation, the SUP is drawing its list of available classifications and products from the WSUS database. In turn, the WSUS database is a brand-new, untouched database that doesn't have the latest list of classifications and products from Microsoft Update.

By preventing the SUP from attempting to update from an outdated WSUS database, you'll speed up the installation and avoid wasting any time during the SUP configuration.

Finally, navigate to Monitoring > System Status > Component Status, and you'll see three new site components that are related to WSUS, as shown in figure 10.5.

	OK	SMS_SOFTWARE_METERING_PROCESSOR	CM01.MOL.SCCMLAB.NET
	OK	SMS_STATE_SYSTEM	CM01.MOL.SCCMLAB.NET
	OK	SMS_STATUS_MANAGER	CM01.MOL.SCCMLAB.NET
	OK	SMS_WINNT_SERVER_DISCOVERY_AGENT	CM01.MOL.SCCMLAB.NET
	OK	SMS_WSUS_CONFIGURATION_MANAGER	CM01.MOL.SCCMLAB.NET
	OK	SMS_WSUS_CONTROL_MANAGER	CM01.MOL.SCCMLAB.NET
	OK	SMS_WSUS_SYNC_MANAGER	CM01.MOL.SCCMLAB.NET
	OK	WINDOWS_INTUNE_SERVICE	CM01.MOL.SCCMLAB.NET

Figure 10.5   WSUS/SUP components are now successfully installed in ConfigMgr.

Now that both WSUS and SUP have been successfully installed, you can move on to configuration.

> **Try It Now—Enable and configure the SUP**
> Follow the steps in this section to enable and configure the SUP server role on CM01. Monitor the log files to ensure that the installation completes successfully.

10.2 Configure software updates in ConfigMgr

To configure the SUP in ConfigMgr, first you'll update the WSUS database so that the SUP has a full list of products and classifications, and then you'll select classifications and products to work with.

First, in the console, navigate to Administration > Site Configuration > Sites, right-click "PS1 – Primary Site 1," and select Configure Site Components > Software Update Point.

Navigate to the Products tab, and as you can see in figure 10.6, the list of products is looking pretty thin on the ground. To resolve this, you'll sync ConfigMgr against Microsoft Windows Update.

> **IMPORTANT** To complete the rest of this chapter, CM01 MUST be able to access the internet. If not, it won't be able to communicate with Windows Update. If CM01 can't access the internet, resolve this before continuing.

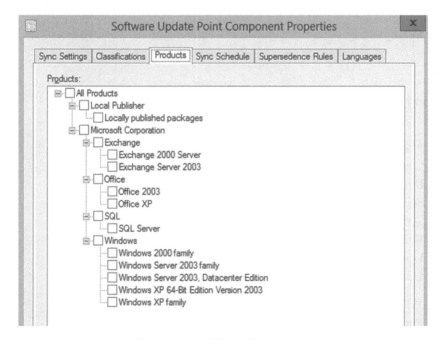

Figure 10.6   That's a pretty bleak list of Microsoft products to patch.

To force CM01 to synchronize against Windows Update, navigate to Software Library > Software Updates > All Software Updates. Then click "Synchronize Software Updates." At this point, CM01 will start to synchronize categories and products against Windows Update. To do this with PowerShell, type `Sync-CMSoftwareUpdate –FullSync $true`.

WHICH LOG?   Open and monitor wsyncmgr.log to see what's happening in real time.

Depending on the speed of your internet connection, the sync will take about 10 minutes. When it's complete, go back into the "Software Update Point" section under "Site Configuration." As shown in figure 10.7, the list of products and classifications now looks different.

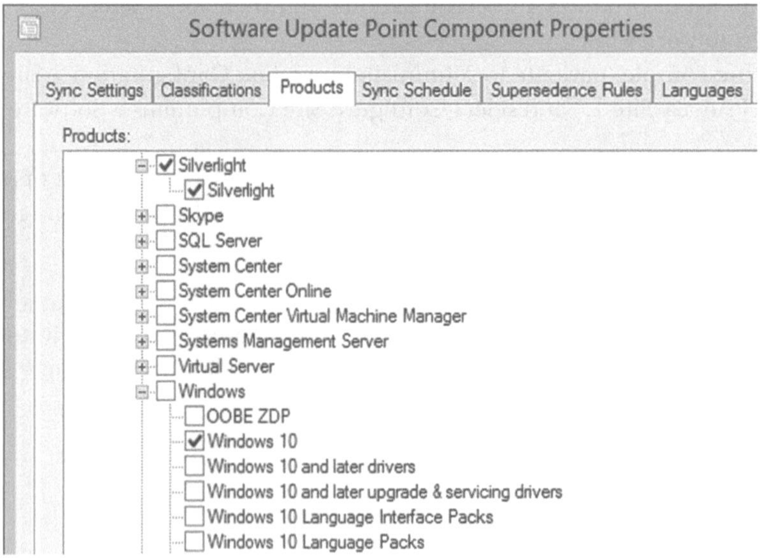

Figure 10.7   A full list of Microsoft products, ready for patching

In the Classifications tab, select the following:

- Critical Updates
- Definition Updates
- Security Updates
- Service Packs
- Update Rollups
- Updates
- Upgrades

Then, under the Products tab, select the following:

- Forefront > Forefront Endpoint Protection 2010
- Silverlight > Silverlight

- Windows > Windows 10
- Windows > Windows Defender

Apply the changes and then go back into Software Library, initiate another updates sync, and monitor the wsyncmgr.log (or use the preceding PowerShell command to initiate the sync). This time, you'll see that much more information is written to the log file as the SUP downloads the metadata for the products and classifications that you specified earlier.

> **TIP** *Metadata* is data about data. For example, metadata about a file might be its size, file type, or the last time it was modified. At this stage in configuring software updates, you've downloaded metadata about each update: name, details, date released, supersedence information, and so on. Synchronizing against Windows Update doesn't automatically download the content into your environment, which, given the size of some updates, is a good thing.

After the process has completed, navigate back to Software Library > Software Updates > All Software Updates, and you'll see a list of software updates that's available, ready for download and deployment.

Try It Now—Synchronize the SUP

Follow the steps in this section to synchronize the SUP against Microsoft Windows Update, ensuring that the sync completes successfully and that the products and classifications are updated.

Think about your own environment: which Microsoft products would you need to enable in the SUP?

10.3 *Download updates into ConfigMgr*

Now that you've configured the SUP to sync updates for the Microsoft products that you're interested in, it's time to move on and download the content for those updates into your environment so that you can deploy updates to your managed clients.

Before you download any content, you want to make sure that you're downloading only content for the specific updates that you're interested in deploying. Otherwise, you can end up downloading, storing, and distributing too much content unnecessarily.

To refine the list of updates, do the following:

1 Navigate to Software Library > Software Updates > All Software Updates.
2 In the far-right corner of the list of updates, click "Add Criteria" and select the following options:
   a Expired
   b Language
   c Product

      d Superseded

      e Update Classification (go back and add Update Classification four more times)

3 This displays additional search filters that you can apply against the update list. Configure each item as follows:

      a Expired: No

      b Product: Windows 10

      c Superseded: No

      d Update Classification: Critical Updates *or* Security Updates *or* Update Roll-ups *or* Updates. (Click "Add" each time to include an extra classification.)

4 Click "Search." The filters apply to the update list, and you'll see only updates for Windows 10 that have neither expired nor been superseded, and that fall within the stated classifications (no definition updates).

5 Select all the updates, right-click the selection, and choose "Create Software Update Group." Call the new group `MoL - Windows 10 Updates`.

6 Navigate to Software Update Groups and you'll see the newly created group listed. Double-click the group to see all the updates you just added.

7 The next step is to download the content for the updates, but to do this you need a location in the environment to physically store the source files. To create a new folder structure and share, type the following in PowerShell:

> **Creates a new folder** ─▷
>
> **Shares the folder** │
>
> **Creates a new subfolder** ─▷

```
New-Item -Path E:\ -Name Updates -ItemType Directory
New-SmbShare -Path E:\Updates -Name Updates -CachingMode None
   -ChangeAccess MOL\Administrator #B
New-Item -Path E:\Updates -Name Windows10Updates -ItemType Directory
```

8 Verify that you can navigate to \\CM01\Updates\Windows10Updates in File Explorer. Navigate to Software Update Groups, right-click the group you created earlier, and select "Download."

9 You're prompted to create a new deployment package to house the software updates. Configure it as follows:

      a Name: Windows 10 Updates

      b Package Source: \\CM01\Updates\Windows10Updates (click Next)

      c Distribution Points: Add > Distribution Point Groups > MoL Lab DPs

      d All remaining settings as default

      e Click "Summary" and then "Next" to start download process

Open the Windows10Updates folder in File Explorer and you'll see it start to be populated with content, as shown in figure 10.8. After the download finishes, you can close the wizard.

> **WHICH LOG?** When you trigger a software update download, the process creates a temporary log file in C:\Users\USERNAME\AppData\Local\Temp\2\ PatchDownloader.log. This shows you the status of every update as it's downloaded. Once complete, the distribution of the deployment package to the DPs can be monitored from distmgr.log.

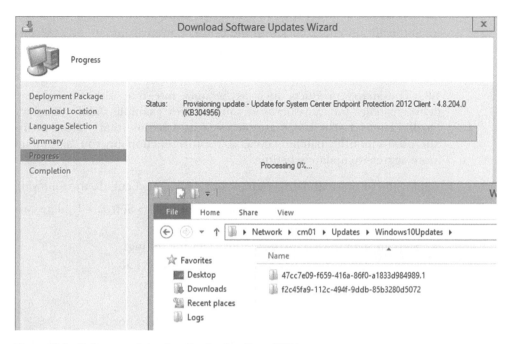

Figure 10.8   Software updates downloading locally to CM01

TIP   The update download process may fail with an error, and the Patch-Downloader.log will have a line that looks like `DownloadContentFiles()` `failed with hr=0x80072ee7` , which indicates a communications problem. To resolve this, open Internet Explorer on CM01 and go to Internet Options > Connections > LAN Settings and untick "Automatically detect settings." Click "OK," close Internet Explorer, and try the process again. What's happening here is that the proxy settings detection in IE are causing the download to fail. Removing the setting fixes the problem.

Try It Now—Download software updates

Follow the preceding steps to download the available updates for Windows 10 to an update package, ready for deployment.

Now that you've downloaded updates to the ConfigMgr environment, it's time to deploy them.

10.4   *Deploy updates to ConfigMgr clients*

To deploy software updates, you'll deploy the deployment group, rather than the deployment package. When a client sees updates within a deployment group that it needs to apply, it will download the content from the distributed package. Another way of looking at it is that the group handles the action, and the package handles the content.

By default, client policy is set to manage software updates and have each managed client automatically check back with the ConfigMgr environment every seven days for new updates. You can make this more aggressive if you like, and given that Microsoft is moving toward a more rapid update release cycle, this is a good idea.

TIP   Third-party products such as Secunia integrate with ConfigMgr to deliver patches for non-Microsoft software (for example, Adobe Reader or Mozilla Firefox). These operate on a release schedule that's different from Microsoft's monthly patching cycle, so for this functionality you might want a more aggressive update schedule.

To deploy the software update group to your managed client, do the following:

1 Navigate to Software Library > Software Updates > Software Update Groups.
2 Right-click Update Group and select "Deploy."
3 Step through the wizard, using the following settings:
   a General > Name > Windows 10 Updates - MoL Lab
   b General > Collection > All Windows 10 Clients
   c Deployment Package > Windows 10 Updates
   d Scheduling > Installation Deadline > As soon as possible
4 On the Summary page, select "Save As Template." Call the template `Windows 10 Updates` and click "Save."
5 Click "Next" to finish the wizard. The updates are deployed.
   At this point, the next time that CLIENT01 runs a check for software updates, it will find the new deployment and process it. But you could be waiting a while, so let's speed things up.
6 Log into CLIENT01 as MOL\Administrator.
7 Navigate to Control Panel > Configuration Manager.
8 Go to the Actions tab, select "Software Updates Deployment Evaluation Cycle," and click "Run Now."
   This forces CLIENT01 to look at the update metadata that resides on the SUP. The ConfigMgr client makes a list of all the updates that the local operating system doesn't have, and reports that back to the ConfigMgr server.

WHICH LOG?   On CLIENT01, the ConfigMgr agent will use the local Windows Update agent to process the updates, so check out C:\Windows\WindowsUpdate.log. After the Windows Update agent has processed the updates, the UpdatesStore.log file in C:\Windows\CCM\Logs will show you how the ConfigMgr client is handling any discovered updates.

9   In the Configuration Manager client, go to the Actions tab, select "Machine Policy Retrieval and Evaluation Cycle" and click "Run Now." This forces the client to pick up the new software updates deployment.
10 Select "Software Update Deployment Evaluation Cycle" and click "Run Now."

11 You should see a pop-up in the top-right corner of the screen, informing you that updates are ready for installation, as shown in figure 10.9.

Figure 10.9   Hey, you! It's time to patch!

12 Click the box and you'll get a more detailed box, as shown in figure 10.10. You see this because you're logged on as a local administrator, which gives you a certain amount of flexibility over when (but not if) the updates will be installed.

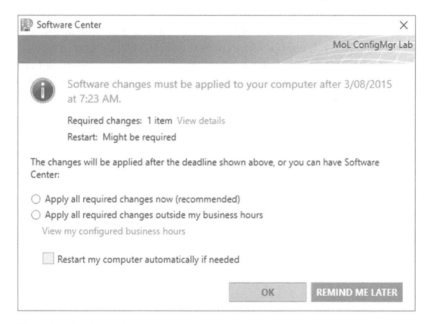

Figure 10.10   As the local administrator, you have some control over update installation.

13 Select "Apply all required changes now" and click "OK." The client starts downloading and installing the updates, and you can monitor the progress in the Software Center.

WHICH LOG?   Although the Software Center will give you an idea of what's going on, for some rich information check out WindowsUpdate.log as well as UpdatesDeployment.log.

This update process may take quite some time, so feel free to wander off and partake of some form of caffeine. As each update is installed, the ConfigMgr client reports back to the Management Point about the status of each update—whether it installed, and if not, what went wrong.

> **Try It Now—Deploy and install updates**
>
> Follow the steps in this section to deploy and install the Windows 10 updates to CLIENT01.
>
> Consider your own environment: would you want to give your users the ability to choose when to install updates, or do updates need to be installed within a certain timeframe?

Congratulations! You've successfully downloaded and deployed Microsoft updates to your managed client. Because of its centralized, highly visible approach to administration, ConfigMgr will enable you to turn the monthly patching process into something that you may not exactly look forward to with breathless, tingling anticipation, but certainly no longer with that deep-seated sense of dread and knee-trembling fear.

And for those of you who don't patch at all, well, now you have no excuse!

10.5 Lab

Add Microsoft Office 2016 updates to the SUP. Create a deployment group and deployment package for Office 2016, but exclude all the updates that relate to the 64-bit version of Office, as the 32-bit version is the most commonly installed.

Preparing to deploy Windows

ConfigMgr is excellent at many tasks, and one of the tasks at its core is deploying Windows. Deployment involves taking a copy of Windows and using ConfigMgr to install it across a wide variety of systems: laptops, desktops, virtual disks, portable media, and virtual machines.

As shown in figure 11.1, this chapter is all about preparing to deploy Windows in your lab. As tempting as it is to jump straight into the deployment, critical resources must be set up first, so that's what you'll be doing.

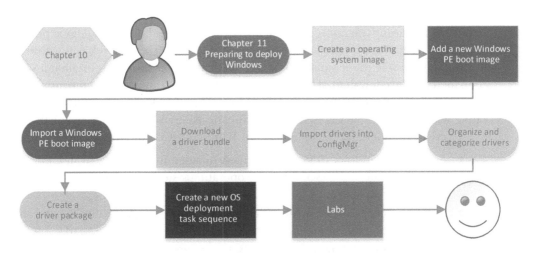

Figure 11.1 By end of this chapter, you'll be ready to deploy Windows by using ConfigMgr.

11.1   *Importing an operating system image*

A Windows operating system image is a self-contained file using the Windows Imaging Format (WIM). A WIM differs from other image formats such as ISO because it's file-based. It's designed to store files and then use an image index to reference those files.

A WIM file can contain multiple image indexes because it has to store each file only once. For example, say you use ConfigMgr or MDT to build a custom image, and then later use the same process to build another image that has extra applications. You can store both images in the same WIM file, but files that are common to both images are stored only once, as shown in figure 11.2. In this way, WIM is an effective and efficient way of building custom images, which is why they're the foundation of operating system deployment (OSD) in ConfigMgr.

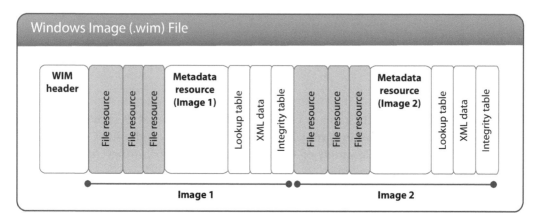

Figure 11.2   You can store multiple Windows images in a single WIM file.

In addition to using operating system images, previous builds of ConfigMgr supported the use of operating system packages to deploy Windows. These are objects within the ConfigMgr console that contain all of the installation files found on original installation media—the equivalent of booting from an ISO or DVD and running the installation wizard. This functionality was replaced in ConfigMgr 2012 R2 SP1 (replaced with operating system upgrade packages, which we won't be using), so now it's images all the way.

To create an operating system image for Windows 10, do the following:

1   Access the Windows 10 ISO that you downloaded in chapter 2 from CM01. You can either mount the ISO within the operating system, or attach it to the VM like an external drive.

2   In File Explorer, create a subfolder under \\CM01\Sources called OS and then another subfolder under OS called Windows 10 x64 Enterprise Gold.

3   From an elevated PowerShell window, type in xcopy F:\sources\install.wim '\\cm01\Sources\OS\Windows 10 x64 Enterprise Gold'. This copies the WIM containing the Windows operating system to a local source on CM01.

4 Navigate to Software Library > Operating Systems > Operating System Images.

5 Right-click "Operating System Images" and select "Add Operating System Image."

6 In the path, enter (don't Browse to) `\\cm01\Sources\OS\Windows 10 x64 Enterprise Gold\install.wim`.

7 Click "Next." On the General page, enter `Windows 10 x64 Enterprise Gold` for the "Name," `10.0.10586` for the "Version," and `Install.wim from original Microsoft installation media (1511 Build)` in the "Comment," as shown in figure 11.3.

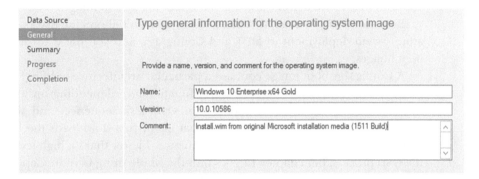

Figure 11.3 Using proper names and descriptions for your images can save a lot of hassle later.

NOTE Given that Microsoft is moving to a much more aggressive release cycle for Windows 10, chances are that the version of Windows 10 you'll be working with will be later than the one used in this book.

8 Click "Summary" and "Next" to complete the import.

To import the OS image using PowerShell, run the following command:

```
New-CMOperatingSystemImage `
-Name 'Windows 10 x64 Enterprise Gold' `
-Description 'Install.wim from original Microsoft installation media' `
—Version '10.0.10240' `
-Path '\\CM01\Sources\OS\Windows 10 x64 Enterprise Gold\install.wim'
```

Try It Now—Import an OS image

Follow the preceding steps to import install.wim from the Windows 10 installation media into ConfigMgr, using either the console or PowerShell.

Think about your own environment. How many custom images do you deploy and support? If you don't already use WIM, would the single-instance file-storage approach help your organization?

For more information on Windows image files, take a few minutes to read this Tech-Net article: http://technet.microsoft.com/en-au/library/cc721962(v=ws.10).aspx.

11.2   *Starting your deployment with WinPE*

If you install a version of Windows from Windows Vista/Server 2008 or later, you'll notice that the installation process starts by loading into an environment where you're presented with a few options, such as which version of Windows you want to install and where you want to install it to. This is Windows Preinstallation Environment (WinPE).

WinPE is a lightweight version of Windows that's used as a staging environment for operating system installations, and is provided as part of the Windows ADK. It can interact with the underlying hardware and communicate over the network to access applications, device drivers, and custom operating system images.

Because WinPE is small, flexible, and bootable, it's always the first part of any operating system deployment in MDT and ConfigMgr, and you use it through the use of boot images.

A ConfigMgr boot image contains a particular architecture of WinPE (either 32-bit or 64-bit) as well as custom scripts and functionality, depending on what you need. The boot image is then assigned to an OSD task sequence, and when the task sequence is deployed against a client, that client first downloads the boot image so that it can process the rest of the task sequence. I know that's a high-level summary of the OSD process, but chapter 12 goes into the whole thing in more depth.

Navigate to Software Library > Operating Systems > Boot Images. As shown in figure 11.4, you'll see two boot images. ConfigMgr creates these automatically by using the Windows ADK during installation.

Icon	Name	Version	Image ID	OS Version
	Boot image (x64)	10.0.10240.16384	PS100005	10.0.10240.16384
	Boot image (x86)	10.0.10240.16384	PS100004	10.0.10240.16384

Figure 11.4   ConfigMgr automatically creates these boot images during installation.

You're going to create a new custom 64-bit boot image suitable for a Windows 10 task sequence:

1 From the Start page on CM01, launch "Deployment and Imaging Tools Environment" using "Run as Administrator." This launches an administrative shell loaded with the ADK tools.

2 Type in `copype amd64 "\\CM01\Sources\OS\WinPE 10 x64"`. This copies all the 64-bit WinPE files to the nominated location (which will be created).

3 Navigate to Software Library > Operating Systems > Boot Images.

4 Right-click "Boot Images" and select "Add Boot Image."

5 On the Data Source page, enter `\\CM01\sources\OS\WinPE 10 x64\media\ sources\boot.wim` as the path and then select "1 – Microsoft Windows PE (x64)" from the drop-down list, as shown in figure 11.5.

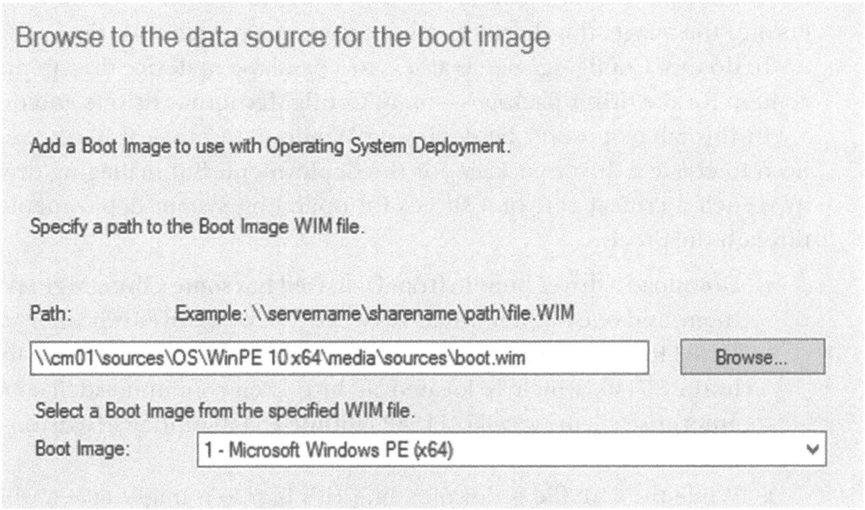

Browse to the data source for the boot image

Add a Boot Image to use with Operating System Deployment.

Specify a path to the Boot Image WIM file.

Path: Example: \\servername\sharename\path\file.WIM

\\cm01\sources\OS\WinPE 10 x64\media\sources\boot.wim   [Browse...]

Select a Boot Image from the specified WIM file.

Boot Image: 1 - Microsoft Windows PE (x64)   ⌄

Figure 11.5   Select the WIM you copied from WinPE as the base of your new boot image.

6   Click "Next." On the General page, enter `Boot Image - Windows 10 (x64)` as the
    "Name" and `10.0.10240.16384` as the "Version" (this is the specific Windows
    version of the boot image).

7   Click "Summary" and "Next" to complete the creation process.

To create the boot image using PowerShell, run the following command:

```
New-CMBootImage `
-Path '\\CM01\Sources\OS\WinPE 10 x64\media\sources\boot.wim' `
-Index 1 `
-Name 'Boot Image — Windows 10 (x64)' `
-Version 10.0.10240.16384
```

> **Try It Now—Create a custom boot image**
> Use the process in this section to create a new custom 64-bit boot image using the
> winpe.wim from the Windows ADK, either via the console or using PowerShell.

11.3   Handling different hardware platforms

One of the abilities of a ConfigMgr operating system deployment is to be able to
deploy the same operating system image across a wide range of hardware platforms.
After all, just because your organization has 10 types of laptops and desktops doesn't
mean you should have to support 10 different images.

ConfigMgr has the ability to detect what type, make, and model of hardware it's
deploying to while processing the task sequence, and then dynamically apply the

correct hardware device drivers. You don't have to embed lots of different device drivers into the image, thus keeping your custom image nice and trim.

To do this, ConfigMgr needs access to a database of device drivers, and the physical content for the driver packages—or, in ConfigMgr terms, drivers and driver packages.

In this lab, you won't be deploying Windows to physical hardware, so you don't need to create a driver package for the deployment. But managing driver functionality is such a critical part of a successful operating system deployment that you'll go through the process:

1 Download a driver bundle from Dell. Dell has some ConfigMgr MVPs working for them, and one of their initiatives was to create a driver repository that's perfectly suited for ConfigMgr. Download the Windows 10 driver bundle for the Dell Latitude E5440, which is located at http://en.community.dell.com/techcenter/ enterprise-client/w/wiki/11542.latitude-e5440-windows-10-driver-pack. Download the CAB file to CM01.

2 While the CAB file is downloading (it's big, so it might take a while), open File Explorer and create the following two folder structures within \\CM01\Sources:

   a \\cm01\Sources\Drivers\Dell Latitude E5440\Windows 10 x64

   b \\cm01\Sources\Driver Packages\Dell Latitude E5440 - Windows 10 x64 - A00

3 After downloading the CAB file, use 7-Zip to open the CAB as an archive and extract the contents of the E5440-Win10-A00-JYW2J.CAB\E5440\Win10\x64\ directory to \\cm01\Sources\Drivers\Dell Latitude E5440\Windows 10 x64, so that it looks like figure 11.6.

4 Navigate to Software Library > Operating Systems > Drivers.

5 Right-click "Drivers" and select "Import Driver."

6 On the Locate Driver page, enter the path as \\cm01\Sources\Drivers\Dell Latitude E5440\Windows 10 x64.

Network ▶ cm01 ▶ Sources ▶ Drivers ▶ Dell Latitude E5440 ▶ Windows 10 x64		
Name ▲	Date modified	Type
audio	8/3/2015 12:54 PM	File folder
chipset	8/3/2015 12:54 PM	File folder
communication	8/3/2015 12:54 PM	File folder
input	8/3/2015 12:54 PM	File folder
network	8/3/2015 12:54 PM	File folder
security	8/3/2015 12:54 PM	File folder
storage	8/3/2015 12:54 PM	File folder
video	8/3/2015 12:54 PM	File folder

Figure 11.6   Extract the contents of the Dell driver CAB file to CM01.

7 Click "Next." The Driver Details page should show device drivers selected and ready for import. Select "Categories" and then "Create" to assign the drivers to the following new administrative categories:

a Windows 10 x64

b Dell Latitude E5540

8 Click "OK." The Driver Details page should look like figure 11.7.

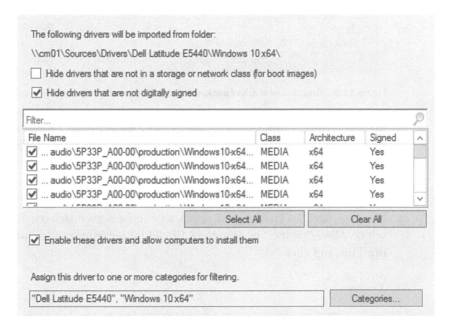

The following drivers will be imported from folder:

\\cm01\Sources\Drivers\Dell Latitude E5440\Windows 10 x64\

☐ Hide drivers that are not in a storage or network class (for boot images)

☑ Hide drivers that are not digitally signed

Filter...

File Name	Class	Architecture	Signed	
... audio\5P33P_A00-00\production\Windows10-x64...	MEDIA	x64	Yes	
... audio\5P33P_A00-00\production\Windows10-x64...	MEDIA	x64	Yes	
... audio\5P33P_A00-00\production\Windows10-x64...	MEDIA	x64	Yes	
... audio\5P33P_A00-00\production\Windows10-x64...	MEDIA	x64	Yes	

[Select All] [Clear All]

☑ Enable these drivers and allow computers to install them

Assign this driver to one or more categories for filtering.

"Dell Latitude E5440", "Windows 10 x64"   [Categories...]

Figure 11.7   Assign administrative categories to your drivers when you import them.

9 Click "Next" and you'll be prompted to add the imported drivers to a driver package. At the moment, you don't have one, so you'll need to create a new one; select "New Package."

10 When the Create Driver Package window opens, enter `Dell Latitude E5440 -Windows 10 x64` for the "Name," and `\\cm01\sources\Driver Packages\Dell Latitude E5440 - Windows 10 x64 - A00` for the "Path," so that the settings look like figure 11.8.

11 Click "Next." The next page prompts you to add drivers to the existing boot images. You don't need to add any drivers to your images, but if you did, you'd consider only storage or network drivers, since these are the only ones that WinPE needs.

12 Click "Summary" and "Next." The driver import process starts.

WHICH LOG?   While the drivers are importing, open the DriverCatalog.log file to monitor the process in action.

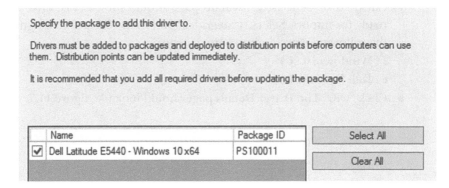

Figure 11.8   Create a new driver package that will house the imported drivers.

13 Move the drivers into their own administrative folder to keep them organized. Right-click "Drivers" and select Folder > Create Folder; call it `Dell Latitude E5440`.

14 Expand the Drivers folder structure and create a subfolder beneath Dell Latitude E5440 called `Windows 10 x64`.

15 Navigate back to Drivers and select all the imported drivers. Right-click and select "Move." Select the Windows 10 x64 folder from the list, as shown in figure 11.9, and click "OK."

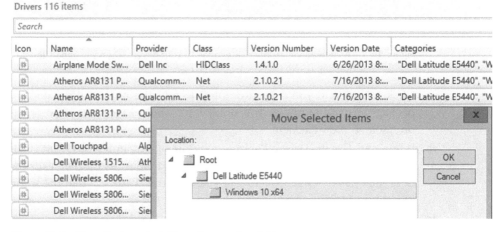

Figure 11.9   Move the imported drivers to a custom folder.

Unlike many other tasks, the process of importing drivers and creating a driver package with PowerShell isn't a one-line process. As a result, rather than print all the code here, you get the code from .\powershell\Import-CMDrivers.ps1.

> **Try It Now—Import device drivers into ConfigMgr**
>
> Follow the steps in this section to download and import device drivers into Config-
> Mgr and create a new driver package.
>
> Think about your own environment. How many hardware platforms do you have to
> support, and how many driver packages would you need to create to support them?
> What would be the best way to organize them so that it makes sense for you and
> your team?

Phew! That's a long process with quite a few moving parts, but hopefully you get a
sense of how important it is, and how ConfigMgr can make the task of supporting
multiple platforms much easier without needing to create and maintain multiple
operating system images or inject a large number of device drivers into a master
image. Finally, you'll move on to bringing everything together in an OSD task
sequence.

11.4 Creating a new task sequence

The time has come, the walrus said, to build a task sequence. Well, maybe not. But
that *is* the time.

A *task sequence* is a logical series of steps and decisions that ConfigMgr uses to successfully deploy Windows on a system. Task sequences can be incredibly complicated
or remarkably simple, depending on your specific needs. In your lab, you'll create a
task sequence from scratch, and then customize it in chapter 12 so that you can
deploy Windows.

To create a new OSD task sequence, do the following:

1 Navigate to Software Library > Operating Systems > Task Sequences.
2 Right-click "Task Sequences" and select "Create Task Sequence."
3 Select the "Install an existing image package" option and click "Next."
4 For the "Name," enter `Deploy Windows 10 x64 Enterprise`. Click the "Browse"
   button next to "Boot image" and then select "Boot Image – Windows 10 (x64)"
   from the list, as shown in figure 11.10.

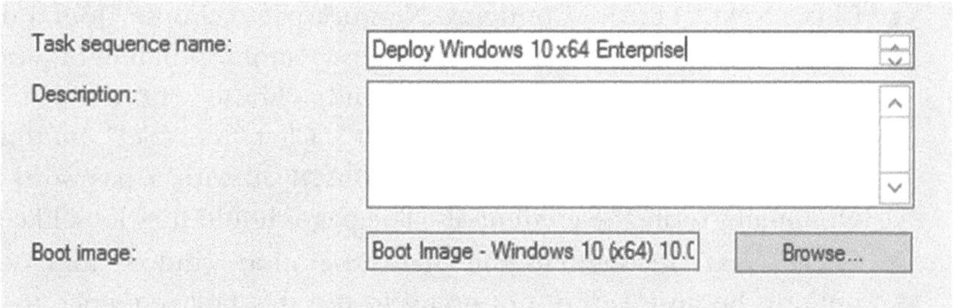

Figure 11.10   Name your task sequence and specify the custom boot image.

5 Click "Next." On the "Windows operating system" page, click "Browse" and choose "Windows 10 x64 Enterprise Gold" from the selection window. Choose "index 1" (there's only one to choose from). Uncheck the "Configure task sequence for use with BitLocker" check box, enable the local administrator account, and enter the password as P@ssw0rd, as shown in figure 11.11. Bit-Locker is Windows drive encryption, used to secure physical hard drives. You won't be enabling it in your lab environment.

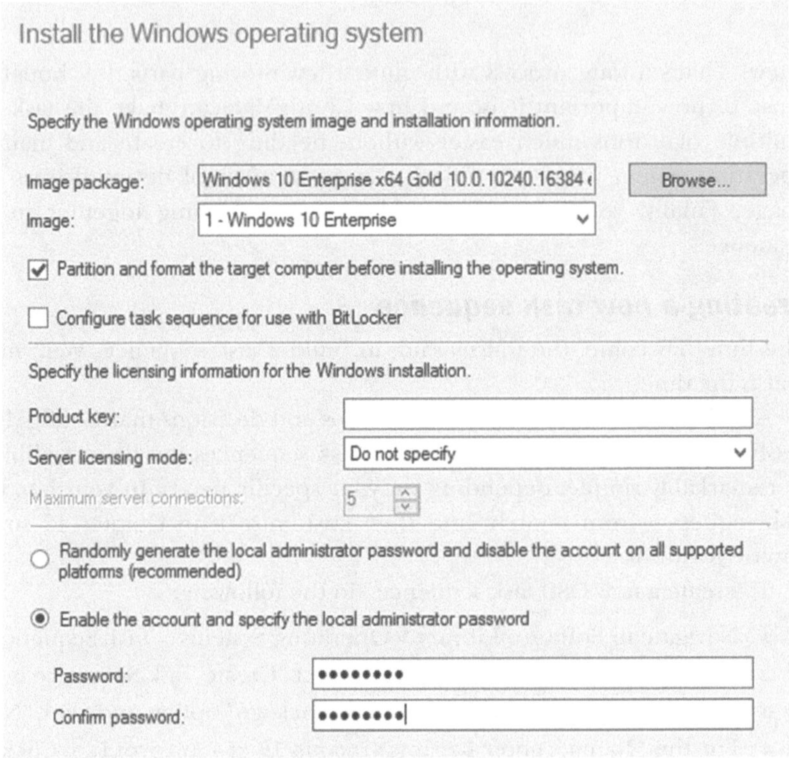

Figure 11.11   Choose the imported OS image to deploy.

6 Click "Next." On the Configure Network page, choose "Join a domain." Click "Browse" for the domain and choose "mol.sccmlab.net," and then select "Browse" for the Domain OU and choose "LDAP://OU=Workstations, OU=MoL,DC=mol,DC=sccmlab,DC=net." Click the "Set" button next to the account, and set the username to MOL\CM_JD with a password of P@ssw0rd. Optionally, verify the credentials. The page should now look like figure 11.12.

7 Click "Next" through to the State Migration window, and deselect all the options, because you're not going to use this task sequence to run user state capture or restore.

8 Click "Summary" and then "Next," and you're finished!

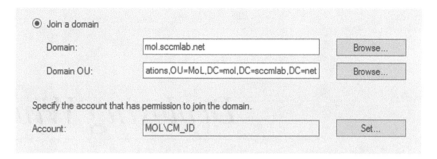

Figure 11.12   Select the appropriate AD account to join the deployed system to the domain.

TIP   This book doesn't deal with user state. It's a core part of performing particular types of operating system deployments, and it can get complex. User state is handled by the User State Migration Tool (USMT), which is also part of the ADK. I recommend spending some time reading up about USMT on TechNet: http://technet.microsoft.com/en-us/library/hh825256.aspx.

As with the drivers and driver package process, creating a task sequence with Power-Shell has a few moving parts, so rather than placing all the code in the book, you can find the code in .\powershell\New-CMLabTaskSequence.ps1.

> **Try It Now—Create an OS deployment task sequence**
> Follow the preceding steps to create a task sequence that will be used to deploy Windows 10. If you're comfortable with the process using the console, then use the PowerShell method, but if you haven't created many task sequences before, go through the console wizard to familiarize yourself with the various options.

Congratulations on making it this far! As you've discovered, you need to consider a load of moving parts when delving into OSD. Chapter 12 builds on what you've done here, and gets Windows deployed. Read on!

11.5   *Lab*

Download a driver CAB file from the Dell website for a different hardware platform. Extract the 64-bit drivers and import them into ConfigMgr, assign them to the correct administrative categories, and create a new driver package.

Deploying Windows

Configuring ConfigMgr to deploy Windows is certainly one of the harder tasks to perform. A successful deployment relies on a lot of moving parts working together properly, and many of them, such as device drivers, networks, server infrastructure, and physical systems, are independent of ConfigMgr itself.

The work you've done in chapter 11 has prepared the lab environment for a Windows deployment, and as you can see in figure 12.1, by end of this chapter that's exactly what you'll have achieved.

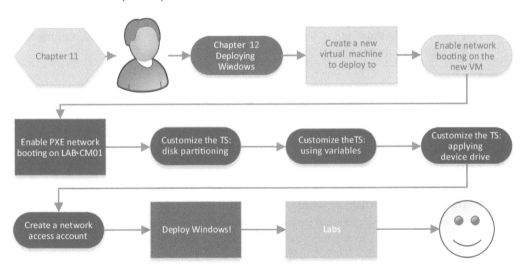

Figure 12.1   The prep work has been done—it's time to deploy Windows!

12.1 Creating a new client system

The first step is to create a new virtual machine to which you'll deploy Windows. This isn't a prerequisite in a normal production environment, but the new virtual machine will provide a fresh platform on which to deploy Windows in your lab. The specs on this virtual machine should be exactly the same as those for CLIENT01, but call this new VM CLIENT02. Follow the same process you used to create the VMs in chapter 2.

> **TIP** If your virtualization host doesn't have enough physical resources, such as RAM, to run all the VMs, you can turn off CLIENT01 because you don't need it for this chapter.

CLIENT02 will be slightly different from the other lab VMs; because you're going to deploy Windows by booting the client from the network, the virtual adapter attached to the VM must support network boot.

Virtual network adapters in most virtualization platforms do support network boot, but the implementation varies. For example:

- VMware-based VMs don't automatically boot to the network, so you have to bring up the VM's boot menu before the system boots from the operating system on the virtual disk.
- Hyper-V–based VMs support booting from the network, but only when you use a legacy network adapter on Generation 1 VMs. Generation 2 VMs support booting from the normal network adapter, as shown in figure 12.2 (don't worry if you're not running Hyper-V, but if you are, then use a Generation 2 VM).

For more information on Generation 2 VMs, read this article on TechNet: http://technet.microsoft.com/en-us/library/dn282285.aspx.

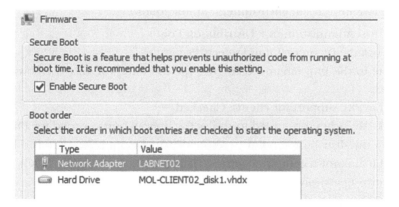

Figure 12.2   Hyper-V Generation 2 VMs natively support network boot.

> **Try It Now—Create a new virtual machine**
>
> Create a new VM called CLIENT02 that has the capability to boot from the virtual network adapter. Power off CLIENT01 if you need to.
>
> Consider your own environment. Do you have any VMs that you can use for ConfigMgr testing? How easily could you provision some?

12.2 Preparing for network booting

When a client machine attempts to boot to the network, the network adapter on the machine (whether physical or virtual) sends out a request on the local network to see whether any systems are configured to respond with boot options. If not, the system attempts to boot to the next configured option, such as the local hard drive.

In a ConfigMgr environment, you can configure a distribution point to act as the responder. Then, based on policy and active deployments, it can instruct the client to boot from a particular boot image and process a task sequence (TS).

To enable a DP to act as a PXE responder (a network service that responds to Preboot Execution Environment requests), you need to enable this feature within the ConfigMgr console. In turn, the DP uses the Windows Deployment Services (WDS) server role, in much the same way as the Software Update Point (SUP) works on top of WSUS.

ConfigMgr can automatically install and configure WDS when you enable PXE on a DP, but it does so using the installation defaults, placing the RemoteInstall folder on the C:\ drive. In your lab, WDS has already been installed with a custom configuration that placed the RemoteInstall folder on the E:\ drive—a larger partition without the operating system.

To enable PXE in your lab environment, do the following:

1. Navigate to Administration > Distribution Points.
2. Right-click the DP on CM01 and select "Properties."
3. Navigate to the PXE tab and configure the following options, as shown in figure 12.3:
   a. Enable PXE support for clients: Checked
   b. Click "Yes" when prompted to review the firewall ports needed for PXE.
   c. Allow this distribution point to respond to incoming PXE requests: Checked
   d. Enable unknown computer support: Checked (and then click "OK")
   e. Require a password when computers use PXE: Unchecked
4. Click "OK" to close the Properties window and enable PXE.

To enable PXE using PowerShell, run the following command:

```
Set-CMDistributionPoint `
-SiteSystemServerName 'CM01.mol.sccmlab.net' `
-EnablePxeSupport $true `
-EnableUnknownComputerSupport $true `
-AllowRespondIncomingPxeRequest $true
```

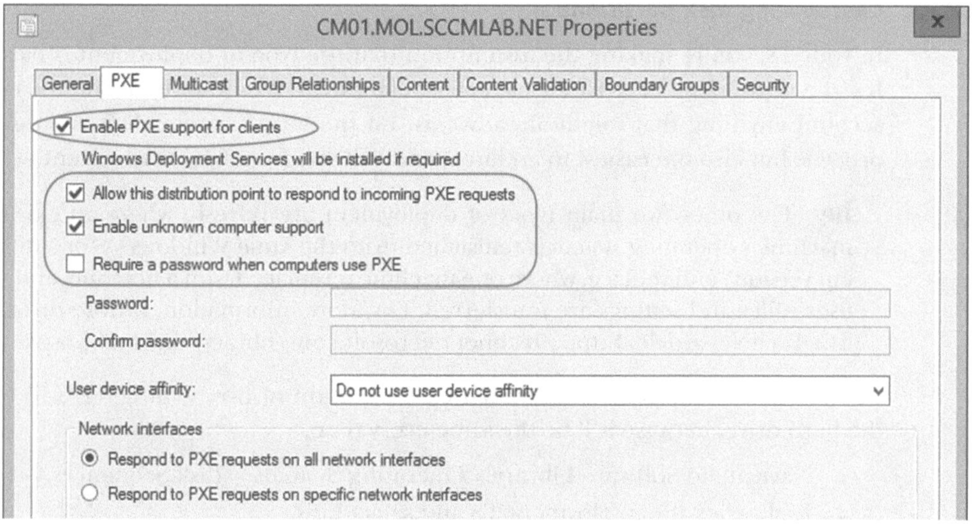

Figure 12.3 Enabling PXE for network booting on a DP

WHICH LOG? After you process the PowerShell command or click OK in the console, PXE will be enabled and configured under the hood. To monitor the process, check out the distmgr.log and SMSPXE.log files. In SMSPXE.log, you'll see that the ConfigMgr boot image packages will be copied to E:\RemoteInstall\SMSImages.

Try It Now—Enable PXE on CM01

Using either the console or PowerShell, enable PXE on the DP on CM01.

Think about your own environment: given that it's generally not recommended to allow clients in remote offices to PXE-boot over a WAN link, how many remote DPs might need to be enabled with PXE?

12.3   Customizing the deployment task sequence

In this section you'll make some changes to the task sequence that you'll use to deploy Windows. Some of these customizations aren't strictly necessary for your lab environment, but because they demonstrate some critical components of TS functionality that you'll use over and over again in production, it's worth spending the time to learn what's going on.

The TS deployment engine is a rich, open framework that can do nearly anything you throw at it. A basic rule of thumb for task sequences is this: if you can define an action, the TS can process it. Let's take a look at how this happens.

12.3.1 Customizing disk partitions

In your TS, you're making the assumption that the type of deployment is bare metal. It's the equivalent of a fresh, clean installation of Windows that doesn't take into account anything that might already exist on the target system. This is a destructive process, but also the easiest to architect and suitable for a lab environment.

> **TIP** The other two main types of deployment are refresh, where an existing machine's operating system is reinstalled (with the same Windows OS or a different version) and replace, where one machine is replaced with a new one, and the user's files and settings are transferred. For more information, browse through this TechNet article: http://technet.microsoft.com/library/dn744288.aspx.

As such, you don't need to do much customization of how ConfigMgr will partition the hard drive, because it'll be the same every time.

1 Navigate to Software Library > Operating Systems > Task Sequences.
2 Right-click the deployment TS and select Edit.
3 You'll see a couple of Partition Disk 0 steps: one for BIOS and one for Unified Extensible Firmware Interface (UEFI) systems. Select each one to see how the disk partitioning is different for each, as shown in figure 12.4.
4 Select "Restart in Windows PE" and choose Add > New Group (from the top of the left pane).
5 Select the new group and rename it `Partition Disks`.
6 Select the step "Partition Disk 0 – BIOS" and click the "Move Up" button to move the step into the new group.
7 Select the step "Partition Disk 0 – UEFI" and move it into the group, as shown in figure 12.5.

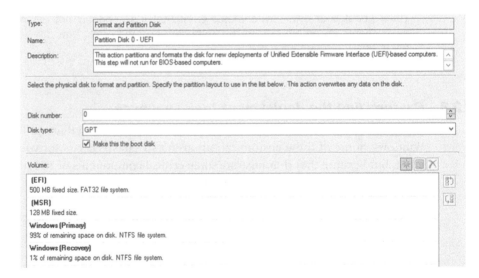

Figure 12.4 Windows disk partitions required for UEFI-based systems

Figure 12.5 Grouping similar steps in the deployment TS

TIP It's generally good practice to use groups in task sequences. Sequences can get long and complex, and groups help with organization and trouble-shooting. Additionally, you can apply logic and functionality at the group level that will apply to all grouped steps and subgroups.

8 Select the step "Partition Disk 0 – BIOS," and in the right-hand section of the window, double-click the "Windows (Primary)" partition in the "Volume" section.

9 In the Partition Properties window under "Advanced Options," enter OSDisk in the "Variable" field, as shown in figure 12.6.

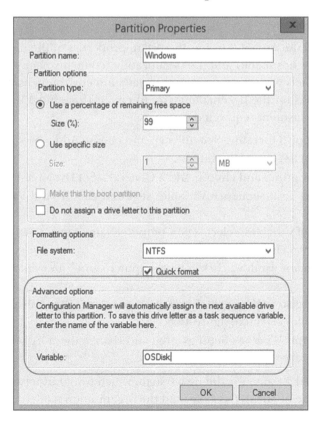

Figure 12.6 Setting a variable to specify which partition Windows will be installed to

10 Select the step "Partition Disk 0 – UEFI" and set the variable for the "Windows (Primary)" partition to "OSDisk" as well. Only one of these steps will run because systems are either BIOS or UEFI (but not both), so using the same variable in two steps is fine.

11 Select the "Apply Operating System" step.

12 From the "Select the location where you want to apply this operating system" drop-down list, select "Logical Drive Letter Stored in a Variable."

13 Type in OSDisk as the variable name, as shown in figure 12.7.

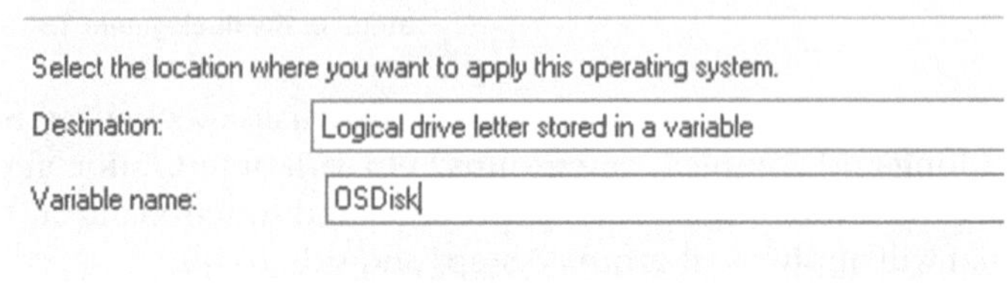

Select the location where you want to apply this operating system.

| Destination: | Logical drive letter stored in a variable |
| Variable name: | OSDisk |

Figure 12.7   Use a variable to specify where Windows will be installed.

Rather than let the TS work out which partition to install Windows to, you've specified it in a way that still allows for dynamic changes.

12.3.2 *Specifying TS variables*

In this section you'll use variables to specify certain properties of the deployment: the computer name (the hostname) and the organization/company name. Defining variables during the TS lets you create a dynamic installation environment that can adapt to different situations on the fly, enabling you to create (hopefully) a single TS that handles all your deployment requirements.

1 Select the "Apply Operating System" step and choose Add > New Group.

2 Call the group Define TS Variables.

3 Select the new group and choose Add > General > Set Dynamic Variables.

4 Select the "Set Task Sequence Variable" step and choose Add Variable > Existing Variable.

5 From the list of variables, select "OSDComputerName" and "OSDRegisteredOrg-Name" and then click "OK."

6 Back in the main window, click "OSDComputerName" and enter CLIENT02 as the value.

7 Select "OSDRegisteredOrgName" and enter MoL ConfigMgr Lab as the value, so that the variables resemble figure 12.8.

8 Select the "Apply Windows Settings" step and change the "Organization Name" to %OSDRegisteredOrgName%.

Here you've specified a name for the new system, which would otherwise receive the default random name of MININT-xxxxxx, and the organization name.

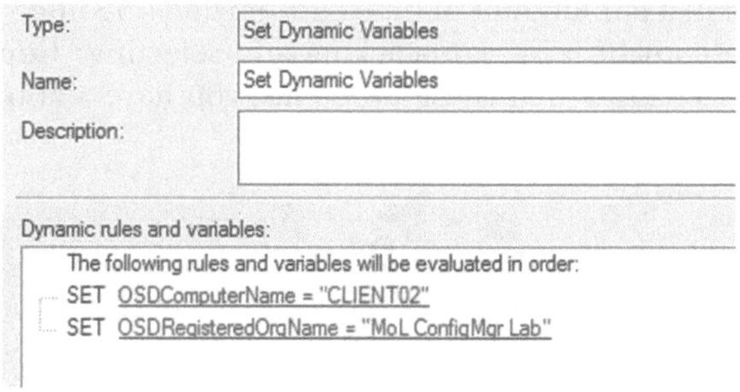

Type:	Set Dynamic Variables
Name:	Set Dynamic Variables
Description:	

Dynamic rules and variables:

The following rules and variables will be evaluated in order:

SET OSDComputerName = "CLIENT02"

SET OSDRegisteredOrgName = "MoL ConfigMgr Lab"

Figure 12.8 Defining dynamic TS variables for deployments

TIP You normally wouldn't hardcode a system name into a deployment TS because it's an inflexible way of specifying the hostname. Rather, you'd use dynamic rules to provide a hostname so that new systems you deploy are named correctly.

12.3.3 Applying device drivers

OK, nearly there. The last step is to make the TS able to deploy Windows to different hardware platforms. In your lab, you won't be deploying to physical hardware (although feel free if you have a spare unit handy). This section uses the Dell driver package that you set up in chapter 11.

1 Select the "Apply Device Drivers" step. You don't want to use this particular method of driver installation, so remove the step.

2 Select the "Apply Network Settings" step and choose Add > New Group. Then rename the group `Apply Device Drivers`.

3 Select the group and then choose the Options tab.

4 Select Add Condition > Query WMI.

5 Make sure that the WMI Namespace is root\cimv2, and then enter the following WQL query: `SELECT * from Win32_ComputerSystem where NOT Model like "%Virtual%"`. This is a negative query, which means that the group will be processed only if the TS is run against physical hardware.

6 Select the group and choose Add > Drivers > Apply Driver Package, and rename the new step to `Dell Latitude E6530`.

7 Click "Browse" and choose the "Dell Latitude E6530 - Windows 10 x64" package.

8 Select the Options tab and add a new Query WMI condition, where the WQL query is `SELECT * from Win32_ComputerSystem where Model like "%E6530%"`. This query will allow the step to run if the TS is run against a Dell Latitude E6530.

Phew—you're done! The task sequence is customized, and you're ready to deploy Windows.

TIP   When you've spent a fair amount of time customizing a TS and you know that it works, make a copy of it by right-clicking and selecting "Copy." That way, if you make later changes that cause problems, you have a known good version to revert to.

Try It Now—Customize the deployment TS

Follow the steps in this section to customize the deployment task sequence steps dealing with disk partitioning, device drivers, and environment variables.

Consider your own environment: what sort of customizations are needed to make a task sequence suitable for deploying Windows?

12.4   Deploying Windows

Now that all the pieces are in place, you're ready to deploy Windows to your new VM.

12.4.1   Making content available from Windows PE

Because the deployment of Windows will start from within WinPE, you need to make sure that WinPE can access the content it needs to run the TS.

By default, content is accessed using the computer account of the ConfigMgr client, but this is no good in WinPE because there's no client available. So you have to specify an account called the Network Access Account (NAA), which WinPE will use to authenticate to CM01 in order to access the content it needs.

To specify the NAA, do the following:

1   Navigate to Administration > Site Configuration > Sites.
2   Right-click "PS1 – Primary Site 1" and select Configure Site Components > Software Distribution.
3   Go to the Network Access Account tab and select "Specify the account that accesses network locations."
4   Click the sunburst icon and choose "New Account."
5   Select "MOL\CM_NAA" as the user name, and "P@ssw0rd" as the account password.
6   Click "OK." The Network Access Account screen should look like figure 12.9.

12.4.2   Deploying the task sequence

The next step is to deploy the TS so that when the VM boots, it will find the active deployment and process it:

1   Navigate to Assets and Compliance > Device Collections.
2   Create a new folder called `Operating System Deployment` (if not already created).
3   Under the root of Device Collections, right-click "All Unknown Computers" and select Add Selected Items > Add Selected Items to New Device Collection.
4   Call the new Collection `Deploy Windows 10 x64` and set the Limiting Collection to "All Systems."

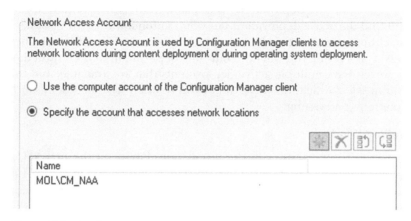

Figure 12.9   Configuring the Network Access Account for WinPE

5   Click "Summary," "Next," and then "Close."

6   The new Collection is created in the root of Device Collections, so move it to the Operating System Deployment folder.

7   Go to Software Library > Operating Systems > Task Sequences.

8   Right-click the deployment TS and select "Deploy."

9   Configure the new deployment as follows:

   a   Collection: Deploy Windows 10 x64

   b   Deployment Settings: Purpose > Available

   c   Make available to the following: Only media and PXE

10   Click "Summary," "Next," and "Close."

11   Select the Deployments tab at the bottom of the console, and you'll see an active deployment ready to go, as shown in figure 12.10.

Figure 12.10   Deploying the task sequence to a device collection

TIP   Because the deployed TS is available rather than required, the system will find the active deployment but won't automatically start booting. When a machine finds an active deployment that's required, it will automatically process it; as a result, you can have only one deployment that's required. You can, however, have multiple active deployments that are available, and this allows you to select whichever deployment you're interested in—useful for lab environments and testing.

12.4.3 Installing Windows

Now you're ready to roll with the installation. Power on the new VM, and it should attempt to boot first from the network. Depending on the type of virtualization platform you're using, you should get a prompt to press Enter or F12 to start the network boot process. Start the process, and the system downloads the custom boot image, as shown in figure 12.11.

```
Loading files...


IP: 192.168.11.214, File: \SMSImages\PS10000D\boot.PS10000D.wim
```

Figure 12.11   Downloading the custom boot image to start the deployment process

WHICH LOG?   You can watch the PXE request happening by monitoring SMSPXE.log.

After the boot image has been downloaded, the WinPE Task Sequence wizard loads. Select the "Deploy Windows 10 x64 Enterprise" task sequence and click "Next." At this point, the TS engine checks every package ID that has been referenced in the task sequence and makes sure that it can find it on an available DP. If package content can't be found, you may see an error like that shown in figure 12.12.

If you see this error, go back to the ConfigMgr console, find the referenced package ID, and make sure it has been distributed correctly. If it has, refresh the content on the

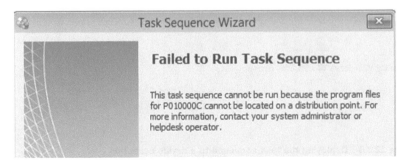

Figure 12.12   WinPE can't find a specific package on a DP.

Figure 12.13 Deploying Windows to a new virtual machine

DP to force an update. Reboot the VM and try the process again. After the TS finds all the relevant content on the DP, the deployment will start, as shown in figure 12.13.

The deployment takes some time, depending on the speed of the underlying hard disk. The full deployment may take up to an hour. You can monitor the progress of the deployment in the console:

1 Navigate to Monitoring > Deployments.
2 Right-click "Deploy Windows 10 x64 Enterprise" and select "View Status."
3 Go to the In Progress tab and select "More Details."
4 As the TS continues, it sends progress information back to CM01. You can see what stage of the TS the system is up to and what messages it's sending back, as shown in figure 12.14.

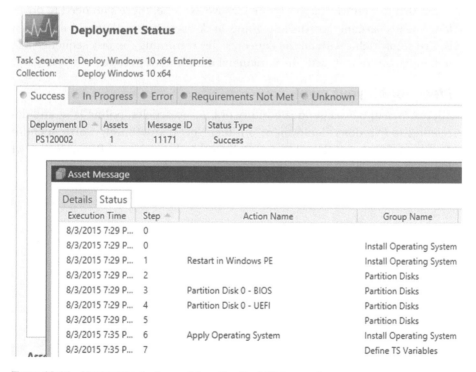

Figure 12.14 Monitor the deployment from the ConfigMgr console.

After the deployment is complete, you'll be able to log in to the newly deployed machine as MOL\Administrator, because CLIENT02 has been joined to the domain during installation.

WHICH LOG?   The entire deployment process is written to the smsts.log file, which is available on the client system in C:\Windows\CCM\Logs, or in X:\Windows\Temp\smstslog in WinPE.

Congratulations! You've successfully deployed Windows to a new system by using ConfigMgr. As you can see, a *lot* of moving parts need to come together correctly for this to work, which is why it can quickly become complex. Windows deployment is an advanced skill, using many technologies that are external to ConfigMgr. After you've done a successful deployment, you've established a firm baseline that you'll be able to come back to and build on time and time again.

> **Try It Now—Deploy Windows**
>
> Follow the steps in this section to deploy Windows to CLIENT02. Check that the deployed system has the correct hostname set and has been joined to the mol. sccmlab.net domain.

12.5   Lab

Given that this entire chapter is one massive exercise, there's no need to do a separate lab. But it's certainly worthwhile going back over the content and making sure that you're comfortable with all the concepts. Try rerunning the task sequence a few times to familiarize yourself with the bare metal deployment process.

12.6   Ideas for on your own

Microsoft maintains a good repository of links to articles, online labs, and downloads relating to Windows deployment on TechNet. It's definitely worth spending some time browsing this excellent resource: http://technet.microsoft.com/en-us/windows/hh974336.

Advanced deployment of Windows with ConfigMgr and MDT

Another chapter on operating system deployment? Nooooooooo...!

Before you head-butt the monitor (again), take a deep breath and fear not. You've already covered the fundamentals of deploying Windows with ConfigMgr. The purpose of this chapter is to unlock advanced deployment scenarios by integrating the Microsoft Deployment Toolkit (MDT) with ConfigMgr so that you can take what you've already learned and run with it, as shown in figure 13.1.

"What are the benefits of integrating MDT and ConfigMgr?" I hear you ask. By using both products together during your Windows deployments, you get access to all the features of both. MDT brings features to the table including extra task sequence variables and user-driven (Lite Touch) installations. Integrating it with ConfigMgr means that you can use MDT's deployment capabilities while still using the power and infrastructure of ConfigMgr.

Yes, you can deploy Windows by using pure ConfigMgr (as you did in chapter 12), but pretty much every organization that uses ConfigMgr for operating system deployment also uses MDT integration. You're overwhelmingly likely to encounter this in every environment outside a lab.

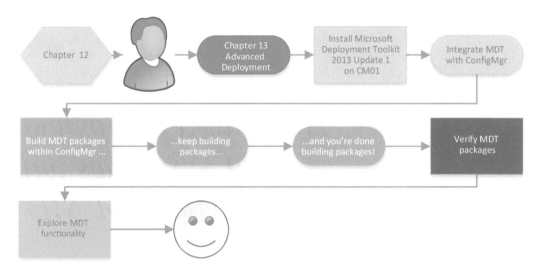

Figure 13.1   You can already deploy, but with MDT you can *really* deploy!

13.1   *Integrating MDT with ConfigMgr*

Integrating MDT and ConfigMgr is a two-step process. First, you'll install MDT on CM01 and get ConfigMgr to recognize it. Then, you'll build all the packages within ConfigMgr that are needed to make use of MDT functionality.

13.1.1   *Installing MDT*

To get MDT and ConfigMgr to talk, you need to install MDT:

1 Log on to CM01 as MOL\Administrator.
2 If the ConfigMgr console is open, close it.
3 Copy across the 64-bit MDT installer from the source MDT machine that you set up in chapter 2 (MicrosoftDeploymentToolkit2013_x64.msi). If you need to download MDT again, you can grab it here: www.microsoft.com/en-us/download/details.aspx?id=50407.
4 Double-click the MSI to launch the MDT installation wizard. You don't need to change any of the installation defaults; click all the way through to the end.
5 Go to the Start page on CM01 and type in `configmgr` to search the installed applications. There will be one result—Configure Config-Mgr Integration—as shown in figure 13.2.

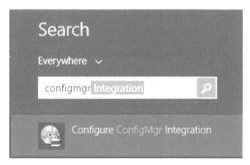

Figure 13.2   Launch the MDT ConfigMgr Integration tool.

6 When the utility launches, the Options page should be automatically configured to install the MDT extensions to ConfigMgr, and both the site server name and site code fields should be prepopulated, as shown in figure 13.3.

INFO The integration between MDT and ConfigMgr happens at the level of the console. Installing MDT makes no changes to the ConfigMgr server, and MDT doesn't need to be launched or configured in any way.

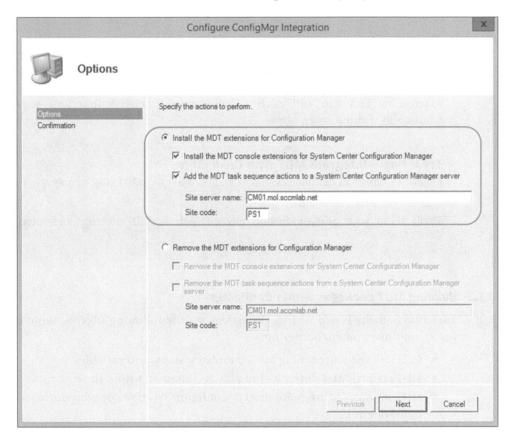

Figure 13.3   The integration utility autodetects the site server and site code details.

7 Click "Next." The utility copies the integration binaries to the locally installed ConfigMgr console. The final message in the utility is, "Operation completed successfully." Click "Finish" to close.

8 Launch the ConfigMgr console and navigate to Software Library > Operating Systems > Task Sequences.

9 Right-click "Task Sequences." You should see a new option, "Create MDT Task Sequence," as shown in figure 13.4.

This proves that MDT is integrated with ConfigMgr. Now to build some functionality.

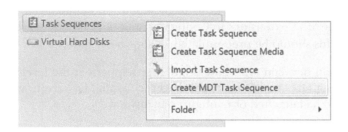

Figure 13.4 The ConfigMgr console has new options for MDT-specific functions.

TIP Because the integration between MDT and ConfigMgr happens at the console level, you need to install and integrate MDT on every system that has the ConfigMgr console installed, assuming that you want to use the MDT extensions. You can still perform all non-MDT-related functions within ConfigMgr without integration.

> **Try It Now—Integrate MDT with ConfigMgr**
>
> Follow the steps in section 13.1.1 to install MDT on CM01 and enable the Config-Mgr integration.
>
> Think about your own production environment: is MDT already integrated with ConfigMgr?

13.1.2 Building MDT packages within ConfigMgr

MDT functionality is exposed to ConfigMgr via the following objects, some of which you're only just now encountering:

- OSD task sequences using MDT templates, steps, and variables
- MDT scripts (MDT core functionality is contained within these scripts.)
- MDT settings (Settings are used to configure Windows options during deployment.)
- MDT-based boot images (Boot images are enhanced with MDT functionality.)

When you integrate MDT and ConfigMgr, the integration process makes no changes to ConfigMgr content, which means that all the resources in the preceding list don't yet exist. You have to create them, and the fastest and simplest way to create all resources necessary for using MDT is to let a wizard do it for you.

You'll create a new MDT-based task sequence to deploy the Windows 10 image. Because it has several package dependencies (as you'll see), the MDT Task Sequence wizard prompts for the location of these packages and lets you create them if they don't already exist. The process is a bit lengthy the first time around, but bear with it:

1 Navigate to Software Library > Operating Systems > Task Sequences.
2 Right-click "Task Sequences" and select "Create MDT Task Sequence."

3 You'll see numerous options in the drop-down list. Select the first option, "Client Task Sequence," and click "Next."

4 Enter MDT Deploy Windows 10 x64 Enterprise as the task sequence name.

5 Under "Join Workgroup or Domain," set the following, as shown in figure 13.5:

   a Domain: mol.sccmlab.net

   b Account: MOL\CM_JD

   c Organization name: MoL ConfigMgr Lab

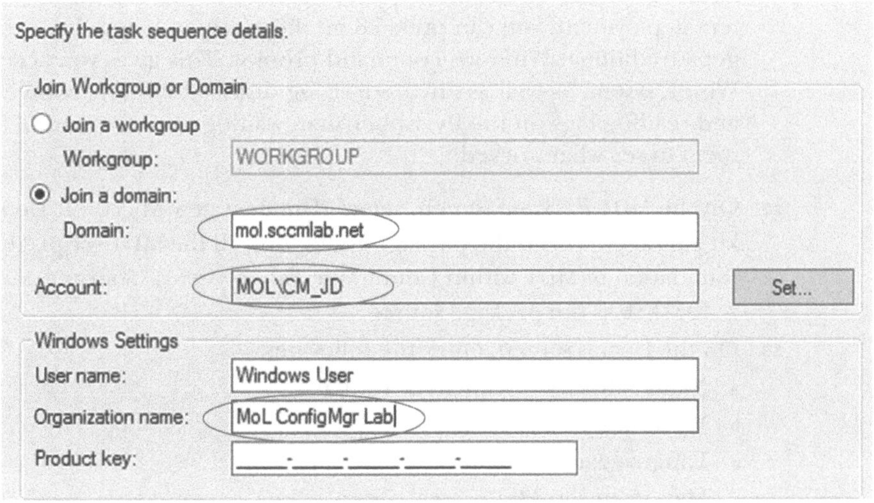

Figure 13.5   Network settings to join Windows to the MOL domain

6 Click "Next." For "Capture settings," choose "This task sequence will never be used to capture an image."

7 Under "Boot Image," select "Create a new boot image package," and enter \\cm01\Sources\Boot\MDT Boot x64 as the UNC path.

TIP You don't need to create the MDT source folders, since the wizard will do this for you.

8 For the boot image "General Settings," enter the following:

   a Name: MDT 2013 Update 2 Boot Image (x64)

   b Version: 10.0.10240.16384

9 For the boot image "Options," select x64 as the platform and set the scratch space to 128 MB.

TIP *Scratch space* is the amount of temporary storage space available to WinPE (remember that a boot image uses WinPE). For an excellent summary about what's happening under the hood, read this blog post by Johan Arwidmark: www.deploymentresearch.com/Research/tabid/62/EntryId/159/WinPE-5-0-scratch-space-in-MDT-2013-and-ConfigMgr-2012-R2.aspx.

10 For the boot image "Components," in addition to "Microsoft Data Access Components" (which should already be selected), select "DISM Cmdlets and Windows PowerShell."

11 For boot image "Customization," select "Enable command support (F8)." You can also make further customizations, such as adding extra files to the boot image (for example, the log viewer utility) or a custom background image—nice for corporate branding.

> **NOTE** Enabling command support means that during an operating system deployment, you can press F8 on the machine being deployed to and get a traditional Windows command prompt. This gives you access to the WinPE system as well as any underlying disks—great for troubleshooting and reading logs on the fly, rather than waiting until the end of a deployment to see what worked.

12 On the MDT Package screen, select "Create a new Microsoft Deployment Toolkit package." This is the package containing all the MDT scripts that provide the foundation of MDT within ConfigMgr. Enter \\cm01\Sources\MDT 2013 Update 2 Toolkit as the package source.

13 On the Details screen, enter the following:
   a Name: MDT 2013 Update 2 Toolkit
   b Version: 1.0
   c Language: en-US
   d Manufacturer: Microsoft

14 For the OS image, click the "Browse" button next to "Specify an existing OS image" and then select the "Windows 10 x64 Gold" image.

15 For "Deployment Method," select "Perform a Zero Touch Installation."

16 For "Client Package," select "Specify an existing ConfigMgr client package" and then choose "Microsoft Corporation Configuration Manager Client Package."

17 For "USMT Package," select "Specify an existing USMT package" and then choose the "User State Migration Tool" package from the package list.

18 For the "Settings Package," select "Create new settings package" and then enter \\cm01\Sources\MDT Settings\Windows 10 x64 as the source folder.

19 Enter the following for the settings details:
   a Name: MDT Settings - Deploy Windows 10 x64
   b Version: 1.0
   c Language: en-US
   d Manufacturer: Microsoft

20 Phew—that's it! Click all the way through to Summary, and click "Next" to start the build process. The boot image, Toolkit package, and settings package are all created by the wizard, as shown in figure 13.6. The process takes approximately 5–10 minutes to complete.

And you're finished! Yes, it's a long and slightly convoluted process, but the great thing is that you need to do it only once. If you were to create another MDT-based task sequence within ConfigMgr, you'd point the wizard to the Toolkit package and boot image that you've already created. If you were deploying a different operating system or architecture, you might need a new MDT settings package, but that's it.

Now it's time to take a look at what you've created.

> **Try It Now—**
> **Build MDT packages**
>
> Follow the (vast number) of steps in section 13.1.2 to create a new MDT-based operating system task sequence in ConfigMgr and build all the packages required for MDT functionality.

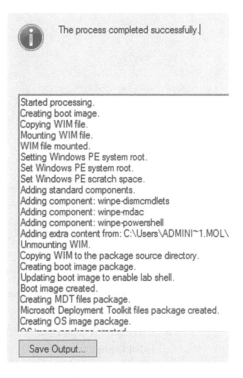

Figure 13.6 The Task Sequence wizard creates all the required MDT packages.

13.2 *Making sure that MDT is awesome*

Let's explore CM01 to see where all these new objects and packages have been created. This will give you a good sense of how MDT functionality is accessed within ConfigMgr.

13.2.1 *Verifying MDT packages*

To verify that the packages required for MDT functionality have been created properly, do the following:

1. Navigate to Software Library > Operating Systems > Task Sequences, and you'll see the new MDT task sequence.
2. Right-click the task sequence and select "Properties." Then go to the Advanced tab. As shown in figure 13.7, you'll see that the task sequence references the newly created MDT boot image.

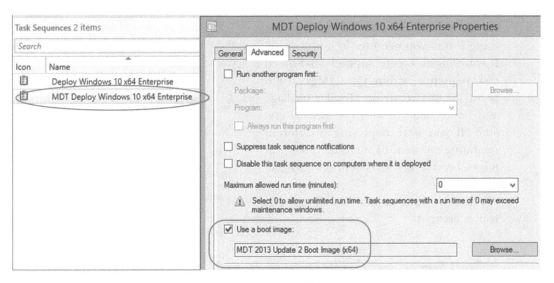

Figure 13.7   New MDT-based task sequence using the new MDT boot image

3   Close the Properties window and navigate to boot images. You'll see that the boot image that the task sequence is referencing is now in the list.

4   Choose Application Management > Packages. As shown in figure 13.8, you'll have two newly created MDT packages.

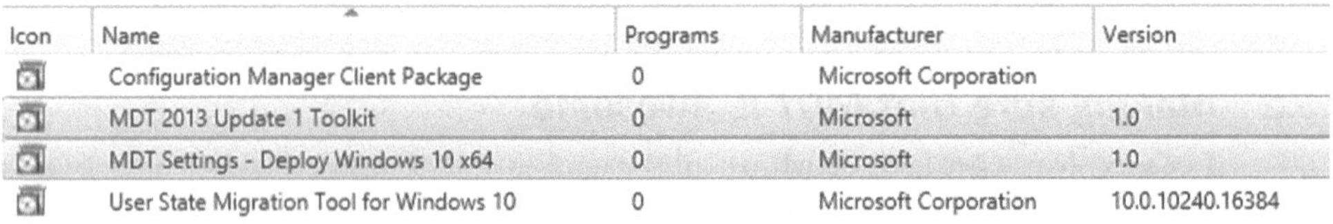

Icon	Name	Programs	Manufacturer	Version
	Configuration Manager Client Package	0	Microsoft Corporation	
	MDT 2013 Update 1 Toolkit	0	Microsoft	1.0
	MDT Settings - Deploy Windows 10 x64	0	Microsoft	1.0
	User State Migration Tool for Windows 10	0	Microsoft Corporation	10.0.10240.16384

Figure 13.8   MDT Toolkit and settings packages for use within ConfigMgr

So, great—you have new packages and a task sequence. But how does all this work together?

13.2.2   *Exploring MDT functionality*

The task sequence is where all of this new functionality merges, so right-click the new MDT deployment task sequence and select "Edit." The first thing you'll notice is that, compared to the standard ConfigMgr task sequence, the MDT task sequence is huuuuuuuuuge. That's because it was built using an MDT deployment template that caters to more deployment scenarios and contains much more logic than the default ConfigMgr templates.

To go through every part of the task sequence in detail would require nearly an entire book by itself. Rather than inflict that on you, this section will draw your attention to the core components of the task sequence.

GATHERING INFORMATION

You'll see that dispersed throughout the task sequence, the step "Use Toolkit Package" appears quite a few times. This task sequence references the MDT Toolkit package that you created earlier. Its function is to download the Toolkit source to the local computer so that it can refer to scripts that are then called in later steps.

For example, you'll see that the gather step is often run immediately after (or soon after) the Toolkit package is downloaded. The gather step runs the ZTIGather.wsf script, which gathers environmental information about the deployment and processes rules contained within the MDT settings package.

As shown in figure 13.9, the information gathered gets written to dynamic task sequence variables that can be called on during the task sequence. This enables you to perform specific actions, such as joining a different Active Directory domain or applying a different machine configuration, based on environmental properties.

Log Text	Component
Property WizardComplete is now = N	Wizard
Property OSCurrentVersion is now = 6.3.9600	ZTIGather
Property OSCurrentBuild is now = 9600	ZTIGather
Property OSVersion is now = WinPE	ZTIGather
Property IsServerOS is now = False	ZTIGather
Property IsServerCoreOS is now = False	ZTIGather
Finished getting OS info	ZTIGather
Getting HAL information	ZTIGather
Property HALName is now = acpiapic	ZTIGather
Finished getting HAL information	ZTIGather
Getting network info	ZTIGather
Checking network adapter: [00000000] Microsoft Hyper-V Network Adapter	ZTIGather
MAC address = 00:15:5D:DD:5C:22	ZTIGather
IP Address = 192.168.10.103	ZTIGather
IP Address = fe80::d157:e211:f9cc:fe40	ZTIGather
Default Gateway = 192.168.10.1	ZTIGather
Property IPAddress001 is now = 192.168.10.103	ZTIGather
Property IPAddress002 is now = fe80::d157:e211:f9cc:fe40	ZTIGather
Property MacAddress001 is now = 00:15:5D:DD:5C:22	ZTIGather
Property DefaultGateway001 is now = 192.168.10.1	ZTIGather
Finished getting network info	ZTIGather

Figure 13.9   The MDT gather step pulls in dynamic information about the deployment.

Using dynamic variables

I recall one customer I worked for who needed to deploy machines to two AD domains. The network was segmented into VLANs, which meant that the machine being deployed had a specific IP address and default gateway, depending on which VLAN the machine was attached to.

I was able to use this environment information to join the machine to the correct domain by extracting the `DefaultGateway001` property and calling it during the task sequence. As a result, rather than needing two task sequences to deploy machines to two AD domains, the customer needed only one task sequence. MDT to the rescue!

HANDLING DIFFERENT SCENARIOS

The last couple of chapters have briefly touched on bare metal, refresh, and replace as concepts in OS deployment. By default, the MDT template caters to these scenarios.

Major section groups in the task sequence come into play, depending on the state of the system being imaged. For example, select the "State Capture" group and switch to the Options tab. As shown in figure 13.10, this group runs if the task sequence variable `_SMSTSinWinPE` is equal to `false`.

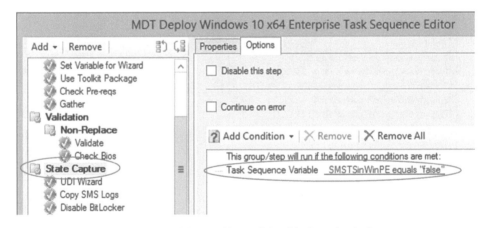

Figure 13.10   Task sequence variables provide conditional logic to the deployment process.

If the task sequence isn't currently running within WinPE, it must be running within the full Windows operating system. Windows and ConfigMgr must already be installed, which means that this isn't a bare metal deployment, but rather a refresh or replace.

Dealing with user state

In a refresh or replace scenario, you're likely to have to deal with backing up and restoring the user state. This is everything that a user may have built up over time on their system through use—documents, settings, and customizations.

Handling user state backups can be a tricky business. Unless you have an operating environment where users can't make any changes and have no choice but to store everything on a central server, chances are you won't know what they may have done on their machines.

As a result, dealing with user state is far more a business concern than a technical problem. Make sure that management sets clear guidelines about what will and won't be backed up. Sometimes it's fine for a user to store nonessential data on their machine, as long as they know that the onus is on them to protect it—although, if a user comes to you in tears because all their wedding photos were erased (which has happened to me), it takes a hard heart to cite company policy back at them (yes, I recovered all their wedding photos).

RICH LOGGING

When a task sequence goes bad, you want all the information possible at your disposal to work out why. This logic is built into the MDT deployment template via the use of the ZTICopyLogs.wsf script.

This takes all the logs generated during the task sequence and drops them on a central network share of your choosing. This action is called right at the end of the state-restore group via the copy-logs step (which is reached after the task sequence has completed successfully) or during the "Gather Logs and StateStore on Failure" group (which is called whenever a step in the task sequence fails).

TIP The location of the log files is controlled by the SlShare task sequence variable (for example, SlShare=\\CM01\Logs). You can define this variable in the CustomSettings.ini file that's part of the MDT Settings package, or you can define it as a step within the task sequence itself.

Try It Now—Exploring MDT functionality

Go through the packages and task sequence created by the MDT wizard. Make sure that you're comfortable with how the various bits and pieces fit together, and what the major sections of the task sequence do.

Understand that in a bare metal deployment (triggered from within WinPE), some of the grouped sections in the task sequence wouldn't run at all. Why?

13.3   *Lab*

Feeling brave? Of course you are!

If you're feeling up to the challenge, perform a bare metal deployment of Windows 10 by using the MDT task sequence. You'll need to deploy the task sequence and make sure that the content for all the dependent packages has been distributed.

Managing Linux clients

14

Ready for another chapter on operating system deployment? Ha-ha, just kidding; I wouldn't inflict that on you! Instead, let's indulge in a change of scene and delve into the (relatively) new world of managing non-Windows clients—specifically, Linux.

ConfigMgr (and SMS, in its previous life) has been all about deploying and managing Windows environments, but with the release of ConfigMgr 2012 Service Pack (SP) 1 came the ability for us ConfigMgr admins to start managing systems running Mac OS X and Linux/UNIX-based operating systems.

Because you're running an up-to-date version of ConfigMgr in your lab environment, you're ready to rock with Linux. As shown in figure 14.1, you'll introduce Ubuntu Server into your lab environment and use ConfigMgr to take control.

14.1 Installing an Ubuntu server

If you've never installed a Linux distribution before, fear not—it's straightforward. ConfigMgr does support various versions of Linux and UNIX, but I've chosen Ubuntu for this lab because it's easy to install and configure.

The first thing you'll need is yet another virtual machine in your lab environment. If you need to power off CLIENT01 and/or CLIENT02 to free up resources for another VM, that's fine. You won't need those systems for the rest of this chapter.

Create a new virtual machine by using the specifications detailed in table 14.1.

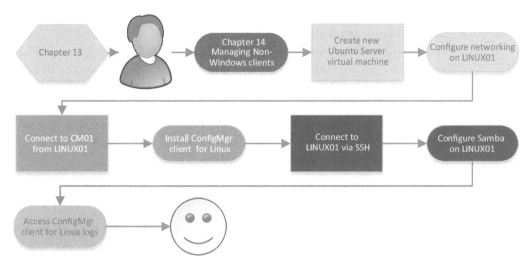

Figure 14.1 This chapter is Linux, Linux, and more Linux!

Table 14.1

VM setting	Setting value
VM Name	LINUX01
CPU	1 × CPU
RAM	1 GB
Hard Disk	1 × 40GB
Network	1 × NIC

Now that you've created the VM, it's time to install Ubuntu by growing a neckbeard, gorging on bulk-buy donuts, and trotting out any other Linux stereotype you fancy!

To get Ubuntu running in the lab environment, do the following:

1 Go to www.ubuntu.com/download/server and download the latest build of Ubuntu Server 14.04 LTS (which stands for *Long-Term Support*). The desktop version of Ubuntu will work too, but the server version is the officially supported build and is also the one you're most likely to encounter in an enterprise environment.

2 The file downloaded should be called ubuntu-14.04.3-server-amd64.iso (or something similar). Attach this ISO to the newly created VM and boot from it.

3 As shown in figure 14.2, the default option is to install Ubuntu Server.

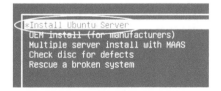

Figure 14.2 Installing Ubuntu Server from the installation ISO

4 Go through the installation options for preferred language, geographical location, and keyboard layout.

5 For the system hostname, enter `linux01` (lowercase), and enter your own name and choose a password for the extra user account. The password you choose here will also be the password set for the root (superuser) administrative account.

6 For the disk partitioning method, select "Guided – use entire disk and set up LVM." There should only be one disk to choose from. Accept all the defaults, and the partition structure is written to disk.

7 Enter HTTP proxy information if you need to (this shouldn't be needed in a home lab environment) and configure image updates as "No automatic updates."

8 When prompted to choose which software to install, select "OpenSSH server and Samba file server" (use the spacebar to select multiple options). Then sit back and let the installation process finish.

9 After the installation is complete, log in to the server by using the username and password you configured during the installation.

10 Now you'll perform a little bit of maintenance and configuration:

11 Download and install all the available critical system updates by using the command `sudo apt-get update` (the `sudo` password is the same password as your user account) and then `sudo apt-get upgrade`. Because this system has never been patched before, this process can take a bit of time, but it's worth it. After completion, reboot the system by using the command `sudo shutdown -r now`.

12 Optionally, configure a static IP address on the system by using the command-line Nano editor and the command `sudo nano /etc/network/interfaces`. Edit the interfaces file to look like figure 14.3, and then save it and exit using Ctrl-X.

13 Finally, reboot the system one last time.

Wow—we do spend a lot of time on preparation, don't we? Never fear; now you can get on to the ConfigMgr piece.

```
# The loopback network interface
auto lo
iface lo inet loopback

# The primary network interface
auto eth0
iface eth0 inet static
        address 192.168.11.212
        gateway 192.168.11.1
        netmask 255.255.255.0
        network 192.168.11.0
        broadcast 192.168.11.255
        dns-search mol.sccmlab.net
        dns-nameservers 192.168.11.200
```

Figure 14.3   Configure a static IP address on your Ubuntu system—it *is* a server, after all.

Try It Now—Install and configure Ubuntu
Follow the steps in this section to create a new virtual machine and install Ubuntu
Server 14.04 on it. Then patch the server and assign it a static IP address.

14.2 Installing the ConfigMgr client for Linux

You have a Linux system ready to go, and your ConfigMgr environment has been
updated, so it's time to get the client installed. By default, the client files for non-
Windows platforms aren't included in the ConfigMgr installation binaries or on the
installation media. Instead, you need to download them separately.

To download the appropriate ConfigMgr client, do the following:

1 Navigate to www.microsoft.com/en-au/download/details.aspx?id=39360.
2 Click the "Download" button, and select "ConfigMgr Client for Linux." Note
   that clients are available for other platforms too, including Mac OS X.
3 Download the ConfigMgr Clients for Linux.exe file to E:\Temp on CM01.
4 Launch the executable. In the folder location to place the extracted files, enter
   E:\Program Files\Microsoft Configuration Manager\XPlat\5.0.7958\Linu x

TIP The folder structure in step 4 doesn't exist in any standard ConfigMgr
implementation. But in your lab environment, E:\ConfigMgr also maps to
\\CM01\SMS_PS1, so by creating a new folder structure here, you're making
the Linux client available via the network. The folder structure also shows
exactly which version of the Linux client is located there.

5 A Linux server needs a little help to grab files directly from a Windows server.
   You need to make the SMS_PS1 share on CM01 appear as part of the Linux
   server by doing the following on LINUX01:
6 Create a new folder in /mnt (the *mount* folder) by using the command sudo
   mkdir /mnt/SMS_PS1.
7 Mount the share on CM01 to the new folder by using the command sudo mount
   –t cifs //cm01/SMS_PS1 /mnt/SMS_PS1/ -o username=administrator. You're
   prompted for the sudo password as well as the Administrator password on CM01
   (which is P@ssw0rd).
8 The mount should complete successfully. Change folders via the command
   cd/mnt/SMS_PS1 and get a directory listing by using ls. You'll see the contents
   of the remote file share, as shown in figure 14.4.

```
james@lab-ubuntu:/$ cd /mnt/SMS_P01/
james@lab-ubuntu:/mnt/SMS_P01$ ls
AdminConsole  CCM      ClientUpgrade  data                   hotfix   install.map
bin           Client   CloudServices  DeviceClientDeployment  inboxes  Licenses
james@lab-ubuntu:/mnt/SMS_P01$ ~_
```

Figure 14.4 Accessing the ConfigMgr server share directly from LINUX01

Looking good! Now you can perform the client installation.

> **TIP**   You can quickly enter file and folder names in Linux by using the Tab key. It tries to work out which file/folder you want based on what's available, like PowerShell.

1   Change the folder to the Linux client installers by using `cd /mnt/SMS_PS1 /XPlat/5.00.7958.1060/Linux`.

2   Get a folder listing by using `ls`. You'll see an install script as well as a few packages for various versions of Linux.

3   Install the client by using the following command: `sudo ./install —mp cm01.mol.sccmlab.net —sitecode PS1 ccm-Universalx64.tar`. This command tells the installer which Management Point and ConfigMgr site code to use, as well as which client package. The installation takes a couple of minutes to complete successfully, as shown in figure 14.5.

```
Registering Providers...
Created /opt/microsoft/omi/./etc/omiregister/root-cimv2/scxcmprovider.reg
Performing post installation cleanup...
Linking startup script...
Initializing data store.  This may take a few minutes...
Installing boot-time scripts...
 Adding system startup for /etc/init.d/ccmexecd ...
   /etc/rc0.d/K20ccmexecd -> ../init.d/ccmexecd
   /etc/rc1.d/K20ccmexecd -> ../init.d/ccmexecd
   /etc/rc6.d/K20ccmexecd -> ../init.d/ccmexecd
   /etc/rc2.d/S20ccmexecd -> ../init.d/ccmexecd
   /etc/rc3.d/S20ccmexecd -> ../init.d/ccmexecd
   /etc/rc4.d/S20ccmexecd -> ../init.d/ccmexecd
   /etc/rc5.d/S20ccmexecd -> ../init.d/ccmexecd
sed: can't read /opt/microsoft/configmgr/bin/reset_policy.sh: No such file or directory
sed: can't read /opt/microsoft/configmgr/bin/reset_hinv.sh: No such file or directory
Starting Configuration Manager...
Installation complete.
james@linux01:/mnt/SMS_PS1/XPlat/5.0.7958/Linux$ _
```

Figure 14.5   The best kind of installation is a successful one!

4   Open the ConfigMgr console on CM01 and go to Assets and Compliance > Devices. You'll see that LINUX01 is listed, but there's no value for client activity. Right-click and select "Approve," as shown in figure 14.6.

And that's it! The ConfigMgr client is installed and active on a Linux system. Congratulations!

> **Try It Now—Install the ConfigMgr client for Linux**
>
> Follow the steps in section 14.2 to install the correct ConfigMgr client for Linux on LINUX01. Make sure that the system appears in the ConfigMgr console and that you approve it.

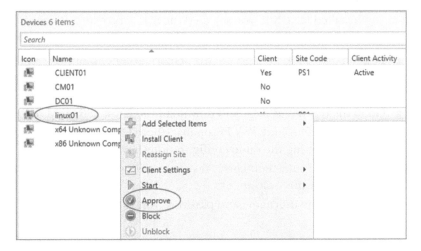

Figure 14.6   You need to manually approve a system that ConfigMgr can't automatically validate.

I approve...

Why did you need to manually approve the new system? Any system that has a valid ConfigMgr client on it and is talking to a site server that can't automatically validate its identity must be manually approved. Any other approach could be a security risk.

You didn't need to do that for the Windows machines because they're part of the same Active Directory domain as CM01; a common platform for identification and authentication is in place. Had they not been on the domain but in a workgroup, you would have had to manually approve them.

Linux servers aren't part of the AD domain, so instead they use certificates to prove their identity. Because the certificate is created and signed during the ConfigMgr client installation, the site server doesn't trust it automatically. In a secure ConfigMgr environment, where the server roles are configured with SSL certificates created and signed by a common certificate authority (more on that later), then a new Linux server can be automatically trusted and doesn't require manual approval.

14.3   Navigating ConfigMgr for Linux

The ConfigMgr client for Linux doesn't have a graphical user interface like the Windows client, so any interaction with the client is done via the command line. This isn't an issue on Linux servers, because most administration is done remotely using a Secure Shell (SSH) connection that enables you to run commands as if you were logged on locally. Let's set up remote administration first.

14.3.1 *Connecting to Ubuntu remotely*

When you installed LINUX01, you selected the SSH server role. It's ready to accept connections, so all you need to do is connect. To connect via SSH, do the following:

1 Log on to CM01 and go to www.chiark.greenend.org.uk/~sgtatham/putty/. PuTTY is a free Telnet/SSH client that has been around for ages, and still does a great job.

2 Go to the download page and download the latest x86 build of PuTTY to CM01.

3 Launch the file, and PuTTY opens (there's nothing to install). Connect to LINUX01 by using the same configuration shown in figure 14.7.

4 Click "Open," and then click "Yes" to store the server's encryption key (you're prompted for this only once).

5 Enter the same username and password you're using to log in to LINUX01, and that's it!

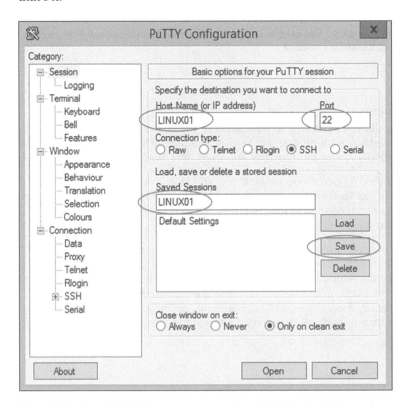

Figure 14.7 Using PuTTY to remotely connect to LINUX01 with SSH

Easy, huh? You'll do the rest of this chapter remotely using PuTTY; that's a realistic admin experience. You can log out of LINUX01 without impacting your SSH session. Use the command `logout`.

14.3.2 *Exploring ConfigMgr logs for Linux*

Before you can explore the ConfigMgr client, you should first check out the log file so you can see what changes are happening in real time. Needless to say, it's not as straightforward as all that. There's no Linux equivalent of CMTrace, so one way (though not the only way) to expose the log files is to create a file share on the Linux server and connect to the log files remotely. Linux uses Samba to serve network shares to Windows computers, and you installed Samba when you installed LINUX01.

To create a new share, do the following:

1 From PuTTY, type in `sudo smbpasswd –a <username>`, where <username> is the user that you're using to log in with. By default, Linux accounts aren't automatically Samba accounts, so you need to assign a Samba password.

2 Edit the Samba configuration by entering `sudo nano /etc/samba/smb.conf`.

3 Add the following lines to the [global] section of the file:

```
oplocks = no
kernel oplocks = no
```

4 Scroll to the end of the smb.conf file and enter the following text block:

```
[configmgr]
path = /var/opt/microsoft
available = yes
valid users = <username>
read only = yes
browseable = yes
public = yes
writable = no
csc policy = disable
```

TIP Note the use of single spaces in the code block. Don't miss these; without them, the share won't be created properly.

5 Use Ctrl-X to save and exit the file. Then restart the Samba service by using `sudo restart smbd`.

6 On CM01, open File Explorer and navigate to \\ubuntu.mol.sccmlab.net\ configmgr. You're prompted for a username and password; enter the Linux username and Samba password that you created earlier.

7 Authenticate, and you should see a folder with a single file: scxcm.log. This is the ConfigMgr log for the Linux client. Launch it with CMTrace. You now have full access to the remote log, as shown in figure 14.8.

Try It Now—Access Linux remotely
Follow the steps in section 14.3 to remotely connect to LINUX01 using SSH, and then create a new Samba share so that you can access the ConfigMgr client logs from CM01.

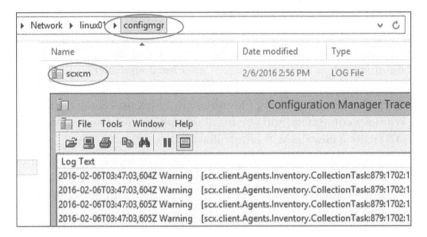

Figure 14.8   Accessing the ConfigMgr client for Linux logs via a remote Samba share— very techy!

Congratulations! If you've never worked with Linux before, you've done well to get through this chapter—it has plenty of new concepts to wrap your head around.

14.4   Lab

Ubuntu isn't the only Linux distro supported by ConfigMgr. Another one that's common in enterprise environments and also relatively easy to set up is CentOS.

So—feeling brave? Good! Have a go at creating another virtual machine in your lab environment called CENTOS, and install the latest release of version 7, which you can download from here: http://wiki.centos.org/Download.

Follow the same process you used for Ubuntu to get the ConfigMgr client installed on CentOS; make sure it's talking back to the site server and that the client is approved.

Deploying to Linux and Mac clients

Now that you have an active Linux-based client in your ConfigMgr lab, we can move on to administrative functions such as inventory and package deployment. As shown in figure 15.1, we'll also spend some time discussing managing clients running Mac OS X. This part of the chapter won't be hands-on like the sections on Linux, because in order to manage OS X clients, you first have to make many infrastructural changes to your environment, which would take another couple of chapters at least. Also, you have to have a Mac handy; otherwise, the whole process is a bit pointless.

We'll go through how OS X management works, however, and you'll learn what you need to do in your own environment to support OS X clients.

15.1 Linux client functionality

The client for Linux and UNIX is substantially lighter than the Windows client when it comes to functionality. Many of the powerful features of the Windows client, such as remote access and operating system deployment, aren't available.

The main functions that the Linux client provides are as follows:

- Hardware inventory
- Software inventory
- Software deployment

Your Linux client is ready to go, so let's get started.

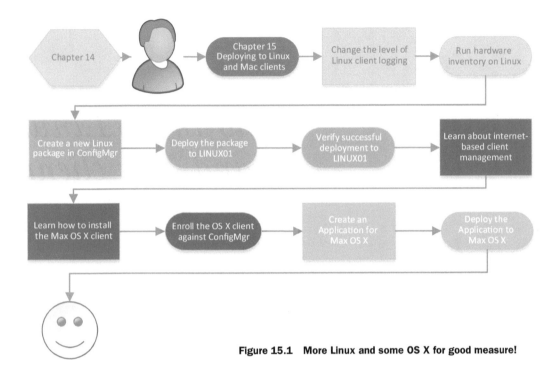

Figure 15.1   More Linux and some OS X for good measure!

15.1.1 *Working with the Linux client*

At times you'll need to stop, start, or restart the ConfigMgr client on a Linux system. A good example of this is if you change the level of logging. By default, the csxcm.log shows you only information-level log entries rather than verbose logging, which is much more useful.

To turn on verbose logging and restart the client for this change to take effect, do the following:

1 On LINUX01, modify the log configuration file using `sudo nano /opt/microsoft/configmgr/etc/scxcm.conf`.

2 Edit the two instances of `INFO` and change them to `TRACE`, as shown in figure 15.2. This causes the client to log verbosely.

3 Exit with Ctrl-X and save the changes.

4 Apply the changes by restarting the ConfigMgr client. To do this, use the command `sudo /etc/init.d/ccmexecd restart`.

5 Take a look at the scxcm.log and you'll see that it's now logging much richer information.

If, for any reason, you want to stop and start the Linux client, use the following commands:

- `sudo /etc/init.d/ccmexecd stop`
- `sudo /etc/init.d/ccmexecd start`

Figure 15.2   Turning on verbose logging for the Linux client

Now that you have a better view of what's happening under the hood, let's move on to inventory.

> **NOTE**   Using verbose logging gives you much more information (with minimal overhead), but your log files can get large and unwieldy. On a Linux distro like Ubuntu, if you're going to use verbose logging, you should also implement log rotation using a utility such as logrotate: www.digitalocean .com/community/tutorials/how-to-manage-log-files-with-logrotate-on-ubuntu-12-10.

15.1.2 Inventorying Linux systems

Linux systems will pick up the hardware inventory settings from the Default Client Settings policy, which is configured to run every seven days. You can force the hardware inventory agent to run by using the command `sudo /opt/microsoft/configmgr/bin/ccmexec —rs hinv` (*hinv* stands for *Hardware Inventory*).

Check out the scxcm.log and you'll see a load of inventory-related log entries whiz past, as the client runs the hardware inventory agent.

> **WHICH LOG?**   In addition to the scxcm.log, you can see the ConfigMgr site server process the incoming hardware inventory in MP_hinv.log, as shown in figure 15.3. On CM01, MP_hinv.log is located at E:\Program Files\SMS_CCM\ Logs.

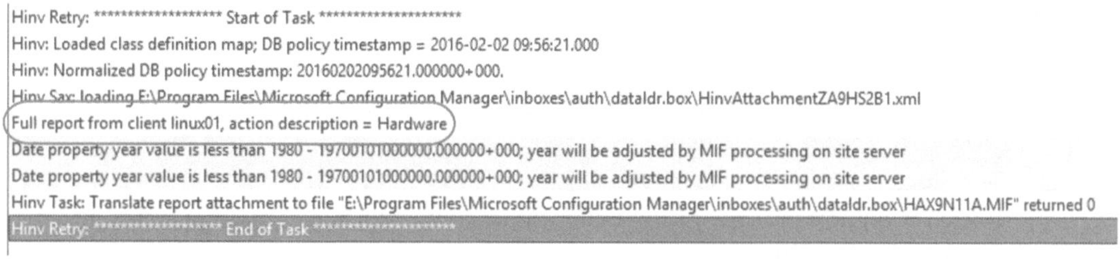

Figure 15.3   The MP_hinv log file shows the incoming hardware inventory report from LINUX01.

Now that the inventory payload has been received, you can view it in the console like any other managed client. In the ConfigMgr console, navigate to Assets and Compliance > Devices. Right-click "LINUX01" and select Start > Resource Explorer.

In the Resource Explorer window, expand Hardware. As you can see, a raft of hardware information is available about LINUX01. Select "Installed Applications." As shown in figure 15.4, all the installed packages and their version details have been gathered.

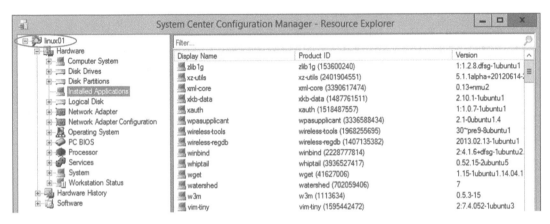

Figure 15.4   Inventory information from Ubuntu available in the ConfigMgr database

How does Windows inventory Linux?

On a managed Windows system, the ConfigMgr client uses Windows Management Instrumentation (WMI) to gather information about the underlying hardware and operating system. The WMI repository in Windows contains a wealth of information that ConfigMgr can use, and that you've already used in queries and operating system deployment.

Microsoft's implementation of WMI on Linux is a Common Information Model (CIM) server called Open Management Infrastructure (OMI). OMI is an open source standard released to the community by Microsoft. For more information on CIM and OMI, read this TechNet article:

http://blogs.technet.com/b/port25/archive/2012/06/29/open-management-interface-omi-open-source-implementation-of-dmtf-cim-wbem-standards.aspx

Now that you know that your Linux client is talking with the ConfigMgr server, let's try to make it do something interesting.

15.1.3 *Deploying Linux packages*

You can deploy software and scripts to managed Linux systems from ConfigMgr. If a Linux package or script supports an unattended installation, chances are that Config-Mgr can deploy it.

The ConfigMgr client for Linux doesn't support the new application model, so anything you deploy to Linux clients is done as a package. In this exercise, you'll deploy a basic package to LINUX01, which will create a text file on the remote client using a shell command:

1   On CM01, open Notepad and save the file as `test.csh`.

>   **TIP**   Note the file extension CSH. When you save the file, make sure that you select Save As Type > All Files. This enables you to change the file extension; otherwise, the file will have a TXT file extension, no matter what.

2   In the text file, enter the line `echo "This is a test!" >> /tmp/testfile.txt`, as shown in figure 15.5. The `echo` command normally outputs to the command window or console, but the `>>` command redirects the output—in this case, to a text file.

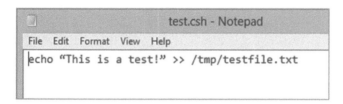

Figure 15.5   The contents of the test script for deployment to LINUX01

3   Save the file to E:\ Sources\Software\Linux\Test Package on CM01. You'll need to create the full folder structure under Software.

4   Next you need to create a new package. In the console, navigate to Software Library > Application Management > Packages.

5   Create a new organizational folder called `Linux`. Then right-click and select "Create Package."

6   Enter `Sample Text File` as the "Name" and `\\cm01\Sources\Applications \Linux Test Package` as the "Source folder," as shown in figure 15.6.

7   Click "Next," and choose to create a Standard program.

8   For the program details, use the following information, as shown in figure 15.7:

   a   Name: Deploy – Sample Text File

   b   Command line: `sh test.csh`

   c   Program can run: Whether or not a user is logged on

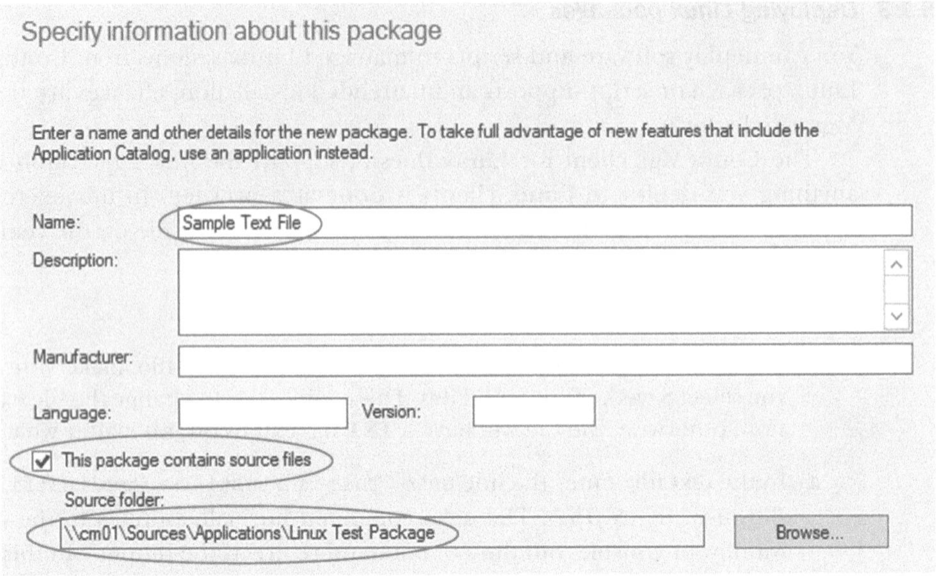

Specify information about this package

Enter a name and other details for the new package. To take full advantage of new features that include the Application Catalog, use an application instead.

Name: | Sample Text File

Description: |

Manufacturer: |

Language: | Version:

☑ This package contains source files

Source folder:
\\cm01\Sources\Applications\Linux Test Package | Browse...

Figure 15.6   Details of the package to deploy to LINUX01

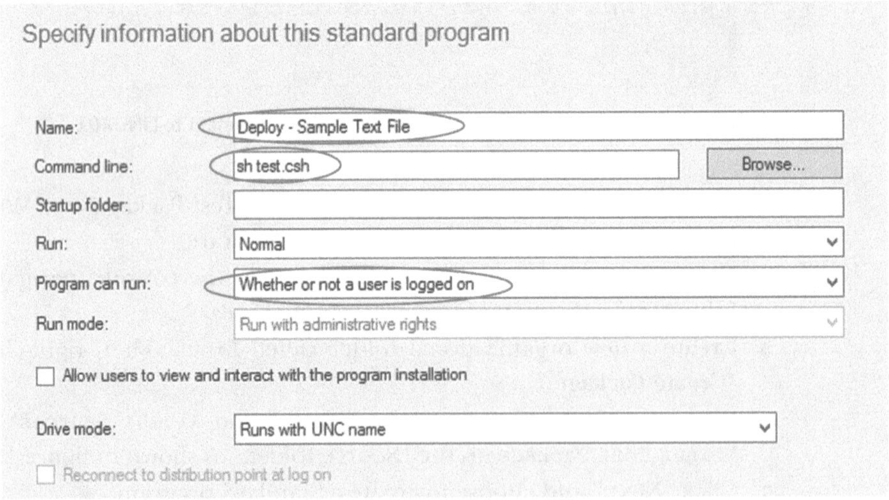

Specify information about this standard program

Name: | Deploy - Sample Text File

Command line: | sh test.csh | Browse...

Startup folder: |

Run: | Normal

Program can run: | Whether or not a user is logged on

Run mode: | Run with administrative rights

☐ Allow users to view and interact with the program installation

Drive mode: | Runs with UNC name

☐ Reconnect to distribution point at log on

Figure 15.7   Details of the program that will be used to deploy the text file

9   In Assets and Compliance > Device Collections, create a new device collection that you'll deploy the package against, using the following details:

a   Name: All Linux Clients

      b Limiting collection: All Desktop and Server Clients

      c Query Rule Name: qry-LinuxOS

      d Query Statement: `select * from SMS_R_System where SMS_R_System` `.Operating SystemNameandVersion like "%Ubuntu%"`

10 Deploy the package against the new device collection. In the Software Library, right-click the Program and select "Deploy." Select "All Linux Clients" as the Collection to deploy to.

11 Distribute the package content to the Distribution Point Group. Step through the wizard until you get to the Scheduling tab. Click "New" to create a new scheduling assignment, and then select "Assign immediately after this event."

12 Step through the rest of the wizard, accepting all the defaults.

13 Log on to LINUX01 and force a download of client policy by using the command `/opt/microsoft/configmgr/bin/ccmexec -rs policy`.

14 Monitor the `scxcm.log`, and you'll see the agent start logging events as the policy is processed.

15 Take a look at the contents of the tmp folder by running ls /tmp. You should see a newly created file called testfile.txt. Check the contents by running sudo nano /tmp/testfile.txt, and the contents should be as shown in figure 15.8.

```
  GNU nano 2.2.6                          File: /tmp/testfile.txt

  This is a test!
```

Figure 15.8 **If you can read this, your deployment worked just fine!**

Congratulations—you've deployed a ConfigMgr Package to Linux! Now for something a bit different...

15.2 *Working with Mac OS X*

This section of the book will be a bit different from those that have come before, in that it's mostly theory rather than hands-on practice. The reason for this change of pace is that managing Mac OS X clients with ConfigMgr would involve quite a bit of infrastructural reworking of our ConfigMgr lab environment—far more than is practical to cover in a single chapter. In fact, it would take a few chapters to cover thoroughly.

    What you'll do, however, is explore how ConfigMgr handles Mac OS X clients, the functionality that the ConfigMgr client for OS X offers, and what the infrastructural dependencies are. This will give you a solid basis for your own investigations.

NOTE If you're interested in some light reading to see how you'd need to change the lab environment, check out this TechNet article: https://technet .microsoft.com/en-us/library/jj591553.aspx.

15.2.1 *Introducing internet-based client management*

Internet-based client management (or IBCM) is a scenario whereby ConfigMgr clients can communicate with their assigned hierarchy even though they aren't on the corporate network. This is achieved by making part of the ConfigMgr server hierarchy accessible via the internet using port forwarding, reverse proxy, or direct connection. Many organizations that implement IBCM place dedicated ConfigMgr server roles in their corporate DMZ rather than expose internal systems to the internet.

The main challenge with IBCM is one of identification: how does a ConfigMgr server know that the internet-based client communicating with it is who it purports to be, and how does the client know that it's talking to a trusted ConfigMgr server? The answer lies in certificates.

To support IBCM, both the ConfigMgr client and the ConfigMgr server must use identifying certificates issued by a trusted certificate authority (CA). The clients must be configured to use a client certificate, while the management point and distribution point roles on the ConfigMgr server must use secure HTTPS communications, protected using an identifying server certificate.

What's the relevance of this for Mac OS X clients? Unlike Linux/UNIX clients, ConfigMgr treats Mac OS X clients as internet-connected systems, regardless of whether they're connected externally via the internet or internally via the corporate network. The infrastructural requirements to support Mac OS X clients are exactly the same as those needed to support internet-based clients.

In the context of our MoL Lab, to support Mac OS X clients, you'd have to do the following:

1 Install and configure a new domain-joined server.
2 Install Active Directory Certificate Services on the new server and configure it to be an enterprise certificate authority.
3 Create and configure multiple certificate templates for use by ConfigMgr clients and servers.
4 Configure Active Directory Group Policy to automatically distribute certificates to domain-joined clients.
5 Then, *either*
  a Configure ConfigMgr communications for HTTPS and reconfigure all existing clients to use HTTPS (since they'd no longer be able to communicate with their assigned primary server).
    or
  b Install a new server to act as a second ConfigMgr site system, with the management point and distribution point roles installed and configured for HTTPS.
6 Oh—and you have to have a Mac handy.

As you can see, that's quite a bit of work to cover in one chapter, and not everyone has a spare Mac lying around.

15.2.2 *Installing the OS X client*

Let's assume that you're working with a ConfigMgr environment that supports Mac OS X. How would you go about installing the client?

Like the Linux/UNIX client, it's not possible to perform a push installation. Rather, you need to make the installation binaries available to each Mac, either by copying them directly to each system or by making them available in a shared location.

The process for distributing and installing the OS X client is as follows:

1 Download the latest OS X client from www.microsoft.com/en-us/download/details.aspx?id=39360. Note that the download is for an MSI rather than an OS X application type.

2 Install the ConfigmgrMacClient.msi on an administrative workstation running Windows, as shown in figure 15.9.

3 In File Explorer, navigate to C:\Program Files (x86)\Microsoft\System Center 2012 R2 Configuration Manager For Mac Client and copy the macclient.dmg file either to a shared location (for example, \\CM01\SMS_PS1\Mac) or directly on to the Mac client.

4 Launch the DMG file and extract the contents to a temporary location.

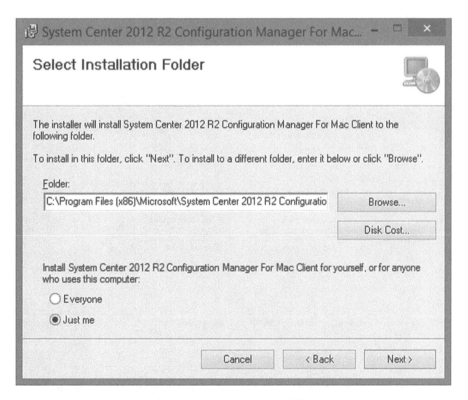

Figure 15.9 The ConfigMgr client for Mac starts life as a Windows MSI.

5   Launch Terminal, navigate to the extracted client files, and install the client by using the command `sudo ./ccmsetup`.

6   Wait for the installation to complete and then reboot the Mac.

7   When you log in again, the enrollment wizard will start automatically. This is the process by which the Mac client enrolls against the ConfigMgr hierarchy and receives a trusted client certificate.

8   Enter the username and password of an Active Directory user account that has permissions to read and enroll the OS X client certificate, as well as the fully qualified name of the site system that's running the enrollment proxy point role (this isn't necessarily the ConfigMgr primary site server).

9   The Mac client receives a new certificate and is enrolled successfully in Config-Mgr. To access the client properties, go to System Preferences > Configuration Manager. Click "Connect Now" to have the client download the latest machine policy, as shown in figure 15.10.

Like the ConfigMgr client for Windows, the client for OS X will talk back to its assigned management point every 60 minutes to retrieve policies.

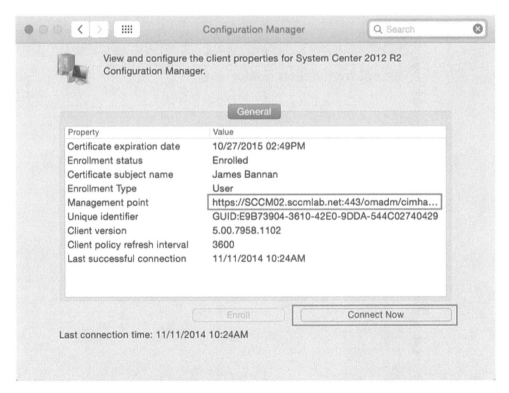

Figure 15.10   The ConfigMgr client properties page gives you a basic amount of information on OS X.

IMPORTANT NOTE The address of the assigned management point uses a fully qualified name. If the OS X client is outside the corporate network (connected to the internet outside the corporate office) and the management point is accessible externally, then the OS X client can be managed both internally and externally.

Even more logs

It wouldn't be ConfigMgr unless there was a log file to look at!

For OS X clients, the ConfigMgr log files are found in two locations: /Library/Application Support/Microsoft/CCM/Logs and ~/Library/Logs. (Note that the ~ is a relative path to the profile folder of the logged-on user; for example, /Users/james/Library/Logs.)

In /Library/Application Support/Microsoft/CCM/Logs, you'll find CCMClient.log. This handles events specific to the client, such as application management. In ~/Library/Logs, you'll find CCMAgent.log (operations such as user logon/logoff), CCMEnroller.log (everything to do with the enrollment process), and CCMPrefPane.log (everything that the user is shown in the Configuration Manager section of System Preferences).

Mac OS X has a built-in utility for reading log files called Console. You can open the log files in Console either by navigating to the log file location in Finder and double-clicking the file (or right-click and select Open With > Console), or going straight to the Console in Utilities.

15.2.3 *Deploying OS X applications*

Applications need to be handled slightly differently in OS X because a fundamental incompatibility exists between how Windows handles applications and how OS X handles them. Without help, OS X can't install Windows applications, and vice versa.

To configure and deploy OS X applications with ConfigMgr, you need to apply a "wrapper" to the original application before importing it into the ConfigMgr console. This acts as an interpretive layer between Windows and OS X, using the ConfigMgr client as an intermediary.

For example, let's say I want to deploy TextWrangler (a free OS X text editor) to all my managed Mac systems. Here's what I'd do:

1   Download the latest version of TextWrangler from www.barebones.com/products/textwrangler. Note that the application format is DMG (disk image).

2   Copy the DMG to a temporary location on a Mac. Then launch Terminal and navigate to the location where the extracted ConfigMgr client files are located. The ConfigMgr client package contains a folder called Tools, as shown in figure 15.11.

3   Use the CMAppUtil utility to apply a CMMAC wrapper to the TextWrangler DMG, specifying both the input file and output path, as shown in figure 15.12.

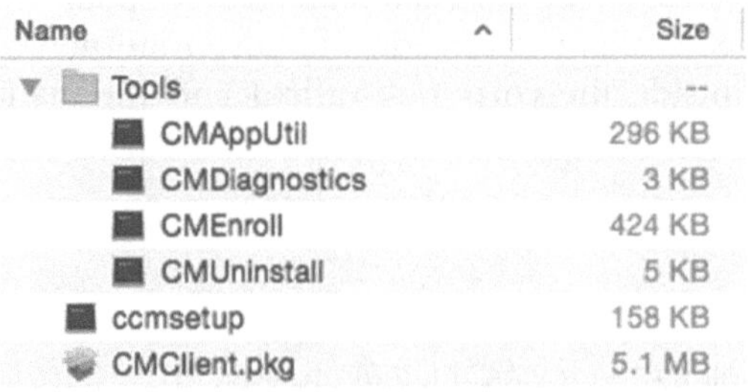

Name	^	Size
▼ 📁 Tools		--
🔲 CMAppUtil		296 KB
🔲 CMDiagnostics		3 KB
🔲 CMEnroll		424 KB
🔲 CMUninstall		5 KB
🔲 ccmsetup		158 KB
🍩 CMClient.pkg		5.1 MB

Figure 15.11 The Tools folder contains some useful utilities for managing the OS X ConfigMgr client.

A tool or two

The utilities contained within the Tools folder are useful for certain local client operations:

- CMAppUtil is used for encapsulating native OS X applications in a CMMAC wrapper for use with ConfigMgr.
- CMDiagnostics creates an archive of all the ConfigMgr client logs that can be sent to a third party for assessment and troubleshooting.
- CMEnroll is used to manually enroll the system against the ConfigMgr enrollment proxy point, rather than using the manual wizard.
- CMUninstall is used to completely uninstall the ConfigMgr client.

```
James-MacBook-Pro:Tools james$ sudo ./CMAppUtil -c ../../ConfigMgr\ Apps/TextWrangler_4.5.11.dmg -o ../../ConfigMgr\
 Apps/
System Center Configuration Manager Application Utility for Mac OS X
Version: 5.00.7958.1102
Copyright 2013 Microsoft Corporation

Checksumming Protective Master Boot Record (MBR : 0)...
Protective Master Boot Record (MBR :: verified    CRC32 $7A10C640
Checksumming GPT Header (Primary GPT Header : 1)...
 GPT Header (Primary GPT Header : 1): verified   CRC32 $231E654C
Checksumming GPT Partition Data (Primary GPT Table : 2)...
GPT Partition Data (Primary GPT Tabl: verified   CRC32 $AF4D0CAB
Checksumming   (Apple_Free : 3)...
                (Apple_Free : 3): verified   CRC32 $00000000
Checksumming disk image (Apple_HFS : 4)...
        disk image (Apple_HFS : 4): verified   CRC32 $7B67CEE8
Checksumming   (Apple_Free : 5)...
                (Apple_Free : 5): verified   CRC32 $00000000
Checksumming GPT Partition Data (Backup GPT Table : 6)...
GPT Partition Data (Backup GPT Table: verified   CRC32 $AF4D0CAB
Checksumming GPT Header (Backup GPT Header : 7)...
 GPT Header (Backup GPT Header : 7): verified   CRC32 $015CF918
verified   CRC32 $0ADF7F54
/dev/disk2              GUID_partition_scheme
/dev/disk2s1           Apple_HFS                    /Volumes/Textwrangler 4.5.11

Creating Cmmac file for /Volumes/TextWrangler 4.5.11/TextWrangler.app
Found detection Methods
Composing the cmmac file output
Output written to ../../ConfigMgr Apps//TextWrangler.app.cmmac.

CMAppUtil successfully processed "TextWrangler.app",
to deploy refer to the product documentation.
James-MacBook-Pro:Tools james$ █
```

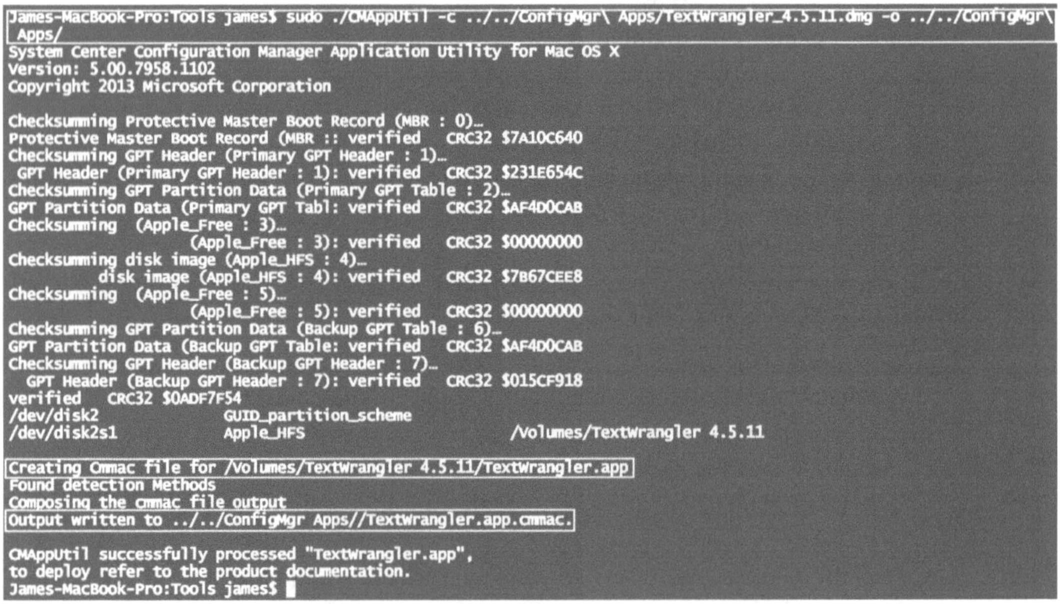

Figure 15.12   Use CMAppUtil to input a native OS X application and output a CMMAC file for ConfigMgr.

4 Look in the specified output folder for a new file called TextWrangler .app.cmmac. Copy this file to a shared location accessible by the ConfigMgr server.

5 In the ConfigMgr console, navigate to Software Library > Application Management > Applications. Right-click and select "Create Application."

6 In the Create Application wizard, in the "Type" drop-down list, select "Mac OS X." Then enter the path to the CMMAC file, as shown in figure 15.13.

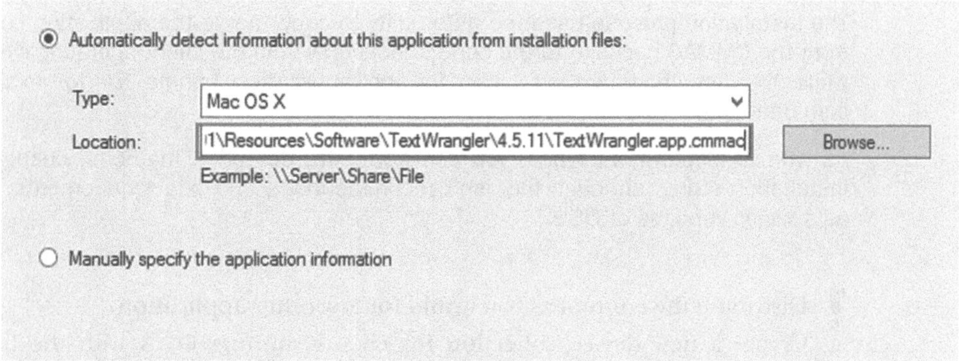

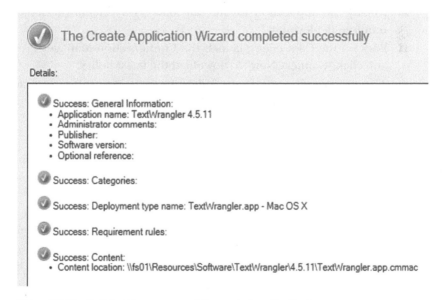

Figure 15.13   Specify the CMMAC file in the Create Application wizard.

7 Give the application an appropriate name (for example, `TextWrangler 4.5.11`). Click "Summary" and then "Next." Ensure that the application has been created successfully, as shown in figure 15.14.

Figure 15.14   Nothing like a successfully created application!

Delving deeper into OS X applications

Although the technologies are different, the concepts behind a successful application deployment are the same for Windows as they are for OS X.

Take a look at the newly created application and check out the properties of the deployment type (one has automatically been created). As with those for Windows-based applications, OS X deployment types use an installation program and detection method to ensure a successful installation.

The installation process uses the ditto utility to copy/merge the application content from the CMMAC package to the correct location within the client operating system, while the detection method looks for the application bundle ID (for example, com.barebones.textwrangler).

As with all deployment types, you can add extra detection methods, change the installation string (although this isn't recommended), and add requirements, such as specific versions of OS X.

8   Distribute the content as you would for any other application.

9   Create a new device collection for clients running OS X with the following properties:

   a   Name: All Mac OS X Clients

   b   Limiting Collection: All Desktop and Server Clients

   c   Membership Rules: Query

   d   Query Criteria: System Resource.Operating System Name and Version is like "%OS X%"

10   Deploy the application to the "All Mac OS X Clients" device collection as a required deployment.

11   Back on the OS X client, launch the Configuration Manager Preferences pane and click "Connect Now" to download the latest policy.

12   The user receives a pop-up indicating that new software is available to be installed, as shown in figure 15.15. The user can choose to delay the installation or install straight away.

And *voilà*! You have software deployed to OS X using ConfigMgr.

Although we haven't covered the concept yet, ConfigMgr can also manage compliance settings for OS X, allowing you to define and enforce certain settings and parameters within the operating system.

At the time of writing, Mac OS X support in ConfigMgr isn't as rich an experience as it is on Windows platforms, but Microsoft has a dedicated development team whose role it is to continue to enhance OS X functionality.

Now, let's take a break from cross-platform management and delve into the murky world of antivirus!

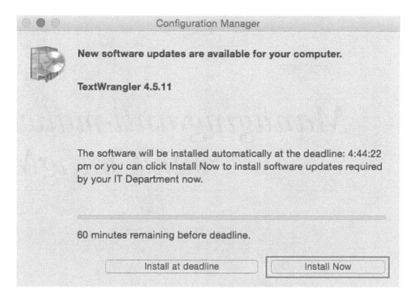

Figure 15.15 The user is informed of new software deployments via a pop-up.

Managing anti-malware with ConfigMgr

Dealing with malware is part and parcel of administering any environment of any size. Because of its prominence as a desktop operating system, Windows has always been a popular target for malware, and the responsibility for ensuring that appropriate countermeasures are deployed and maintained often falls to desktop and server administrators.

ConfigMgr has the ability to natively act as the center of your anti-malware solution, using System Center Endpoint Protection (or SCEP, for short). SCEP used to be Forefront Endpoint Protection (or FEP), which was a separate product, but this was integrated into ConfigMgr 2007 via a manual installation process. ConfigMgr 2012 and later bring both products together seamlessly, using skills and investments that you've already made in your environment.

Anti-malware on Windows 10 is handled differently from previous versions of Windows. With Windows 8.1 and earlier (including Server 2012 R2), SCEP installs as a discrete application that's managed via ConfigMgr. On Windows 10, the SCEP installation process integrates with Windows Defender, which is already present on the operating system. In this chapter, as shown in figure 16.1, you'll take control of Windows Defender and manage it directly using ConfigMgr, and then get a feel for reporting and incident management.

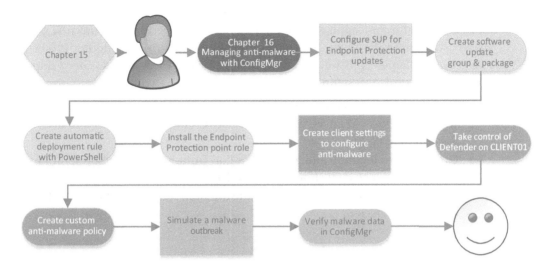

Figure 16.1 By the end of this chapter, your anti-malware will be up and running.

16.1 *Enabling System Center Endpoint Protection*

SCEP functionality in ConfigMgr relies on interdependent features to form a coherent solution. At a high level, these are as follows:

- *Endpoint Protection client*—This is the locally installed client that handles all anti-malware functions on the managed system.
- *Endpoint Protection server role*—This provides a communication channel between the Endpoint Protection client (on the ConfigMgr server) and the ConfigMgr database. It also creates default policies and SCEP settings.
- *Software updates*—The SUP brings down SCEP client updates and anti-malware definitions so that they can be made available to managed systems.
- *Distribution points*—These are where managed clients access SCEP updates and definitions, just like all ConfigMgr-distributed content.

First, you need to look at software updates, since this is a prerequisite before you enable the Endpoint Protection role. You'll also be using CLIENT01, so if this virtual machine has been powered off, you'll need to turn it back on.

16.1.1 *Configuring software updates*

In theory, you don't absolutely have to use your ConfigMgr SUP to manage SCEP updates. You could use ConfigMgr to deploy and manage SCEP but have all your managed clients go out to the internet for updates. In a small managed environment, this might not be a bad idea, but in the vast majority of cases, you'll want to use the ConfigMgr hierarchy to distribute the content as you get full control and visibility over what's happening, which you don't get with internet-based updating.

By default, when ConfigMgr distributes the SCEP client, the client is configured to look at ConfigMgr for its updates, which is why you need to configure this first. You've already configured the SUP to download updates for Forefront Endpoint Protection in a previous chapter; this will also bring down updates for System Center Endpoint Protection. To verify this setting:

1   Navigate to Administration > Site Configuration > Sites.
2   Right-click "PS1 – Primary Site 1" and select Configure Site Components > Software Update Point.
3   Go to the Products tab and ensure that Forefront > Forefront Endpoint Protection 2010 is selected, as shown in figure 16.2.
4   Go to the Classifications tab and ensure that (among others) "Definition Updates" is selected.

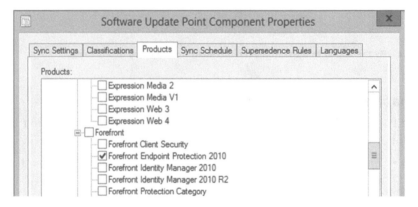

Figure 16.2   **Make sure that the SUP is configured correctly before enabling Endpoint Protection.**

Unlike updates for most other products, updates for anti-malware products (especially definition updates) are released frequently—sometimes more than once per day. Clearly, you don't want to have to manually administer this frequency of updating, so your next step is to create an automatic deployment rule (ADR), so that ConfigMgr does the heavy lifting for you.

The first step in creating an ADR for Endpoint Protection is to create a software update group (SUG). To make sure that you're working with the latest update metadata from Microsoft, it's worth performing a manual sync against Windows Update. To do this:

1   Navigate to Software Library > Software Updates > All Software Updates.
2   In the ribbon, select "Synchronize Software Updates."
3   Monitor the WSyncMgr.log file in CMTrace until the sync is complete.

    Depending on the speed of your internet connection and the last time you performed a sync, the whole process can take up to 15 minutes to complete.

4 Navigate back to "All Software Updates" and select the "Add Criteria" drop-down arrow next to the "Search" field.

5 Select the categories and category values as detailed in table 16.1.

Table 16.1   Search categories for the latest SCEP definitions

Category	Value
Date Released	Is on or after 1 last day
Expired	No
Product	Forefront Endpoint Protection 2010 *or* Windows Defender
Superseded	No
Update Classification	Definition Updates

HINT   Searches are powerful tools, but re-creating them every time can be a soul-destroying exercise in wasted time. Save your searches by using the "Save Current Search As" button in the ribbon. In this case, save it as "Latest Antimalware Definitions."

6 Perform the search, and as shown in figure 16.3, the result should be two software updates.

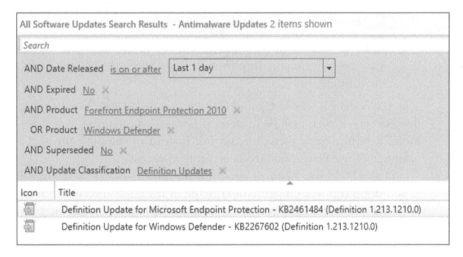

Figure 16.3   The tighter the search, the more accurate the results.

7 Right-click the update and select "Create Software Update Group." Call the group `Antimwalware Definitions`.

8 Navigate to Software Updates > Software Update Groups, and you'll see the newly created group. Right-click "Antimalware Definitions" and select "Download."

9 You'll create a deployment package to hold the downloaded update content. Step through the wizard by using the information in table 16.2.

NOTE You'll need to create the folder AntimalwareDefinitions in E:\Updates before creating the deployment package. To do this by using PowerShell, the command is `New-Item -Path 'E:\Updates' -Name 'AntimalwareDefinitions' -ItemType Directory`.

Table 16.2 **Create a software update deployment package with this information**

Deployment package property	Value
Name	Antimalware Definitions
Package Source	\\CM01\Updates\AntimalwareDefinitions
Distribution Point Group	MOL Lab DPs
Distribution Priority	High
Download software updates from the Internet	Selected
Language	English

WHICH LOG? Monitor the download progress in PatchDownloader.log, which is normally found in the .\AppData\Local\Temp\2 folder of the logged-on user (for example, C:\Users\Administrator.MOL).

10 After the download is complete, you can create the ADR. Navigate to Software Updates > Automatic Deployment Rules, and select "Create Automatic Deployment Rule."

The ADR wizard is one of ConfigMgr's longest ones (yay!) because there's a lot to tell the site server, such as how to determine which updates to download, where to put them, how to deploy them, and so on. Instead of stepping through every step and option, let's use PowerShell to speed up the process.

All the code you need to generate the ADR is available in .\powershell\Create-ADREndpointProtection.ps1. Grab the file or the code and run it on CM01.

After you've run the script, in Software Update > Automatic Deployment Rules you'll see a new ADR called "ADR – Endpoint Protection Definitions." To run the rule, right-click the ADR and select "Run Now." Monitor the progress of the rule until complete.

WHICH LOG? When you want to keep an eye on automatic deployment rules, the RuleEngine.log file is the one you want.

Once the rule is complete, navigate back to Software Updates > Software Update Groups. There will be a newly created group called "ADR – Endpoint Protection Definitions" that was created by the ADR engine. This is the group the engine will be using from this point onward, so you can go ahead and delete the group you created earlier called Endpoint Protection Definitions.

OK—you're finished! Anti-malware updates are now residing in your ConfigMgr environment, and you have a rule to make sure that this keeps happening. Now you can move on and get SCEP active.

Timing your sync

You've fudged the Endpoint Protection ADR a bit, in that although it's configured to run every day, the SUP isn't set to run automatically. What are the implications of this?

Well, an ADR assesses software update metadata that resides within the ConfigMgr database, so if that metadata isn't being updated (because the SUP updates only manually), then the ADR is always assessing its rule against stale data.

In the case of your lab environment, the ADR is an example of what you'd do in an enterprise environment, with the exception that you'd schedule the ADR to run after a successful SUP sync, to ensure that the ADR is always working with the latest update metadata.

16.1.2 *Enabling the Endpoint Protection server role*

Thankfully, compared to setting up the SUP component, enabling SCEP on the ConfigMgr server is straightforward.

As mentioned earlier, the Endpoint Protection server role established a communications channel between the SCEP client and the ConfigMgr database. This is done by installing SCEP on the ConfigMgr server that will host the Endpoint Protection role. The installation happens automatically when you enable the role; there's nothing manual to be done.

To enable the Endpoint Protection server role, do the following:

1 Navigate to Administration > Site Configuration > Servers and Site System Roles.
2 Right-click "CM01" and select "Add Site System Roles."
3 Click through the wizard pages until you get to the System Role Selection page, and then select "Endpoint Protection point."
4 You'll get a warning about setting up ConfigMgr to download Endpoint Protection updates. You've already done this, so accept the warning and click "Next."
5 Accept the SCEP license terms and click "Next."
6 On the Microsoft Active Protection Service (MAPS) page, select "Do not join MAPS" and then click through to the end of the wizard.

WHICH LOG? The Endpoint Protection point role installation is over quickly. Look at the EPSetup.log to watch installation progress, and to verify that SCEP is being installed on the ConfigMgr server (you'll see it in the taskbar as well).

It takes a few minutes for SCEP to be installed on CM01, and for that time the taskbar remains red. Don't panic—it's because the anti-malware engine definitions are out-of-date. SCEP automatically updates itself, and the application icon changes to green.

Now that's complete, you can focus on deploying SCEP to your managed clients.

16.1.3 *Configuring Endpoint Protection on clients*

You can install SCEP manually on managed clients, or use a traditional Active Directory group policy or a ConfigMgr application/package deployment. But you have another option available, which is to use ConfigMgr-driven client settings.

> **TIP** Any client can install SCEP manually, because the installer is made available via the SMS_<SITE> share. Navigate to \\CM01\SMS_PS1\Client and you'll see the SCEPInstall.exe client installation package. On a client that already has the ConfigMgr client installed, you'll find the same installer already present in C:\Windows\CCMSetup; it gets pushed down as part of the client payload.

Using client settings, you can direct ConfigMgr to install SCEP on any managed system that doesn't already have it. To get SCEP deployed, do the following:

1 Navigate to Administration > Client Settings.
2 Right-click and select "Create Custom Client Device Settings."
3 For the settings name, enter `Endpoint Protection Settings`, and tick the "Endpoint Protection" check box.
4 Configure the Endpoint Protection settings by using the values in table 16.3, and then click "OK."

Table 16.3   **Configuration for Endpoint Protection client settings**

Endpoint Protection setting	Value
Manage Endpoint Protection client on client computers	Yes
Install Endpoint Protection client on client computers	Yes
Automatically remove previously installed anti-malware software	Yes
Allow Endpoint Protection client installation and restarts outside maintenance windows	No
For Windows Embedded devices...	Yes
Suppress any required computer restarts after the Endpoint Protection client is installed	Yes
Disable alternate sources for the initial definition update on client computers	Yes

5 Right-click the newly created settings and select "Deploy."
6 Select the "All Windows 10 Clients" device collection and click "OK."

Now that the settings have been created and deployed, let's verify that they work.

7 Navigate to Assets and Compliance > Device Collections and select "All Windows 10 Clients."

8 Right-click the collection and select Client Notification > Download Computer Policy.

9 Log on to CLIENT01 and open Task Manager. In the Processes tab, you should see the SCEPInstall.exe package start after a minute or two, as shown in figure 16.4. This shows that SCEP is being installed.

▷	Microsoft Windows Search Inde...	0.8%	3.2 MB	0.1 MB/s	0 Mbps
▷	Microsoft® Volume Shadow Co...	0%	0.6 MB	0 MB/s	0 Mbps
	RDP Clipboard Monitor	0%	1.4 MB	0 MB/s	0 Mbps
	SCEPInstall Package (32 bit)	0%	2.9 MB	0 MB/s	0 Mbps
	SCNotification (32 bit)	0%	2.7 MB	0 MB/s	0 Mbps
▷	Spooler SubSystem App	0%	1.1 MB	0 MB/s	0 Mbps
▷	Windows Media Player Network...	0%	1.0 MB	0 MB/s	0 Mbps
	Windows® installer	0%	1.7 MB	0.1 MB/s	0 Mbps
▷	Windows® installer	0%	3.3 MB	0.1 MB/s	0 Mbps

Figure 16.4   The client has found the Endpoint Protection settings and is installing SCEP.

16.2 *Using anti-malware policies*

SCEP client functionality is managed by anti-malware policies. These policies determine client behavior such as schedule scans, update locations, and exclusion settings.

Whenever the SCEP client is deployed using ConfigMgr client settings, a default policy is also installed. You can see this on CLIENT01:

1 Log in to CLIENT01.

2 Launch Windows Defender from the Start menu.

3 When the Windows Defender client opens, navigate to Help > About. As shown in figure 16.5, the client has a default policy configured.

To take a look at what settings this default policy contains, you can open the policy in the ConfigMgr console:

1 Navigate to Assets and Compliance > Endpoint Protection > Antimalware Policies.

2 Right-click "Default Client Antimalware Policy" and select "Properties."

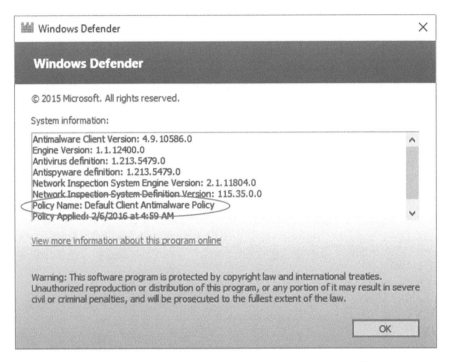

Figure 16.5   SCEP/Defender is installed with a default policy already configured.

Here you can browse through the various settings that make up the default policy. Scheduled scan settings are of particular importance to any organization because of their intensive nature.

For example, it might seem like a great idea for a security-conscious admin to force a full scan every day at 9:00 a.m., but that will be offset by the company-wide lack of productivity that seems to cripple everyone just as they're trying to start the workday.

You'll create a custom anti-malware policy that allows the client to send report data to Microsoft via MAPS, as well as have a more aggressive definitions-update policy. To create the custom policy, perform the following steps:

1 In Antimalware Policies, right-click and select "Create Antimalware Policy."
2 For the name, use `Custom Workstation Antimalware Policy`.
3 Select "Microsoft Active Protection Service" and then "Definition Updates."
4 For the MAPS settings, change the membership type to "Advanced membership."
5 For the definition update settings, change "Force a definition update" to "Yes," change the update sources to just "ConfigMgr" and "Microsoft Update" (as shown in figure 16.6), and change the "If Configuration Manager is used as a source" to "36 hours."
6 Click "OK." Then right-click the newly created policy and select "Deploy."
7 Select the "All Windows 10 Clients" device collection.

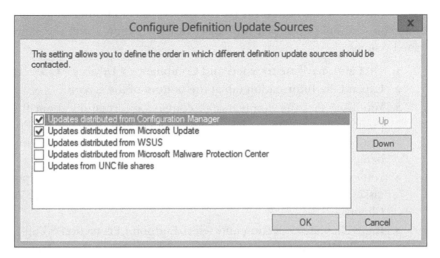

Figure 16.6   Use the anti-malware policy to specify from where clients can update.

8   Navigate back to Assets and Compliance > Device Collections. Select the "All Windows 10 Clients" collection and trigger a client policy update.

9   Back on CLIENT01, verify that the SCEP agent has received a policy update by opening the SCEP agent and going to Help > About. As shown in figure 16.7, the new policy is now being applied as well as the default policy. This is because the new policy overrides the default policy, but only a small number of settings are being overridden.

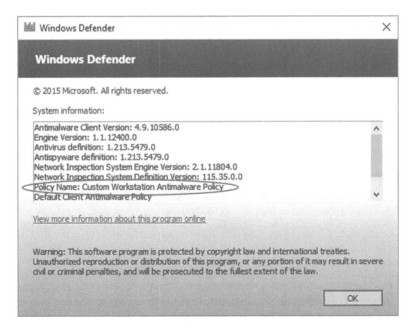

Figure 16.7   New policy is being applied to the SCEP agent

This SCEP client information is passed back to the computer object in ConfigMgr so that you can build up a rich repository of information about the state of your managed systems:

1   On CM01, navigate to Assets and Compliance > Devices > CLIENT01.

2   Expand the Information tab at the bottom of the screen.

3   You'll see that the Summary tab contains information about the client's Endpoint Protection status. The Malware Detail and Antimalware Policies tabs give extra information about whether the client is infected, and which policies are being applied.

4   You can also use the ConfigMgr console to perform basic Endpoint Protection tasks. Navigate to Assets and Compliance > Device Collections > All Windows 10 Clients.

5   Right-click the collection and select Endpoint Protection > Full Scan. This triggers the Windows Defender client on all systems in the collection to perform a full scan.

6   Back on CLIENT01, ensure that the Windows Defender client is running a full scan.

Now that you know your managed clients are receiving the anti-malware policy successfully and that information is flowing back and forth, let's see how Defender handles a malware outbreak.

16.3 *Dealing with malware outbreaks*

Defender is deployed, updates are merrily downloading, and you're sitting back in your chair, confident that things are good. Then the malware hits.

Computers in your organization *will* get hit with malware. Whether through malicious intent or because a user clicked the wrong link, your anti-malware product will be called on to protect your managed systems. When malware is detected, how does Defender react?

To test this, you're going to have to get your hands dirty. You don't want to introduce live malware into your lab environment, so instead you'll use a testing tool that a decent anti-malware product will *think* is malware, but that's harmless.

Testing anti-malware

Anti-malware is much like backups: you hope you never need them, but you're grateful that you have them when the need arises.

The problem is that if you have an anti-malware solution (or a backup solution) that you haven't tested, you're incurring a massive risk. A nonfunctional solution is much worse than no solution at all.

In the same way that you should have a disaster-recovery testing process in place for backups, you should also regularly test anti-malware to ensure that it's still capable of performing its function.

The team over at EICAR (formerly the European Institute for Computer Antivirus Research) has such a utility available. It will allow you to simulate a malware outbreak in the lab environment and see how both SCEP and ConfigMgr respond. Let's get started:

1. On CLIENT01, open Internet Explorer and navigate to www.eicar.org/85-0-Download.html. Four files are available for download, each designed to test a different malware vector:

   a. eicar.com

   b. eicar.com.txt

   c. eicar_com.zip

   d. eicarcom2.zip

2. Attempt to download each file in turn (I used the secure HTTPS download links).

   As shown in figure 16.8, each time you attempt to download one of the files, Defender produces a pop-up that alerts you to the fact that a threat was detected, but that automatic action was taken.

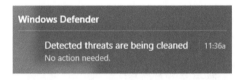

Figure 16.8   Have no fear; Defender is here.

3. After you've tried to download each file (they'll all fail), open the Defender client and then navigate to the History tab.

4. Select "All detected items" and then "View details." As shown in figure 16.9, the Defender agent has intercepted each item and quarantined it, protecting the operating system.

5. Click "Remove all" to delete each instance.

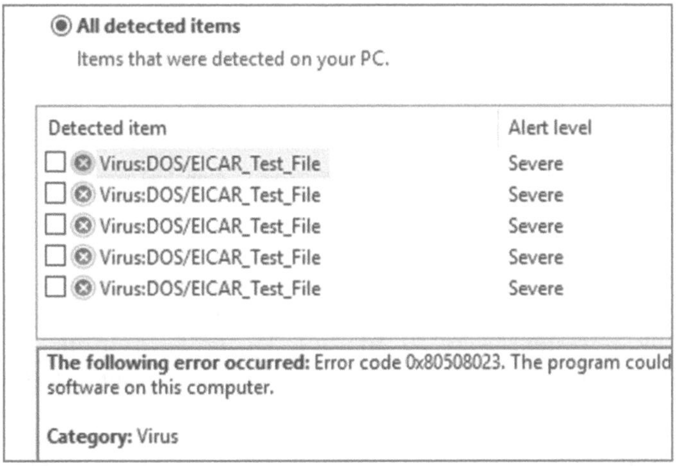

Detected item	Alert level
⊙ All detected items	
Items that were detected on your PC.	
☒ Virus:DOS/EICAR_Test_File	Severe
☒ Virus:DOS/EICAR_Test_File	Severe
☒ Virus:DOS/EICAR_Test_File	Severe
☒ Virus:DOS/EICAR_Test_File	Severe
☒ Virus:DOS/EICAR_Test_File	Severe

The following error occurred: Error code 0x80508023. The program could
software on this computer.

Category: Virus

Figure 16.9   Defender intercepted and automatically quarantined the EICAR test file.

The Defender agent continually sends any information about detected malware back to the ConfigMgr server, so that you as the administrator are fully informed and can take appropriate action as necessary.

To see what's going on in ConfigMgr, navigate to Monitoring > Endpoint Protection Status > System Center Endpoint Protection Status. As shown in figure 16.10, malware information from CLIENT01 will have been passed back up to the ConfigMgr server.

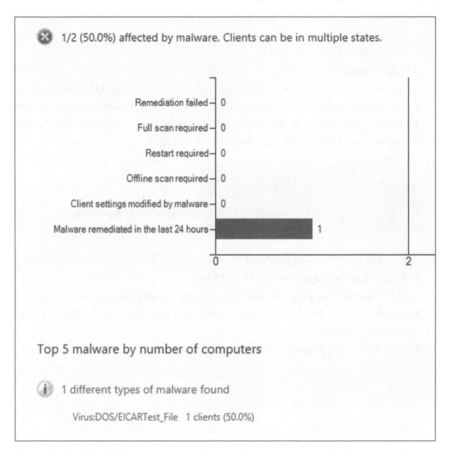

Figure 16.10   The SCEP status page in the console gives you a graphical overview of malware outbreaks.

TIP   If you don't see any information in the status page, it's likely that ConfigMgr hasn't processed it yet. Anti-malware monitoring/status information is automatically refreshed every 20 minutes. To force a refresh, select "Run Summarization" in the ribbon. You can also change the summarization schedule and make it more or less aggressive.

Navigate to Monitoring > Endpoint Protection Status > Malware Detected. Here you'll see a breakdown of the types of malware detected in various device collections. If you suspect that a file has been incorrectly quarantined (a false positive), you can select "Restore files quarantined by this threat," which will move the quarantined file(s) back to their original position. Obviously, be careful with this feature!

If detected malware is definitely a false positive and you want to whitelist it, select "Allow this threat," and the next time clients refresh the policy, they will no longer quarantine the file(s).

It's important to note just how central the ConfigMgr client is to this whole solution; without a healthy client, the foundation of your entire management solution is compromised. So that's the focus of the next chapter: getting healthy and staying healthy.

16.4 Labs

Antivirus doesn't belong just on managed workstations; it's vitally important to ensure that servers are protected too. But servers don't function the same as workstations (obviously), so an anti-malware policy that's appropriate for one is unlikely to be suitable for the other.

For example, you don't want servers talking out to the internet to pick up definition updates. Servers shouldn't be able to access the internet at all unless there's a specific reason to do so. But with servers, you have more flexibility about when you can schedule full scans, since they're on all the time (all being well!), so you could even schedule a full scan every day. Alternatively, you may want to exclude certain local files (like database files and log files on a SQL server) from being constantly scanned by the anti-malware agent.

For this lab, create a new, custom anti-malware policy suitable for servers. Then create a client settings policy for servers that will deploy SCEP to DC01 (the operating system is Windows Server 2012 R2, so it'll be SCEP rather than Defender). Make sure that SCEP is automatically installed and that the correct policies are applied.

Making sure clients
are healthy

17

You might have the healthiest, most finely tuned ConfigMgr server hierarchy in existence, but if your clients are chronically unhealthy, then you may as well not be bothering. It should be clear by now that the ConfigMgr client is the real workhorse in your environment. The ConfigMgr server and database are where all the administration happens, but without a fleet of healthy clients ready to do your bidding, you're rather like a general standing in front of an army, shouting at soldiers who have all gone to sleep.

So in this chapter, as shown in figure 17.1, you'll examine the common causes and symptoms of client health problems, how to detect them, and how to remediate them.

Ready to delve into client health? Good—let's get started.

17.1 Understanding common client health issues

Back in the days of Configuration Manager 2007, many admins made heavy use of so-called health-check collections. These were device collections that reported on different aspects of client behavior, such as how many clients had failed to send through inventory or how many reported having the client installed but were marked inactive.

With Configuration Manager 2012 and later, you don't need to use health-check collections anymore, because the console gives you an easy way to keep an eye on what's going on, and because the client has a self-healing function, designed to keep things running smoothly.

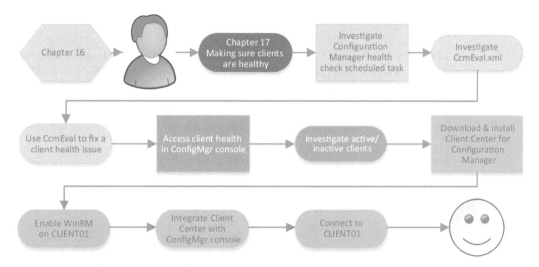

Figure 17.1 **In this chapter, you'll get healthy and stay healthy.**

Looking at how the self-healing function works gives good insight into the various things that can derail ConfigMgr client operations:

1 Log into CLIENT01 and navigate to Control Panel > Administrative Tools > Task Scheduler.

2 In Task Scheduler, navigate to Task Scheduler Library > Microsoft > Configuration Manager.

As shown in figure 17.2, three built-in scheduled tasks are automatically created when the ConfigMgr client gets installed. The one you're interested in is the Configuration Manager Health Evaluation task.

1 Select the "Configuration Manager Health Evaluation" task and then select the Actions tab.

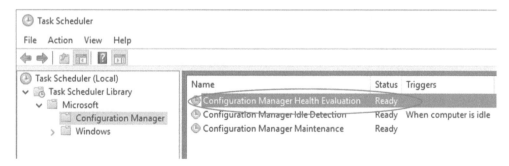

Figure 17.2 **ConfigMgr health evaluation is a standard Windows scheduled task.**

As you can see, this task has only one action: to run C:\Windows\CCM\Ccm-Eval.exe, an executable that also gets installed along with the ConfigMgr client. The behavior of CcmEval.exe is driven by CcmEval.xml; this details exactly what gets checked for and how remediation happens.

2 Open a Windows PowerShell administrative window (click "Start," right-click "Windows PowerShell," and choose "Run As Administrator") and then enter the following commands, as shown in figure 17.3:

```
[xml]$xml = Get-Content C:\Windows\CCM\CcmEval.xml
$xml.ClientHealth.HealthCheck | Select-Object Description
```

```
                               Administrator: Windows PowerShell
PS C:\Users\Administrator> [xml]$xml = Get-Content C:\Windows\CCM\CcmEval.xml
PS C:\Users\Administrator> $xml.ClientHealth.HealthCheck | Select-Object Description_
```

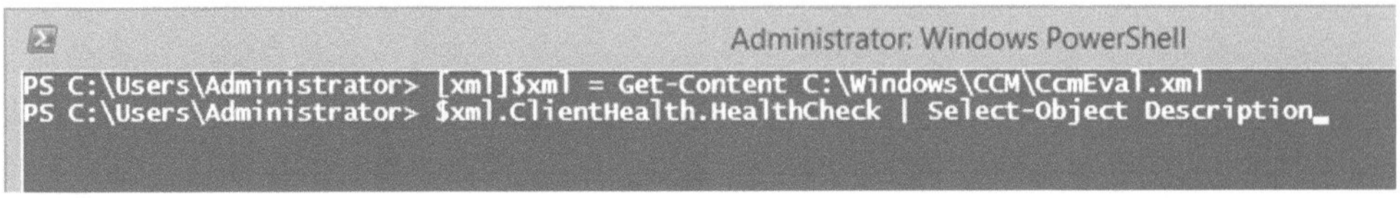

Figure 17.3 Use PowerShell to import and investigate the structure of an XML file.

The output looks identical to the items in the following list, which contains potential issues that the health evaluation checks for:

- Verify WMI service exists
- Verify/remediate WMI service startup type
- Verify/remediate WMI service status
- WMI Repository read/write test
- Verify/remediate client WMI provider
- WMI repository integrity test
- Verify BITS exists
- Verify/remediate BITS startup type
- Verify/remediate client prerequisites
- Verify/remediate client installation
- Verify SMS Agent Host service exists
- Verify/remediate SMS Agent Host service startup type
- Verify/remediate SMS Agent Host service status
- WMI Event Sink test
- Microsoft Policy Platform WMI integrity test
- Verify/remediate Microsoft Policy Platform service existence
- Verify/remediate Microsoft Policy Platform service startup type
- Verify/remediate Antimalware service startup type
- Verify/remediate Antimalware service status
- Verify/remediate Network Inspection service startup type
- Verify/remediate Windows Update service startup type

- Verify/remediate Windows Update service startup type on Windows 8
- Verify/remediate Configuration Manager Remote Control service startup type
- Verify/remediate Configuration Manager Remote Control service status
- Verify/remediate Configuration Manager Proxy service startup type
- Verify/remediate Configuration Manager Proxy service status
- Verify/remediate SQL CE database is healthy

As you can see, many potential issues could cause problems for the ConfigMgr client. It's important to note that some issues—for example, the SMS agent host service being set to disabled—would cause the client to stop functioning completely. But because CcmEval.exe runs independently of the ConfigMgr client, it's an issue that can be automatically resolved.

To see how CcmEval works, let's break something. The software updates component of the ConfigMgr client is in turn dependent on the Windows Update service. If this service is disabled, the client can't scan for or apply software updates; this is one of the conditions that CcmEval is configured to test for and remediate. To disable the service, use the following PowerShell snippet:

```
Set-Service wuauserv -StartupType Disabled
```

Verify the change by entering the following:

```
(Get-CimInstance `
-Class Win32_Service `
-Filter "Name='wuauserv'").StartMode
```

The output lets you know that the service is now disabled. To trigger the remediation scan, navigate back to the Configuration Manager health evaluation task in the Task Scheduler. Right-click the task and select "Run."

WHICH LOG? CcmEval.exe logs its output to CcmEval.log in the \Windows\ CCM\Logs folder on the client.

As shown in figure 17.4, CcmEval detects that the Windows Update startup type is incorrect. It attempts to remediate it and is able to do so successfully.

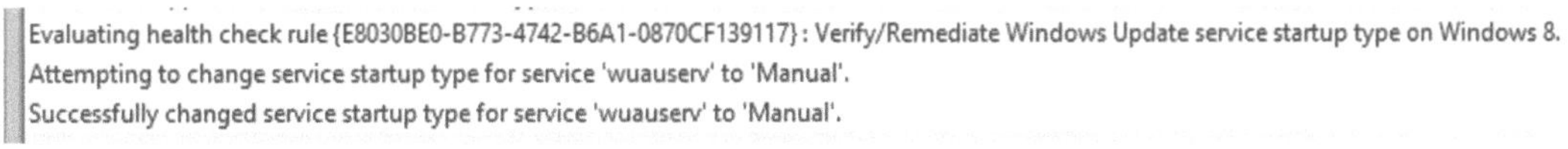

Evaluating health check rule {E8030BE0-B773-4742-B6A1-0870CF139117}: Verify/Remediate Windows Update service startup type on Windows 8.
Attempting to change service startup type for service 'wuauserv' to 'Manual'.
Successfully changed service startup type for service 'wuauserv' to 'Manual'.

Figure 17.4 CcmEval is designed to test for and remediate common client heath issues.

To verify that the startup type for the service has indeed been changed, run the following:

```
(Get-CimInstance `
-Class Win32_Service `
-Filter "Name='wuauserv'").StartMode
```

The output reads *Manual,* which is what it was set to before you changed it. Now that you've seen how health is managed at the client level, let's look at how it's handled from an administrative perspective.

17.2 *Administering client health*

Understanding how client health and remediation works on a single system is important, but it's an inconvenient way to administer an entire environment of managed systems. To do this, you need to get an overall picture of client health from within the ConfigMgr console.

Client activity, as well as the results of the CcmEval health and remediation checks, is sent back to the ConfigMgr primary site server and rolled up into the database. You can then get a regularly updated overview of the state of client health across your ecosystem. To have a look at what's happening in your lab environment, navigate to Monitoring > Client Status.

As shown in figure 17.5, this pane gives you an overview of client activity and health. The collection field on the far right of the pane (not visible in the figure) lets you select a different device collection to view statistics for.

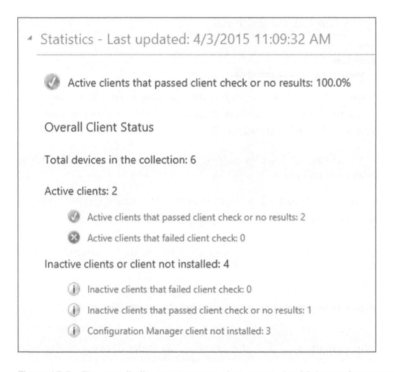

Figure 17.5 The overall client status pane alerts you to health issues in your environment.

Clients are organized into two main categories: active and inactive. The definition of each is as follows:

- *Active*—The ConfigMgr client is installed and is talking to the ConfigMgr hierarchy.
- *Inactive*—The ConfigMgr client has been installed at some point but, for reasons currently unknown, isn't talking to the ConfigMgr hierarchy.

NOTE Only active clients are considered in overall health statistics of your environment. A client can be inactive for legitimate reasons, so it's inaccurate to have them count as unhealthy.

Let's examine each major health category in more depth.

17.2.1 Active clients

Active clients are, in turn, organized into two subcategories:

- Active clients that passed the health check, or no results
- Active clients that failed the health check

The first category represents your healthy clients. An active client that has passed back no health check results may have been only recently installed, or may have been installed in a remote location and is talking to a different management point. In this situation, health check information will eventually pass back into the ConfigMgr database, but for the time being the client can't be considered unhealthy.

The second category is the one that needs your constant attention. Active clients that have failed their health check are considered unhealthy. More than that, being categorized as unhealthy indicates that CcmEval has been unable to remediate the issue(s), and that the client needs direct intervention.

To get more detail about which devices are healthy or unhealthy, click either one of the links. This redirects you to a "sticky node" under Assets and Compliance > Devices, as shown in figure 17.6.

Assets and Compliance		Active clients that passed client check or no results from All Desktop and Server Clients 4 items				
▲ 🖥 Overview		Search				
👥 Users	Icon	Name	Client	Site Code	Client Activity	Client Check Result
▲ 🖥 Devices	🖳	linux01	Yes	PS1	Active	No Results
📖 Active clients that passed client check	🖳	DC01	Yes	PS1	Active	Passed
🖳 User Collections	🖳	CLIENT02	Yes	PS1	Active	No Results
▲ 📦 Device Collections	🖳	CLIENT01	Yes	PS1	Active	Passed

Figure 17.6   These sticky nodes show you which devices are fine and which are having problems.

Another way to view the status of all active clients is to use PowerShell:

Searches the ConfigMgr
database for devices

```
Get-CMDevice |
Where-Object {$_.ClientActiveStatus -eq '1'} |
Select-Object Name,LastActiveTime,ClientCheckPass,LastClientCheckTime |
Sort-Object -Property Name |
Format-Table —AutoSize
```

**Returns only devices
with active clients**

**Formats the output
for readability**

**Returns a limited list
of client properties**

This returns all active clients regardless of their health status, along with information about their last activity and health checks.

17.2.2 *Inactive clients*

Inactive clients are arranged into the same categories as active clients (passed health check/no results or didn't pass health check), plus one more—Configuration Manager client not installed.

A client may be inactive for various reasons, and many of them are perfectly legitimate, with no implications for client health. Some examples are as follows:

- Systems that were provisioned for testing and then decommissioned.
- Servers that reached end-of-life and were decommissioned.
- Notebooks that have been off-site or powered off for a lengthy period of time (for example, the allocated user is on leave or sabbatical).
- The device has been imported via ConfigMgr discovery methods, but won't be managed by ConfigMgr.

Sometimes, however, an inactive client is indicative of a wider problem that needs resolution. For example, if all the systems at a branch office become inactive unexpectedly, then there's definitely an issue somewhere that needs investigation.

As with the active clients, click any of the links in the statistics pane, and this will take you to the relevant sticky node in the Assets and Compliance section of the console. Alternatively, to get a report with PowerShell, use the following code:

**Returns
only known
devices with
inactive
clients**

Searches the ConfigMgr
database for devices

```
Get-CMDevice |
Where-Object {$_.ClientActiveStatus -ne '1' -and $_.Name -notlike "*Unknown*"} |
Select-Object Name,DeviceOS,ClientType,LastActiveTime,LastClientCheckTime |
Sort-Object -Property Name |
Format-Table —AutoSize
```

**Returns a limited list of properties
related to client activity**

**Formats the output
to be easier to read**

This returns all the inactive clients, along with whether they're supposed to have the client installed, as well as some pertinent information to help you identify them, as shown in figure 17.7.

```
PS P01:\> Get-CMDevice | `
Where-Object {$_.ClientActiveStatus -ne '1' -and $_.Name -notlike "*Unknown*"} | `
Select-Object Name,DeviceOS,ClientType,LastActiveTime,LastClientCheckTime | `
Sort-Object -Property Name |
Format-Table -AutoSize

Name        DeviceOS                        ClientType LastActiveTime       LastClientCheckTime
----        --------                        ---------- --------------       -------------------
LAB-CM01    Microsoft Windows NT Server 6.2
lab-ubuntu  Ubuntu 14.04 x64                1          1/21/2015 1:01:34 AM


PS P01:\>
```

Figure 17.7 Use PowerShell to easily query all inactive clients.

Now that you know how to find out the general state of client health across the organization, what can you do to remediate problems when they arise?

17.3 *Using Client Center for Configuration Manager*

Based on the scenarios you've already looked at, you're likely to encounter two main problems with client health:

- The client is installed but is nonfunctional in some way, and the auto-remediation isn't fixing the problem.
- The client is either installed but is completely corrupted, or was installed and now isn't.

You're going to flesh out your lab environment with tools that will help you remediate these problems—either by fixing them, or by making sure that they never happen in the first place.

When a client is in a nonfunctional state, experiencing a problem that can't be fixed with CcmEval, then this is the point at which you, as the administrator, need to get involved. Often this means remoting on to the problem system or troubleshooting it physically.

These approaches are fine, but are generally inefficient. In both cases, you need to start digging into the root cause of the problem, and often this process involves disrupting the system's user. To streamline the process, you'll use the Client Center for Configuration Manager.

Client Center, a tool developed by Swiss MVP Roger Zander, enables you to remotely connect to a ConfigMgr client by using Windows Remote Management (WinRM), get a comprehensively deep view of the ConfigMgr client, and initiate remediation actions if necessary. Best of all, it doesn't interrupt the user, so problems can be tackled with a minimum of fuss.

To install and configure Client Center:

1 On CM01, open Internet Explorer and go to https://sccmclictr.codeplex.com/.

2 Download the latest version (v.1.0.2.3 at the time of writing).

3 Shut down the Configuration Manager console.

4 Launch the Client Center for Configuration Manager 2012_x64_V1.0.2.3.exe installer (the installation is extremely quick).

5 Right-click the newly created application icon on the desktop and select "Run As Administrator."

6 Client Center opens. Select the blue drop-down arrow on the left side of the application and navigate to Console Extensions > Register Console Extension, as shown in figure 17.8.

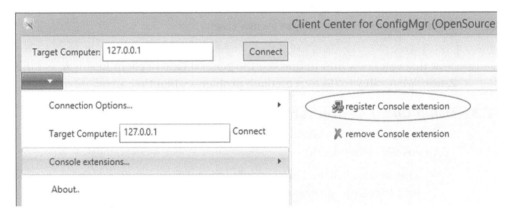

Figure 17.8 Register Client Center with the console for ease of administration.

7 Close Client Center and then log on to CLIENT01.

8 Open an administrative PowerShell window and enter `winrm quickconfig`.

9 Say "Yes" to all the prompts. As shown in figure 17.9, Windows Remote Management will now be configured and running on CLIENT01.

10 On CM01, open the Configuration Manager console and navigate to Assets and Compliance > Devices.

11 Right-click "CLIENT01" and select "Client Center." The application opens and automatically connects to CLIENT01 using WinRM.

As shown in figure 17.10, Client Center is divided into four main sections: Monitoring, Inventory, Software Distribution, and Agent Settings. The application ribbon contains Agent actions such as triggering a software inventory update or an update scan cycle.

Because the tool is absolutely comprehensive, it's worth having a quick tour through the major sections so as not to get lost.

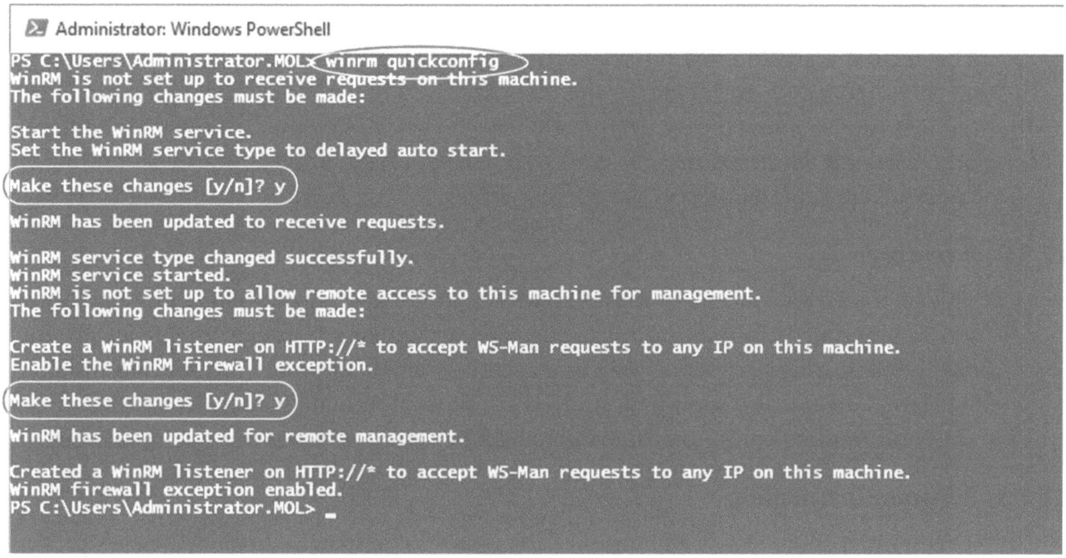

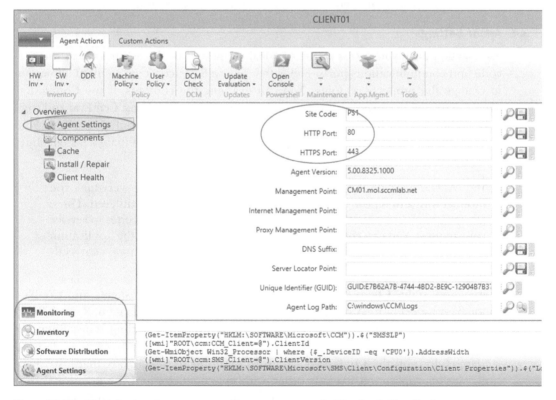

Figure 17.9 Enable and configure WinRM on the remote client for Client Center to function.

Figure 17.10 Client Center gives you access to every component of the ConfigMgr client.

17.3.1 Monitoring

This section is a gold mine for system health and logging. You can view all the services on the remote system (including the ones that are critical for ConfigMgr), and all the services can be stopped or started from here as well. You can see all running Windows processes, kill any active process, and start a new process. You can start event monitoring as well as remotely access the client log files.

17.3.2 Inventory

This section gives you everything to do with software and hardware inventory as well as software update information, including missing updates. You can trigger an installation of all missing updates, as well as a repair or uninstall or any inventoried installed software. You can also see which desired configuration management (DCM) baselines are being applied (more on that later) and what power settings the system is using.

17.3.3 Software Distribution

This section shows you which applications have been installed using ConfigMgr and which advertisements for applications and packages have been made available to the system. You can also see the execution history of application installs, and can modify service windows, including adding new ones or removing existing ones.

17.3.4 Agent Settings

This section gives you access to the physical properties of the agent such as the site code and communications ports. Fields that have a Save icon next to them allow you to change the property remotely. You can examine the contents of the ConfigMgr agent cache and perform maintenance, view the results of the latest CcmEval and trigger another scan, or initiate a repair/uninstall/reinstall of the ConfigMgr client. You can also repair critical Windows components such as WMI, and initiate a system shutdown/reboot.

> **TIP**   As you navigate through Client Center, you'll notice that every time you interact with a function, one or more lines of PowerShell are rendered. These are the commands that Client Center is running behind the scenes to service your request. You can copy these code snippets straight out of the application into your own PowerShell projects; it's a great way to quickly access correctly formatted PowerShell.

Pretty good, right? Client Center gives you robust access to investigate and troubleshoot every aspect of the ConfigMgr client and find out what's going on. Remediation can be as simple as forcibly restarting a service up to and including reinstalling the entire client.

Hopefully, now the ConfigMgr client isn't an obscure magic box that just "does stuff." It's an application like any other, with dependencies and the occasional bad hair day. But now you have enough information and resources to find out exactly what's wrong and why it's happening, and fix it.

Prepare your systems for Client Center

The download page for Client Center lists prerequisites that you need to meet in order for the application to run successfully. The only requirements on the remote system are local administrator access and WinRM.

You don't want to have to connect to every machine in your environment and run `winrm quickconfig` just to use Client Center. Fortunately, there's a straightforward way for you to enable and configure WinRM across your entire environment using Group Policy.

Head over to Group Policy MVP Alan Burchill's blog for all the details: www.grouppolicy.biz/2014/05/enable-winrm-via-group-policy/

This segues nicely into our next chapter. Client health, or "the state of our environment," is one of those things that you, as the ConfigMgr administrator, will often be called on to report on, which brings us into the wonderful world of ConfigMgr reporting.

17.4 Labs

The Configuration Manager console combined with Client Center gives you all the power you need to fix a recalcitrant ConfigMgr client. But if things get to that stage, you're being pulled away from whatever other huge list of tasks you're already working on. What you need is another solution that works in the background on your behalf, mitigating client issues before you need to get involved.

Enter the ConfigMgr client startup script by Enterprise Client Management MVP Jason Sandys. This machine script runs on every domain-joined machine each and every time the system boots. If the client isn't installed or working correctly, the script takes action. The advantage of this approach, in addition to your existing toolset, is that as long as the machine can log on to the domain, the ConfigMgr client is being actively targeted. (If the machine can't log on to the domain, you have more serious issues that have nothing to do with the client.)

For this lab, do the following:

1 Download the client startup script from http://blog.configmgrftw.com/configmgr-client-startup-script/ and configure it appropriately for your lab environment.

2 Create a new Group Policy Object on DC01 that will run the configured script (if you're not sure how to do this, here's the relevant TechNet article: https://technet.microsoft.com/en-au/library/cc770556.aspx).

3 Deploy the GPO to CLIENT01.

4 Uninstall the ConfigMgr client from CLIENT01.

5 Reboot CLIENT01 and make sure that the client startup script runs and reinstalls the ConfigMgr client.

Reporting in ConfigMgr

Everything you do in Configuration Manager generates data. Collections, deployments, inventories, and everything else generates data, which is written into the ConfigMgr database, ready for use.

At some point, you're going to want to query that data for business reasons: How many of the managed systems received the latest updates? Have there been any antimalware outbreaks in the last week? You can use the console to access this data, but what about nontechnical users who need report data, or setting up processes for automatically generating relevant reports on a schedule? This is where Configuration Manager reporting comes into play.

As shown in figure 18.1, this chapter is all about enabling reporting within ConfigMgr, working with reports, scheduling them, and creating custom reports.

By the end of this chapter, you'll have configured your lab environment for reporting and you'll have a solid understanding of how ConfigMgr reporting works and can be customized for your own purposes.

18.1 Enabling Reporting Services

To be able to use reports in your ConfigMgr environment, like the one shown in figure 18.2, you first have to enable the reporting services point.

This is a ConfigMgr server role that uses SQL Server Reporting Services (SSRS), which is already installed on CM01 (this happened during the initial virtual machine build).

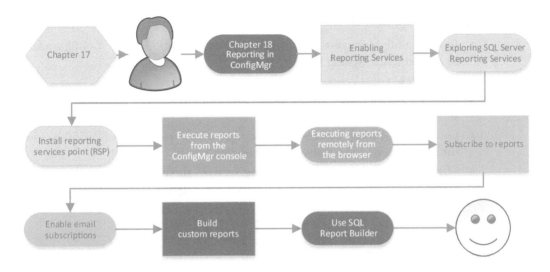

Figure 18.1   Reports, reports, and more reports!

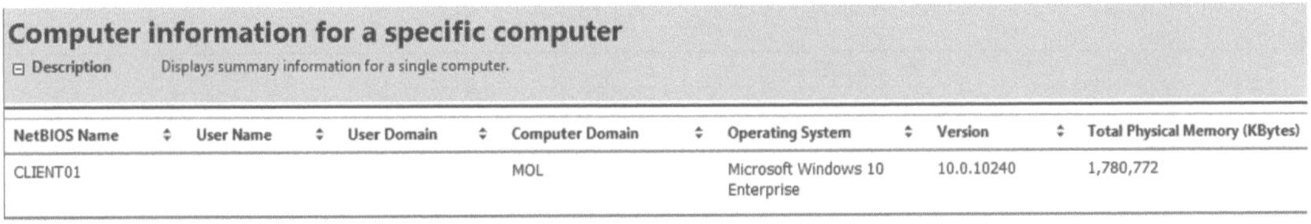

Computer information for a specific computer

⊟ Description   Displays summary information for a single computer.

NetBIOS Name ⇕	User Name ⇕	User Domain ⇕	Computer Domain ⇕	Operating System ⇕	Version ⇕	Total Physical Memory (KBytes)
CLIENT01			MOL	Microsoft Windows 10 Enterprise	10.0.10240	1,780,772

Figure 18.2   Reports give you easy access to ConfigMgr data.

Exploring SSRS

You can use the installation of SQL Server Management Studio on CM01 to have a dig around in SSRS, although at this stage there's not much to see.

On CM01, open SQL Server Management Studio, and when the Connect to Server dialog box opens, change the server type from "Database Engine" to "Reporting Services." Leave all other options the same.

The only node of reporting services on CM01 that has anything in it is Security; notice that the roles are different from those found in a SQL database server.

For more information on SSRS, spend a bit of time browsing through this MSDN article: https://msdn.microsoft.com/en-us/library/ms159106.aspx.

To install the reporting services point(RSP), do the following:

1 In the ConfigMgr console, navigate to Administration > Site Configuration > Servers and Site System Roles.

2 Right-click "CM01" and select "Add Site System Roles."

3 Click through to the "System Role Selection" page, and then tick "Reporting services point."

4 On the "Reporting services point configuration" page, click "Verify" to check the connection to the SSRS instance on CM01.

5 Leave the folder name and reporting services server instance name the same. For the username, select Set > New Account > MOL\CM_SR. The configuration should look like figure 18.3.

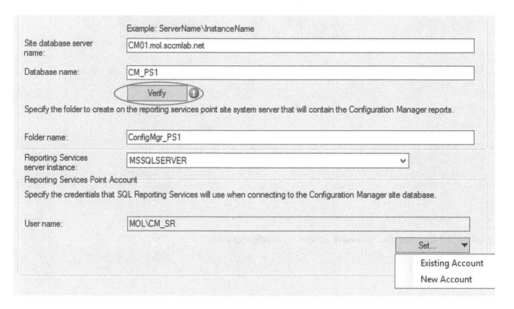

Figure 18.3   The configuration for the reporting services point installation

> **IMPORTANT NOTE**   In a lab environment, you could use an existing account, such as the network access account, as the reporting services account. Best practice is to have a dedicated account for each discrete ConfigMgr role, so that there's no overlap of security boundaries and you minimize the risk of too few accounts having too many privileges.

6 Click through to the end of the wizard, and the RSP installation will commence in the background.

WHICH LOG? The installation of the RSP gets logged to srsrpMSI.log and srsrpsetup.log, respectively. After the RSP is up and running, ConfigMgr populates the SSRS instance with all of the included reports; this activity gets logged to srsrp.log, and the process takes a few minutes to complete.

After the reports have been copied to the reporting point, you can check out the new reports in the console by navigating to Monitoring > Reporting > Reports, as shown in figure 18.4.

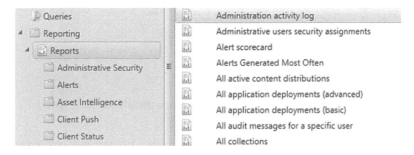

Figure 18.4 You're now ready to run reports.

Expand the Reports node and you'll see a load of new organizational folders. Select the topmost node (Reports) and you'll get a full list of the 468 built-in reports that are now available in the RSP. Now you can start using reports.

18.2 *Executing reports*

Executing a report from the console is a simple process: find the report you're interested in, right-click the report, and select "Run." Easy, right?

Let's take a report that most admins and managers are interested in as an example: software update compliance (indicating the number of clients that have installed the updates deployed to them). To run this report, do the following:

1 Navigate to the report folder Software Updates – A Compliance.
2 Right-click the report "Compliance 1 – Overall compliance" and select "Run."
3 As shown in figure 18.5, the report requires parameters in order to run. Select "MoL - Windows 10 Updates" for the "Update Group," and "PS100014 - All Windows 10 Clients" for the "Collection."
4 Select "View Report" to execute the report with the selected parameters.

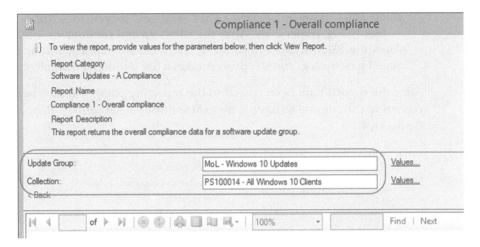

Figure 18.5   Select the input parameters in order to run the compliance report.

5 As shown in figure 18.6, the report renders with a breakdown of the compliant and noncompliant systems in the specified collection. You have only a single system in your lab, and at this stage it doesn't matter whether it's compliant.

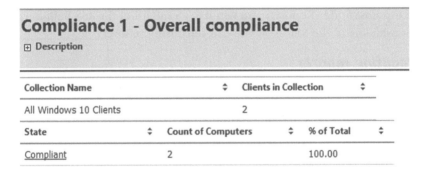

Figure 18.6   A report showing the state of compliance in your lab environment

6 Note that the entries under "State" are underlined. These are hyperlinks, which are links to existing, predefined reports. Click either "Compliant" or "Noncompliant" (depending on your report).

7 This causes a new report to be rendered: Compliance 7 – Computers in a specific compliance state for an update group. The report has been automatically populated with the parameters you selected for the first report, with the addition of the compliance state as an input.

8 The device name (CLIENT01) is also a hyperlink to another report. Click the name, and a new report is rendered: Compliance 5 – Specific computer. This report gives a full rundown of every update that has been deployed against the system and the corresponding compliance state. Note that you can narrow the results further by specifying the Vendor and/or Classification.

This shows the power of ConfigMgr's reporting model. The built-in reports are linked in such a way that you can start your report at a high level and then drill down as necessary. You could have run either of the linked compliance reports directly if you knew exactly what information you were after. This is handy for users who need to view ConfigMgr data but who don't have in-depth knowledge of the state of the current environment.

On that note, how would nonadministrative users access ConfigMgr reports? You don't want to have to hand out remote logon access to the server, or deploy the console to every person who might want to run a report.

The good news is that you don't have to. Because ConfigMgr reporting is built on top of SSRS, all of the reports are automatically available via a browser. To see this in action, do the following:

1 Log on to CLIENT01 as MOL\Administrator and open Internet Explorer.

2 Navigate to http://cm01/Reports, and when the SQL Server Reporting Services page loads, select the ConfigMgr_PS1 folder.

3 Select "Details View" (top-right corner) to change the view away from the tiled layout (easier to read).

4 In the "Search" field, enter Compliance 1. There will be two results: the report you want, and Compliance 7 (which refers to Compliance 1 in its description). Click "Compliance 1 – Overall compliance" to run the report.

5 Drill down through the reports as you did in the console.

TIP When running web reports, it's unclear where to change the parameter values. At the top of the report, directly underneath the report path is an arrow that triggers Show/Hide Parameters, as shown in figure 18.7. Select that and you'll see the report's parameter fields.

Figure 18.7 Use this drop-down to show or hide report parameters.

So now that you have your reports and know how to access them, what do you do with them?

18.3 *Subscribing to reports*

Reports give you the ability to quickly access comprehensive data about your Config-Mgr environment. You won't need to frequently access some of these reports, whereas you should run others regularly so that you have a constant view of what's happening day to day. This is where subscriptions are incredibly valuable.

Subscriptions allow you to automatically run a report on a schedule, and deliver it via various mechanisms so that you always have access to the latest report data without having to run each report manually. A good example of this is anti-malware definitions—a report that runs daily. Viewing the compliance state of your anti-malware agents will alert you to any issues before they become real problems.

To create a new report subscription, do the following:

1 In the console, navigate to Monitoring > Reporting > Reports > Software Updates – A Compliance.
2 Right-click the report "Compliance 1 – Overall compliance" and select "Create Subscription."
3 For the Subscription Delivery options, use the information in table 18.1 to populate the subscription parameters.

NOTE   Creating a new report subscription requires you to create a new folder on CM01 called E:\Reports. Share the folder as reports so that the UNC path \\CM01\Reports is valid.

Table 18.1 Subscription delivery options

Delivery method option	Option value
Report delivered by	Windows File Share
File name	Windows10UpdateCompliance
Add file extension when created	Ticked
Path	\\CM01\Reports
Render format	Xml file with report data
User Name	MOL\Administrator
Password	
Overwrite option	Increment file names as newer files are added

4 Click "Next" and create a Subscription schedule with the following parameters:
   a Weekly
   b Repeat after 1 week
   c On day: Monday
   d Start time: 8:30 a.m.

5 Click "Next" and specify the following report parameters:
  a Update Group: MoL - Windows 10 Updates
  b Collection: PS100014 - All Windows 10 Clients
6 Click through to the end, and you've created a new subscription.
7 Navigate to Reports > Subscriptions, and you'll see the newly created subscription.

Based on the schedule you created, an XML file is created in \\CM01\Reports each week—which is great, but what if you wanted something a little more convenient?

Subscriptions can be delivered to your mail inbox, but before this is available as a delivery option, you have to give ConfigMgr the ability to talk to a mail server. To enable this functionality, do the following:

1 On CM01, go to Start > Reporting Services Configuration Manager.
2 Connect to CM01\MSSQLSERVER and navigate to Email Settings.
3 Enter a sender address and the name of a valid Simple Mail Transfer Protocol (SMTP) server. Select "Apply" and close the RS Configuration Manager.
4 Back in the ConfigMgr console, go to Monitoring > Reporting > Subscriptions.
5 Right-click the subscription and select "Properties." Change the "Report delivered by" option from "Windows File Share" to "Email."

You can now send out regular reports by email, to yourself or to whoever else in the organization needs a regular update on what's happening in ConfigMgr.

Working with SMTP

The email settings options in SSRS don't give you many options to work with. It assumes that the SMTP server is an on-premises mail server that you can configure to allow mail relay from the SSRS server. In many organizations, this may indeed be the case, but not always and almost certainly not in a lab environment.

You can configure Internet Information Services (IIS) on Windows Server to act as a simple mail relay for SMTP. You can configure your application to talk directly to the local SMTP service, and then the service handles the communication with the SMTP server that you want to use.

For example, Office 365 and Google Mail both provide SMTP services, but you would need to configure your own mail relay locally in order to use them with SSRS. Read this TechNet article for a more detailed walk-through: https://technet.microsoft.com/en-us/library/dn592151(v=exchg.150).aspx

---

You've seen how to work with the built-in ConfigMgr reports, but what if you need something a bit more customized?

18.4 *Building custom reports*

The built-in reports in ConfigMgr are designed to cover a wide range of reporting scenarios, but there will always be a requirement for custom reporting. Different users within different companies are interested in lots of different types of data, presented in a variety of ways, and the built-in reports can't possibly cater to every scenario.

Because ConfigMgr reporting is built upon SSRS, with a bit of knowledge you can easily create your own custom reports to meet any internal business need.

For example, let's look at the endpoint report "Antimalware overall status and history." This gives you the state of your SCEP clients over a given period of time, usually one week. This is a useful report to schedule because it can provide a running commentary on the health of your anti-malware deployment, making you quickly aware of potential problems. The issue with this report is that if you go to schedule it, you'll find that the input parameters for the report include the start and end dates. This is fine for a one-off report, but if you schedule the report, you would want to specify a dynamic time frame (for example, "Last 7 days"). Unfortunately, the built-in report doesn't give you that option. This is where creating a custom report will deliver the result you need.

To write a custom report, do the following:

1 Choose Monitoring > Reporting > Reports > Endpoint Protection.
2 Right-click "Antimalware overall status and history" and select "Edit."
3 This causes SQL Server Report Builder to download (from SSRS) and run, as shown in figure 18.8.

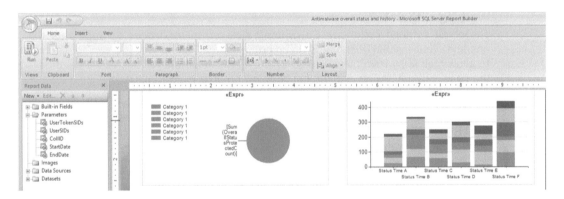

Figure 18.8   Using SQL Server Report Builder to create a custom ConfigMgr report

4 On the left side under "Report Data," expand "Parameters" and select "Start-Date."
5 Right-click "StartDate" and select "Parameter Properties."
6 On the General tab, change the "Select parameter visibility" option from "Visible" to "Hidden."

7 On the Available Values tab, select "Get values from a query":

   a Dataset: DateRange

   b Value field: StartDate

   c Label field: StartDate

8 Click "OK" to save the changes, and then repeat the process with the EndDate parameter:

   a Dataset: DateRange

   b Value field: EndDate

   c Label field: EndDate

9 Select the SQL Server image in the top-left corner and choose "Save As."

10 Save the report in the original folder as `Antimalware overall status and history - Last 7 days` and close Report Builder.

11 Go back into the console and refresh the reports in the Endpoint Protection folder; you'll see the newly created report.

12 Run the report. The only parameter you need to input is the Collection. The start and end date fields are hidden and automatically populated from the DateRange dataset. You can create a subscription to this report, and the start and end dates will be calculated based on the day on which the report runs.

TIP Whenever you're working with a built-in resource such as a report (or any resource in any application), it's best practice to make a copy and save all your changes to the copy. That way, you'll always have an untouched original, in case you ever need to roll back custom changes.

Congratulations! You've successfully created a custom SQL report, and you're finished with reporting.

18.5 Labs

As you saw earlier, SSRS doesn't have a complex system for sending email. For this lab, try configuring the installation of IIS on CM01 to support SMTP relay. Then configure that SMTP instance to talk to an external SMTP service, such as Office 365, Google Mail, or your own ISP. Finally, configure both SSRS and Configuration Manager (Administration > Site Configuration > Sites > PS1 > Configure Site Components > Email Notification) to send email via the SMTP service on CM01.

19

Keeping an eye
on your clients

You're successfully deploying applications and packages, but do you know whether your users are using them? Or, you've deployed an application successfully, but the help desk keeps getting calls from users whose settings have mysteriously changed ("I didn't change anything, honest"), and the application no longer works. What's happening?

As shown in figure 19.1, in this chapter you'll drill down deeper into what's happening on the client with both software metering and compliance.

These aspects of ConfigMgr have little to do with the end-user experience and lots to do with you being the best ConfigMgr admin you can be. At the end of this chapter, nothing will be hidden from your laser gaze!

19.1 *Enabling software metering*

Let's imagine that Paint.NET is an expensive application (it's free, but let's pretend that it isn't), and your company is spending loads of money each year on licensing. Management wants you to find out who's using the product, to see whether a case can be made for reducing the license count (and thus cost) while still ensuring that users who are using it can continue to do so.

The software metering agent is a discrete component of the ConfigMgr agent that can monitor which applications are being used. On CLIENT01, launch the ConfigMgr client properties from the control panel, and you'll see Software Metering listed under Components. Software metering is handled at the client level, with

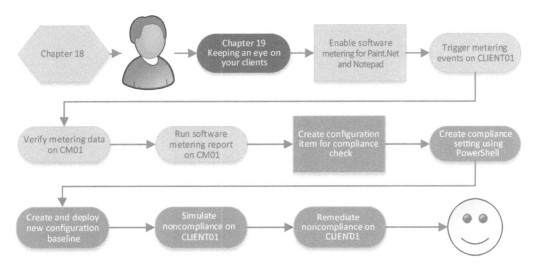

Figure 19.1 Be Big Brother with metering and compliance.

the server dictating which information needs to be collected and how often it should be sent back to the central database.

Software metering is dependent on software inventory, so you do have to enable software inventory on your clients in order to use metering. To see how they interact, on CM01 open the console and navigate to Assets and Compliance > Software Metering. As shown in figure 19.2, the console has already been populated with information about inventoried applications, such as filenames and version details.

Icon	Name	Original File Name	File Name	File Version
	Microsoft OneDrive - OneDrive.exe - 17.3. (1033)	OneDrive.exe	OneDrive.exe	17.3.*
	Microsoft® Windows® Operating System - ApplicationFrameHost.exe - 10.0....	ApplicationFrameHost.exe	ApplicationFrame...	10.0.*
	Microsoft® Windows® Operating System - cmd.exe - 10.0. (1033)	Cmd.Exe.MUI	cmd.exe	10.0.*
	Microsoft® Windows® Operating System - conhost.exe - 10.0. (1033)	CONHOST.EXE	conhost.exe	10.0.*
	Microsoft® Windows® Operating System - control.exe - 10.0. (1033)	CONTROL.EXE	control.exe	10.0.*
	Microsoft® Windows® Operating System - DllHost.exe - 10.0. (1033)	dllhost.exe	DllHost.exe	10.0.*
	Microsoft® Windows® Operating System - DllHost.exe - 6.3. (1033)	dllhost.exe	DllHost.exe	6.3.*
	Microsoft® Windows® Operating System - dwm.exe - 10.0. (1033)	dwm.exe.mui	dwm.exe	10.0.*

Figure 19.2 Software metering rules are automatically generated via software inventory.

For each inventoried application, a metering rule has been automatically created, but each rule is disabled. To take a closer look at a metering rule, find the rule created for Paint.NET, right-click the rule, and select "Properties." As you can see in figure 19.3, the main components of the rule are the name of the executable and the file version. Note also that wildcards can be used instead of absolute values—so, for example, if you wanted to monitor any version of Paint.NET 4, you could change the version string to `4.*`.

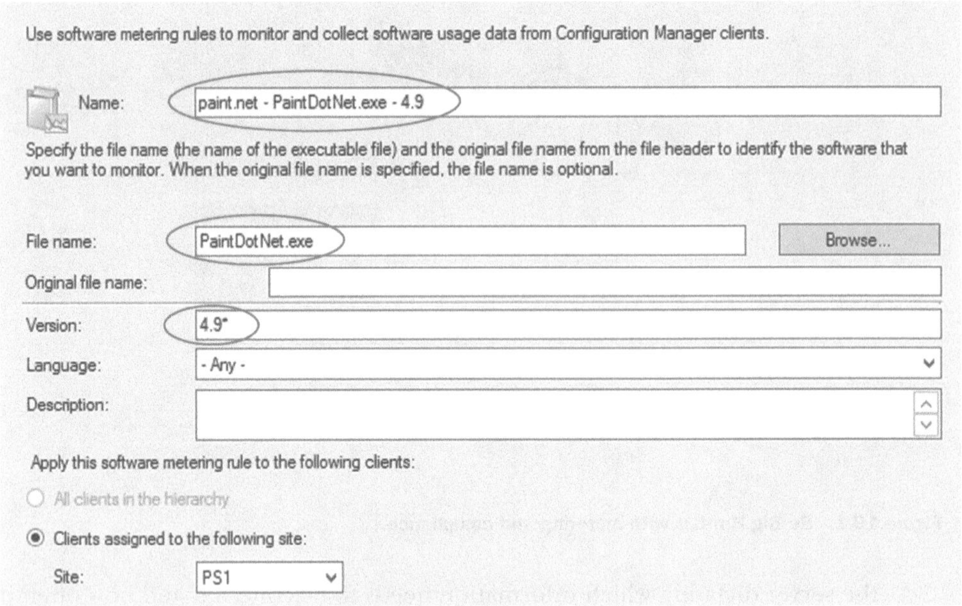

Use software metering rules to monitor and collect software usage data from Configuration Manager clients.

Name: paint.net - PaintDotNet.exe - 4.9

Specify the file name (the name of the executable file) and the original file name from the file header to identify the software that you want to monitor. When the original file name is specified, the file name is optional.

File name: PaintDotNet.exe   Browse...

Original file name:

Version: 4.9*

Language: - Any -

Description:

Apply this software metering rule to the following clients:

○ All clients in the hierarchy

● Clients assigned to the following site:

Site: PS1

Figure 19.3   Metering rules are automatically populated from inventory data.

To enable this metering rule, right-click the rule and select "Enable." Do the same for the rule for Notepad.exe (you now have two rules enabled). To see the rules in action, do the following:

1 Log on to CLIENT01 and trigger a Machine Policy Retrieval & Evaluation Cycle from the ConfigMgr agent properties (the new metering rule represents a change in machine policy).
2 Make sure that Paint.NET is installed but not launched.
3 Launch both Paint.NET and Notepad. You won't see anything obvious, but as with everything in ConfigMgr, the logs are busy behind the scenes.

   WHICH LOG? Software metering events on the client are logged in mtrmgr.log. This log shows that every active process is assessed to see whether there's an active metering rule that matches the process name and version. If there is, the log will show "Found match against RuleID <number>," where the <number> is the assigned ID to the metering rule. If not, the log shows "No matching rule found for process <number>," where <number> is the Windows process ID.

4 Looking in mtrmgr.log, you should see entries for PaintDotNet.exe and Notepad.exe with matching metering RuleIDs, as shown in figure 19.4. Close the applications and note that process termination is also logged.

   By default, the ConfigMgr client collects this metering information and sends it back to the central server (via the associated management point) every

New rule PS100026 received successfully	mtrmgr
New rule PS100027 received successfully	mtrmgr
Creation event received for process 2944	mtrmgr
Process ID 2944 is for process C:\Program Files\paint.net\PaintDotNet.exe	mtrmgr
Found match against RuleID PS100026	mtrmgr
Tracked usage for process 2944	mtrmgr
Creation event received for process 4504	mtrmgr
Process ID 4504 is for process C:\windows\system32\notepad.exe	mtrmgr
Found match against RuleID PS100027	mtrmgr
Tracked usage for process 4504	mtrmgr

Figure 19.4   Launching a metered application triggers an event in the metering logs.

seven days. You can change this in Client Settings, or you can force the issue to watch the process in action.

5   On CLIENT01, launch the Configuration Manager agent and go to "Actions." Run the "Software Metering Usage Report Cycle" action.

WHICH LOG?   When clients send software metering reports back to the ConfigMgr hierarchy, the events are logged in swmproc.log.

6   On CM01, launch swmproc.log to see the software metering events logged on CLIENT01 get uploaded to the server, as shown in figure 19.5.

Log Text	Component
Inbox notification tiggered, pause for 10 seconds....	SMS_SOFTWARE_METERING_PROCESSOR
Moving up to 2048 usage data files to the processing queue.	SMS_SOFTWARE_METERING_PROCESSOR
Moved 1 .MUX files from the inbox to the processing queue.	SMS_SOFTWARE_METERING_PROCESSOR
Moved 0 .MUV files from the inbox to the processing queue.	SMS_SOFTWARE_METERING_PROCESSOR
Started the No. 1 usage processing thread, thread ID = 790	SMS_SOFTWARE_METERING_PROCESSOR
Main thread waiting for file change notification or timeout after 60 minutes.	SMS_SOFTWARE_METERING_PROCESSOR
New usage processing thread started, current usage processing thread count: 1	SMS_SOFTWARE_METERING_PROCESSOR
Processed 1 XML files and 0 VAR files.	SMS_SOFTWARE_METERING_PROCESSOR
Disposition: 1 ok, 0 retry, 0 corrupt.	SMS_SOFTWARE_METERING_PROCESSOR
4 records added to database.	SMS_SOFTWARE_METERING_PROCESSOR
Usage processing thread terminating, current usage processing count: 0	SMS_SOFTWARE_METERING_PROCESSOR

Figure 19.5   Software metering data is uploaded to the ConfigMgr server for central processing.

Now that your clients are uploading metering data into the ConfigMgr database, you want to be able to get a visual overview of what's happening, and this is where reporting comes in. Navigate to Monitoring > Reporting and expand the Reports node. You'll see a dedicated Software Metering category. To run a report on the active metering rule, run the "Report Computers that have run a specific metered software program" using the following values:

- Rule name: Microsoft Windows Operating System - NOTEPAD.EXE - 10. (1033)

- Month: latest value (for example, 5)
- Year: latest value (for example, 2015)

You'll see that the report gives a rundown on the number of metered events, and average metrics such as the amount of time the application has been used and the average duration of each use. It's worth spending some time going through the software metering reports to see the various options for extracting metering data. In your lab environment, the reports will be pretty barren as there's little data, but in a production environment, the metering reports will quickly start showing rich historical data.

19.2 *Configuring compliance*

Compliance is something of a dark art, and not many organizations understand it fully or implement it effectively. The idea behind compliance is to generate a working set of rules that define how managed systems in your environment are supposed to look or function, and then have a compliance platform (ConfigMgr, in this case) regularly test these rules and remediate noncompliance.

To show how compliance works, let's create a fictional scenario. Your users regularly complain to the help desk that they can't print. On investigation, the help desk discovers that the Windows Print Spooler service has been stopped. Starting the service resolves the problem. Something is obviously causing this to happen, and that needs investigation, but by using compliance, you can both get a sense of the scale of the problem and minimize user impact and help-desk calls. To do this, you'll follow these steps:

1 Create a configuration item (CI).
2 Add the CI to a configuration.
3 Deploy the baseline.

19.2.1 *Configuration Items*

Let's start with a configuration item. This setting defines the rule or rules that you want to test for, and how to remediate noncompliance (if appropriate). One or more items are then combined into a baseline for deployment (more on that later).

To create a rule for your users' printing problem, do the following:

1 Navigate to Assets and Compliance > Compliance Settings > Configuration Items.
2 Right-click and select "Create Configuration Item."
3 Name the item `Windows Print Spooler Service` and click "Next."
4 For the Windows version, unselect all versions except "All Windows 10 and higher." Click "Summary" and then "Next to finish."

   Now you have a newly created CI, but without any settings or rules, it won't do much. Let's make it more functional.

5 Right-click the CI and select "Properties."

6 Go to the Settings tab and select "New."

7 Configure the new Setting's General tab with the following values:

   a Name: Print Spooler Running State

   b Setting Type: Script

   c Data Type: String

   d Add Script, Discovery Script, Script Language: Windows PowerShell

   e Discovery Script, Code: `(Get-Service -Name Spooler).Status`

8 Navigate to the Compliance Rules tab and create a new rule, configured as follows:

   a Name: Print Spooler Service Running

   b Rule Type: Value

   c Value returned by the specified script: Running

   d Report noncompliance: Checked

   e Noncompliance severity: Warning

9 Click "OK" to everything and close the CI.

Confused? Don't be. You've created a new setting that's defined using a simple PowerShell script. To see what the script will do, log on to CLIENT01 and run `(Get-Service -Name Spooler).Status` in an elevated PowerShell window. The script queries the status of the print spooler service, which should return a value of "Running." This is the value you provided to indicate compliance.

19.2.2 *Configuration baselines*

Now that you have a CI, you want to apply it to a configuration baseline (CB) and deploy it in your lab environment. A *configuration* is a collection of one or more CIs that define a particular set of compliance rules and remediation steps. The CB is the bit that you deploy; you can't deploy CIs directly to clients. You can have multiple baselines deployed to clients—for example, you might have a baseline for desktop systems and another one for servers, or another one for a particular set of file and registry settings that affect one business-critical application.

Before you can apply a CB to an existing CI, you have to create a new CB:

1 Navigate to Configuration Baselines, right-click, and select "Create Configuration Baseline."

2 Configure the new baseline with the following properties:

   a Name: All Lab Clients

   b Configuration Data, Add: Configuration Item

   c Configuration Data, Name: Windows Print Spooler Service

3 Click "OK," and the new CB should look like figure 19.6.

4 Navigate to Administration > Client Settings.

5 Right-click "Default Client Settings" and select "Properties."

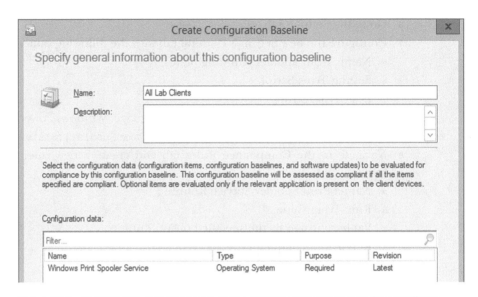

Figure 19.6   Configuration baselines contain the settings you want to test for compliance.

6   Navigate to the "Computer Agent" section and change "PowerShell execution policy" to "Bypass" (which is nasty, of course—in production you should sign your scripts!).

7   Navigate back to "Compliance Baselines," right-click the "All Lab Clients" CB, and select "Deploy."

8   Deploy the baseline using the following properties:

   a   Collection: All Windows 10 Clients

   b   Simple schedule: Every 1 day

9   Run a machine policy retrieval on CLIENT01 to allow the system to pick up the changes.

19.3   Seeing compliance in action

Now that you've defined and deployed your baseline, you'll replicate the printing problem described earlier and see how ConfigMgr will handle it and remediate it.

Log on to CLIENT01 and launch the Configuration Manager client. Then navigate to the Configurations tab. As shown in figure 19.7, you should see the CB that you assigned to the device collection.

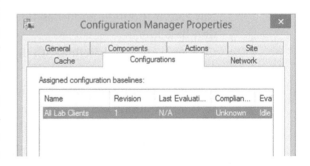

Figure 19.7   The ConfigMgr client is aware of which configurations have been deployed.

The baseline will be evaluated based on the schedule you specified during the deployment (once per day), but you can force an evaluation. Highlight the baseline and select "Evaluate." The baseline properties will change, and the baseline should be returned as "Compliant."

WHICH LOG? You can monitor the compliance activities of the agent in the DCMAgent.log and DCMReporting.log files.

Navigate back to CM01 and go to Configuration Baselines. The deployed baseline should show a Compliance Count of 1, indicating that compliance has been checked on at least one client and that the client was indeed compliant. If you don't see that, select "Run Summarization" from the toolbar and refresh the console. Now that you know your scripts and baselines are working, let's break something:

1. On CLIENT01, open an elevated PowerShell window and type in `Stop-Service –Name Spooler`. This stops the print spooler service.

2. Verify the service status by entering `Get-Service –Name Spooler`. The "Status" should be "Stopped."

3. Evaluate the baseline again; the result reads "Non-Compliant."

4. Back on CM01, refresh the baseline. The compliance count changes to 0, and the noncompliance count changes to 1.

    OK, so you can use this compliance rule to get a picture of the number of systems that have this problem. You can use this data to work out how widespread the problem is and take appropriate action. But let's assume that what you want is to not worry about the state of the print spooler service at all, and that ConfigMgr should automatically remediate noncompliance. You have the option to tell your Configuration items to remediate noncompliance, but you have to tell ConfigMgr exactly how to do this. So let's give ConfigMgr some more information.

5. On CM01, navigate back to "Configuration Items," right-click the Windows Print Spooler Service CI, and select "Properties."

6. Go to the Compliance Rules tab, select the single rule, and delete it.

7. Go to the Settings tab and edit the Print Spooler Running State setting.

8. Add a remediation script using the following values:

    a. Script language: Windows PowerShell

    b. Code: `Start-Service –Name Spooler`

9. Click "OK." Go back to the Compliance Rules tab and create a new rule with the following properties:

    a. Name: Print Spooler Service Running

    b. Value returned by script > Equals > Running

    c. Run the remediation script: Checked

10. Click "OK" and shut down the CI.

11. Trigger another machine policy update on CLIENT01.

12. Evaluate the baseline; the compliance changes to Compliant.

13   Select "View Report" and scroll to the end of the report. As shown in figure 19.8, you'll see that the compliance script returns a value of "Stopped," which causes the remediation script to run. The compliance script then returns a value of "Running," which means that the baseline is now compliant again.

Remediated Rule:

Rule Name	Rule Description	Setting Name	Setting Type	Setting Description	Instance Data			
					Expression	Instance Source	Previous Value	Remediated Value
Print Spooler Service Running		Print Spooler Running State	Script		Equals Running	Property = Line[0]	Stopped	Running

Figure 19.8   Automatic remediation of noncompliance is successful.

14   In PowerShell, use `Get-Service –Name Spooler` to verify that the service is running again.

15   Check on CM01 that the compliance count has changed back.

Congratulations; you've navigated your way through compliance! When creating CIs, you'll notice that a wealth of options are available for you to build items—files and file properties, registry values, and SQL queries—plenty to let you troubleshoot what's relevant in your environment.

And talking of troubleshooting, let's move on and take a look at how to figure out when things are going badly.

19.4   Labs

How secure is your production environment? How does the configuration of your enterprise operating system compare to Microsoft's recommended best practices? Don't know? ConfigMgr can help you work it out.

You may have noticed that the ConfigMgr console has an option to import configuration data, rather than just creating a new configuration item or baseline. Where can you import configuration data from? Well, another ConfigMgr environment, certainly, but you can also import compliance baselines from Microsoft Security Compliance Manager (SCM).

SCM is a solution accelerator that lets you access Microsoft's recommended configuration settings for a variety of operating systems and applications. You can use these default baselines to create your own custom baselines, and you can import them into ConfigMgr to evaluate your managed environment.

For this lab, perform the following tasks:

1   Download Microsoft Security Compliance Manager, and install it on CM01 (you can use the existing SQL Server instance).

2   Launch SCM and download the latest baselines from Microsoft.

3   Export the Win8.1 Computer Security compliance baseline as an SCCM 2007 DCM CAB file (at the time of writing, there are no compliance baselines for Windows 10, but the ones for Windows 8.1 will work).

4 Import the CAB file into ConfigMgr as compliance data.

5 Verify that the compliance items and compliance baseline have been created successfully.

6 Deploy the Win8.1 Computer Security compliance baseline to the All Windows 10 Clients Collection (don't enable remediation).

7 Evaluate and report on the deployed baseline.

What to do when *things go wrong*

The full title of this chapter should be, "What to do when things go wrong and it's not ConfigMgr's fault, regardless of what anyone else says." As you've seen over the course of this book, ConfigMgr depends on the wider technical environment for much of its own functionality, and sometimes things don't work the way they're supposed to.

ConfigMgr does a decent job of informing you when things aren't going as well as they should be, so as you can see in figure 20.1, this chapter is all about listening carefully to what your environment is telling you.

We'll also cover scenarios in which problems elsewhere in the environment could be causing problems for ConfigMgr. It's by no means an exhaustive list, but it'll give you a solid basis for more-advanced troubleshooting.

20.1 Assessing site health

ConfigMgr constantly monitors and assesses all roles and components within the hierarchy, and if you want to get a quick overview of the health of your environment, this is the place to start.

In the ConfigMgr console, navigate to Monitoring > System Status > Site Status. As shown in figure 20.2, this pane shows the health of all of the site system roles currently installed in the hierarchy.

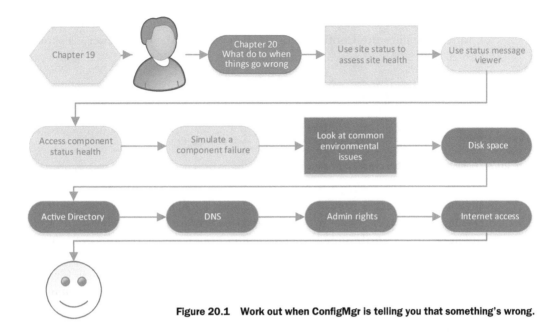

Figure 20.1 Work out when ConfigMgr is telling you that something's wrong.

TIP If your lab environment had secondary site servers connected to the primary, the roles installed on those servers would show up in this console pane on the primary as well. Information about secondary site servers is passed up to the primary site database for storage and assessment.

	Icon	Status	Site System	Site System Role
▶ ⬜ Alerts				
🔍 Queries	✓	OK	\\CM01.mol.sccmla...	Software update point
▶ ⬜ Reporting	✓	OK	\\CM01.mol.sccmla...	Site server
⬜ Site Hierarchy	✓	OK	\\CM01.mol.sccmla...	Application Catalog we...
	✓	OK	\\CM01.mol.sccmla...	Reporting services point
◢ ⬜ System Status	✓	OK	\\CM01.mol.sccmla...	Site database server
⬜ Site Status	✓	OK	\\CM01.mol.sccmla...	Site database server
⬜ Component Status	✓	OK	\\CM01.mol.sccmla...	Management point
⬜ Conflicting Records	✓	OK	\\CM01.mol.sccmla...	Distribution point
⬜ Status Message Queries	✓	OK	\\CM01.MOL.SCCM...	Component server
⬜ Deployments	✓	OK	\\CM01.mol.sccmla...	Application Catalog we...
⬜ Client Operations	✓	OK	\\CM01.mol.sccmla...	Endpoint Protection point
▶ ⬜ Client Status	✓	OK	\\CM01.mol.sccmla...	Service connection point
⬜ Database Replication	✓	OK	\\CM01.mol.sccmla...	Distribution point

Figure 20.2 ConfigMgr constantly monitors site role health.

To see the underlying status of each role, right-click a role and select Show Messages > All, which launches the Configuration Manager Status Message Viewer, as shown in figure 20.3.

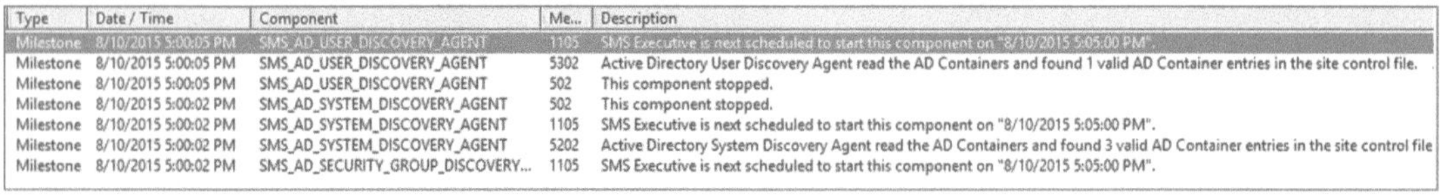

Type	Date / Time	Component	Me...	Description
Milestone	8/10/2015 5:00:05 PM	SMS_AD_USER_DISCOVERY_AGENT	1105	SMS Executive is next scheduled to start this component on "8/10/2015 5:05:00 PM".
Milestone	8/10/2015 5:00:05 PM	SMS_AD_USER_DISCOVERY_AGENT	5302	Active Directory User Discovery Agent read the AD Containers and found 1 valid AD Container entries in the site control file.
Milestone	8/10/2015 5:00:05 PM	SMS_AD_USER_DISCOVERY_AGENT	502	This component stopped.
Milestone	8/10/2015 5:00:02 PM	SMS_AD_SYSTEM_DISCOVERY_AGENT	502	This component stopped.
Milestone	8/10/2015 5:00:02 PM	SMS_AD_SYSTEM_DISCOVERY_AGENT	1105	SMS Executive is next scheduled to start this component on "8/10/2015 5:05:00 PM".
Milestone	8/10/2015 5:00:02 PM	SMS_AD_SYSTEM_DISCOVERY_AGENT	5202	Active Directory System Discovery Agent read the AD Containers and found 3 valid AD Container entries in the site control file.
Milestone	8/10/2015 5:00:02 PM	SMS_AD_SECURITY_GROUP_DISCOVERY...	1105	SMS Executive is next scheduled to start this component on "8/10/2015 5:05:00 PM".

Figure 20.3   Behind every status are a *lot* of status messages.

You can show messages from a given time range or click "Skip" to show everything. Showing all messages results in a lot of data returned, and probably quite a bit of white noise, so it's worth using the View > Filter option to narrow the results in terms of message severity, ConfigMgr component, and so on.

It's important to note that the Status Message Viewer shows all messages for a given site, rather than for a particular site role, so if you're attempting to troubleshoot a particular role (for example, the Application Catalog isn't loading properly), you'll need to filter the results accordingly; or instead of Site Status, navigate to Monitoring > System Status > Component Status.

The Component Status pane gives you a breakdown of all the various ConfigMgr components across the entire hierarchy, both monitored and unmonitored, as shown in figure 20.4.

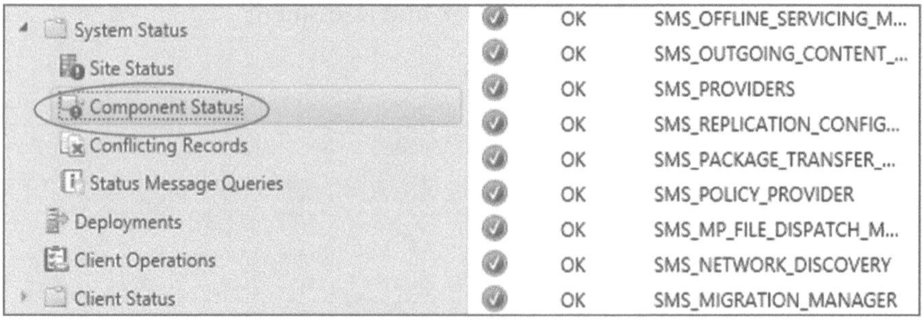

Figure 20.4   Get a quick traffic-light health view of your hierarchy.

Components are unmonitored when they're not installed or not in use. For example, the SMS_NETWORK_DISCOVERY component is unmonitored because you didn't enable Network Discovery in your lab environment. To see how status monitoring works, let's break something and watch what happens:

1 On CM01, go to Start and launch SQL Server Reporting Services Configuration Manager.

2 Connect to the ReportServer instance on CM01, and then on the main page, select "Stop." This stops the SQL Reporting server, while leaving the main SQL database service running.

3 Go back to the ConfigMgr console and navigate to Monitoring > System Status > Component Status.

4 Right-click "SMS_SRS_REPORTING_POINT" and select Show Messages > All. As shown in figure 20.5, you'll see a warning status along with a couple of informational messages about the problem, suggesting resolution steps.

	Milestone	SMS_SRS_REPORTING_POINT	4610	Component Status Summarizer set the status of component "SMS_SRS_REPORTING_POINT" running on computer "CM01.MOL.SCCMLAB.NET" to Warning.
	Milestone	SMS_SRS_REPORTING_POINT	4608	Component Status Summarizer detected that component "SMS_SRS_REPORTING_POINT", running on computer "CM01.MOL.SCCMLAB.NET", has reported 1
	Milestone	SMS_SRS_REPORTING_POINT	7403	The report server service is not running on Reporting Service Point server "CM01.MOL.SCCMLAB.NET"; start the service to enable reporting.

Figure 20.5 Status messages are logged when a problem is detected.

5 Open the srsrp.log file, and you'll see regular errors logged as the health of the Reporting Services point (which relies on SQL Reporting Services) is checked every minute. Scroll up to the first instance of the error, and you'll see a log entry that begins "STATMSG: ID=7403." This is the event that created the status message you read in step 4.

6 Back in the console, refresh the Component Status page. You'll see that the SMS_SRS_REPORTING_POINT component is in a Warning state. If the service stays offline and enough error status messages are logged, this will change to "Error state" and the Reporting Services point role will also be flagged as unhealthy.

7 To fix the issue, turn the ReportServer service back on, and check the srsrp.log to make sure that the change has been picked up.

8 Back in Component Status, right-click "SMS_SRS_REPORTING_POINT" and select Reset Counts > Error. This changes the number of logged errors against this component back to zero. In a couple of minutes, the component status reverts to "OK."

TIP The component status would have reset on its own within 24 hours. Manually resetting the error counts gets you back to square one faster, and is also useful for troubleshooting if you're seeing a lot of errors over a short period of time.

In the real world, this scenario is feasible. SQL Server Reporting Services is a dependency of ConfigMgr, and it's possible for this service to be in an error state or otherwise unavailable, thus impacting ConfigMgr. In a larger environment, it's not uncommon for the SQL infrastructure to be controlled by a dedicated department, or for SQL roles such as reporting and analytics to be hosted on dedicated servers or server clusters. In these more complex environments, you, as the ConfigMgr admin, might not be responsible for these systems, but it's in your best interest to have as much trouble-shooting information in hand as possible to assist with a speedy resolution.

On that note, let's take a look at some common issues that you'll have to be aware of, regardless of whether you have to fix them!

20.2 *Understanding common environmental issues*

Stuff goes wrong in any environment, and even if it's not your fault (unless, of course, it is), it can still be up to you to work out what's going on. Especially if it impacts ConfigMgr.

This section goes through some common scenarios that can impact ConfigMgr functionality, how you can work out what's going on, and what you can do to fix it. It's certainly not a comprehensive list, but it'll give you some good ideas for any scenario you encounter.

20.2.1 *Disk space*

Low disk space on the ConfigMgr server can cause some real problems, the same as with any server-based application. ConfigMgr has some built-in alerts to monitor the disk that hosts the site database file, because if *that* runs out of space, it can bring the entire application grinding to a halt.

> **TIP** To find the exact path of the site database and log files, open SQL Server Management Studio, connect to the site database server, right-click the site database (for example, CM_PS1), select "Properties," and navigate to "Files."

But low disk space can also impact other roles, such as the distribution point. If there isn't enough space to distribute a new application to a DP, clients talking to that DP either won't pick up the content, or might pick it up from a secondary DP across a WAN link (which is painful).

As shown in figure 20.6, ConfigMgr does keep track of the available free space on disks that are available for use by the distribution point role (in the Administration section), but it won't generate an alert when this space gets too low.

CM01.MOL.SCCMLAB.NET			
Icon	Drive	Total Disk Space (MB)	Free Disk Space (MB)
🖭	C	60,000.00	34,175.20
🖭	E	246,271.00	214,629.41

Figure 20.6 ConfigMgr will keep an eye on free space on disks used by distribution points.

Additionally, ConfigMgr doesn't keep track of available space on any other disk attached to the server. For example, you might have a dedicated disk for the Config-Mgr installation binaries; if this runs out of space, you're in trouble, and ConfigMgr won't tell you about it before it happens.

You can keep a watchful eye over disk space manually, but a better solution is to have it done automatically. The ConfigMgr agent will do the job of monitoring free disk space if you install the ConfigMgr agent on each server in the hierarchy. You'll also need to enable the agent to gather free-space information as part of hardware inventory:

1 In the console, navigate to Administration > Client Settings.
2 Modify an existing client policy or create a new one.
3 Select Hardware Inventory > Set Classes.
4 Expand "Logical Disk (SMS_LogicalDisk)" and select "Free Space (MB)," as shown in figure 20.7.
5 Save and apply the policy.

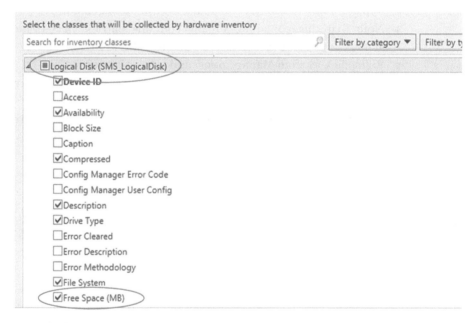

Figure 20.7   Need to gather more data? Just tick a box!

ConfigMgr will now collect free-space information for each disk as part of the regular hardware inventory scan. You can use this information to build device collections, or use the built-in free-space reports in Monitoring > Reporting > Reports > Hardware > Disk.

TIP It's fine for a lab environment, but installing the ConfigMgr agent on server operating systems requires a specific license, and you don't want to assume that you're covered. Make sure you're allowed to install the agent before doing so. Another option for quicker, real-time monitoring of server disk space is to use System Center 2012 Operations Manager R2 (SCOM).

20.2.2 *Active Directory*

When you install the ConfigMgr client by using one of the many methods available on a domain-joined system, the default behavior of the client is to browse to a specific spot in Active Directory to retrieve all the relevant information about which Config-Mgr hierarchy it should be associated with, which management boundary it falls in, and which management point it should be talking to.

This information doesn't just appear in Active Directory (AD) auto-magically. ConfigMgr has to physically put it there, and in order to do that, each publishing server has to have the necessary permissions. To see how this works, do the following:

1 Log on to DC01 and launch Active Directory Users and Computers.
2 Select View > Advanced Features.
3 Expand mol.sccmlab.net > System > System Management.
4 Note that this container already contains entries: mSSMSSite and mSSMS-ManagementPoint. These have been added by CM01.
5 Right-click "System Management" and select "Properties."
6 Select the Security tab and find the entry for the ConfigMgr server's AD computer object (for example, CM01$, as shown in figure 20.8).
7 Note that the computer object has the equivalent of full control permissions over the container. This is required for the primary site server to publish information to Active Directory.

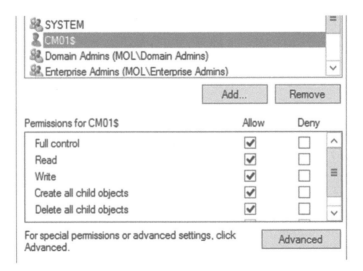

Figure 20.8   The ConfigMgr primary server AD computer account has full control over the System Management container.

TIP Every primary site server and central administration site (CAS) server in your environment needs explicit permissions to this container in order to publish site information. This can be done using an AD security group rather than individual security entries.

By default, the System Management container doesn't exist in Active Directory. It has to be created especially for ConfigMgr. Additionally, the AD schema has to be extended in order to accommodate the ConfigMgr-specific entries. Neither of these functions is performed automatically by ConfigMgr at any stage of installation or operation. They have to be actioned manually (or programmatically).

If you're seeing issues in your ConfigMgr environment where domain-joined clients are failing to talk back to the site/management point with which they're supposed to be associated, you can ask the following questions:

- Is the primary site server publishing information to the System Management container?
- If not, does the primary site server have permissions?

  or
- Has the System Management container been created?

The ClientLocation.log file on the affected clients will also give you a good idea of exactly what's going on.

20.2.3 DNS

ConfigMgr is a domain-joined system, and Active Directory is highly dependent on domain name resolution (DNS) for healthy functionality, so if there's a problem with DNS, then you'll almost certainly have wider problems to deal with beyond ConfigMgr.

But what clues can you get from ConfigMgr that something is wrong with DNS? In the scenario with multiple site servers in your hierarchy (for example, secondary site servers, remote distribution points, and so forth), you may see the console reporting that the roles on these remote servers are in an unhealthy state. Each site server in any hierarchy relies on DNS to establish reliable communications with every other server, and if this can't happen, the hierarchy is effectively broken.

The test is to run a name-resolution check from each side of the communication channel, for example:

- On CM01, launch a command window and type `PING REMOTE01.mol .sccmlab.net`.
- On REMOTE01, launch a command window and type `PING CM01.mol .sccmlab.net`.

In each case, the local server should be able to use DNS to resolve the remote server's name to its assigned IP address (for example, 192.168.11.200), as shown in figure 20.9. If it can't resolve the IP address or it resolves the incorrect IP address, then you know you have a DNS problem. The problem could be with the DNS server itself, or possibly

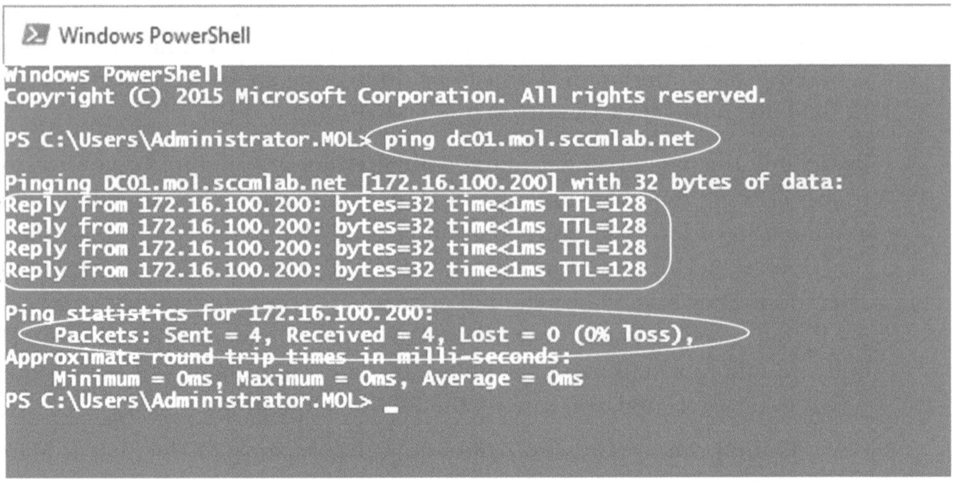

Figure 20.9   You want to see healthy name resolution; otherwise, ConfigMgr gets sad.

that DNS has been incorrectly configured on one or more of the servers. Either way, ConfigMgr won't be happy until you resolve it.

In another scenario, DNS is working properly, but DNS scavenging isn't being used. When a domain-joined client receives a dynamic IP address from a DHCP server, it registers its hostname in DNS against that dynamically assigned IP address, so that other systems on the network know how to communicate with it. Over time, each client receives different IP addresses, so DNS scavenging is used to make sure that DNS contains only the most up-to-date records (such as making sure everyone knows your current cell number).

When DNS scavenging isn't used, ConfigMgr gets confused. Targeted deployments still go out, but either go to the wrong clients or vanish into the ether. Remote management sessions may fail to connect or, most confusingly to everyone concerned, will connect to the wrong client. Confirming that DNS is the root cause of the problem in this scenario requires the same approach as the first scenario: log on to each affected system and run name-resolution tests.

You can see whether DNS scavenging is enabled in your environment by doing the following:

1   Log on to DC01 and launch the DNS management snap-in.
2   Expand DC01 and select mol.sccmlab.net.
3   Under forward lookup zones, right-click "mol.sccmlab.net" and select "Properties."
4   On the General tab, select "Aging."
5   As shown in figure 20.10, "Scavenge stale resource records" should be enabled. Enable it if it isn't.

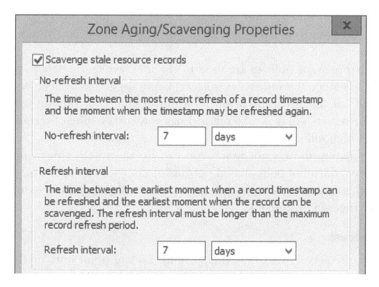

Figure 20.10   DNS scavenging is a must for avoiding problems with out-of-date records.

TIP   In larger environments with multiple zones, you can enable and configure scavenging for all zones by right-clicking the DNS server instead of the zone. But this affects all zones, so don't use this approach if you require granular per-zone scavenging settings.

TIP   When troubleshooting DNS, it can be useful to create manual entries in a system's HOSTS file, since you're directly controlling how a system resolves a particular name. Just make sure that you clean up after yourself; the local HOSTS file takes precedence over every other name-resolution method!

20.2.4 Admin rights

To do its job, the ConfigMgr primary site server needs full administrator rights over itself as well as every other server that sits beneath it in the hierarchy. Normally, this is done manually by adding the computer object account (for example, MOL\CM01$) into the local administrators group, but it can also be done using Group Policy. The latter is the recommended approach, because it can be centrally controlled and audited.

TIP   When giving an account local administrator access, avoid the temptation to add that account to the Domain Admins group. The Domain Admins group does automatically have local administrator access to every domain-joined system, but this approach gives the account far too much privileged access, to the extent that it could be considered a security breach.

Problems can crop up when Group Policy or some other mechanism is used to configure local administrators membership, and that mechanism doesn't take ConfigMgr permissions requirements into account. It's possible for ConfigMgr to be working perfectly, and then have the rug pulled out from under it by an improperly configured policy.

If this happens, or policies are used to change/revoke the default permissions on the local file system, then site roles will start being flagged as unhealthy, content distributions will fail, and anything involving actions initiated by the site server to itself or to other site servers will be problematic. Logs may show explicit "Access denied" error messages, which will assist in narrowing down the problem.

Unfortunately, there's not much you can do to prevent this from happening if you're not in control of policy-based permissions in your environment. Just make sure that the relevant admins check with you as the ConfigMgr admin before making significant changes in production.

20.2.5 *Internet access*

ConfigMgr site servers that host the software update point and/or the asset intelligence synchronization point role(s) need to be able to talk out across the internet to Microsoft in order to get the latest metadata and update content. In some organizations, this isn't a problem; you can give the server the ability to talk straight out. That's certainly the simplest approach, but for many organizations this is unacceptable; only specific servers have direct internet access, and all others either have no access, or access via a forward proxy.

To configure a site server to communicate through a proxy, do the following:

1 Navigate to Administration > Site Configuration > Servers and Site System Roles.
2 Select the relevant site system (for example, CM01.mol.sccmlab.net).
3 Select the Site system role at the bottom of the pane, right-click, and select "Properties."
4 In the Proxy tab, enter the relevant proxy server details and credentials, as shown in figure 20.11.

In the event that you have to configure ConfigMgr to talk through a proxy server, you may run into problems where the proxy is acting as a bottleneck, perhaps because it's blocking access to specific Microsoft URLs, or because it's caching content locally and processing it before releasing it to the ConfigMgr server. Whatever the cause of the problem, ConfigMgr is unaware of what's happening on the proxy server and will see it as a general failure to access the internet.

In cases like this, you'll need to work closely with your networking team to figure out what's going on. All enterprise network proxies allow for real-time troubleshooting, so the team should be able to see exactly what's happening and how to resolve it.

> **TIP** Keeping a close eye on the wsyncmgr.log will let you know quickly if you have an internet access problem.

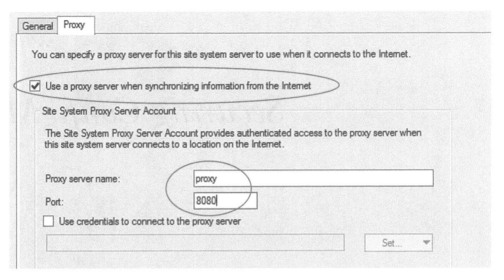

Figure 20.11 ConfigMgr needs internet access, but a proxy server will work just fine.

As I mentioned earlier, this isn't a comprehensive list of things that can go wrong and impact ConfigMgr. Almost as many things can go wrong as there are environments for them to go wrong in! But you now have a good idea of how external factors can derail your day, and some of the things you can do about it.

20.3 Labs

As you learned earlier in the chapter, disk space can be a real problem for ConfigMgr when it all runs out, but apart from the disk(s) that hosts the site database and log files, ConfigMgr doesn't do any active monitoring of free space.

This lab is all about remedying that. Modify the hardware inventory classes to include free space, and then deploy the policy and the ConfigMgr agent (if necessary) to CM01 so that you're now collecting free-disk-space data. Create a new device collection based on this data (for example, All Site Servers with <10% Free Space), and then run a report to make sure that the data is being collected properly.

If you're feeling brave and have enough resources available in your lab environment, try spinning up an instance of System Center Operations Manager (SCOM), install the SCOM agent on CM01, and configure SCOM to collect free-space data.

If you don't have enough free resources to install SCOM in your lab (fair enough if you don't!), you can also try signing up for a trial of Azure, and enable Operations Management Suite (OMS). Install the OMS agent on CM01 and collect free-disk-space data.

Securing ConfigMgr

21

In a large organization, many people can use ConfigMgr at the same time for different tasks. For example, some people may be responsible for deploying applications and patches to workstations, and a different team may be performing the same tasks for servers. One team may use ConfigMgr to connect remotely to managed workstations to support users, whereas another team may be responsible for the entire ConfigMgr hierarchy.

Often each member of all of these teams has the same level of internal access to ConfigMgr: Full Administrator. Why? Because it's considered "easier" to give people more access than they need rather than work out what access they need and provide only that much. Easier, that is, until a desktop admin rolls out Microsoft Office to all the servers, and then management wants to know how that happened (and starts casting bowel-twisting looks in *your* direction).

Fortunately, ConfigMgr has a comprehensive and granular internal security structure, and as shown in figure 21.1, you'll use this to apply the principle of least privilege to all ConfigMgr users.

There's no denying that sometimes crafting and assigning granular permissions can be painful. Trying to keep track of what's happening where takes practice and patience. Figure 21.2 illustrates what you're trying to achieve in this chapter: building up permissions one layer at a time gives you great control over who can access what, without crippling people's productivity.

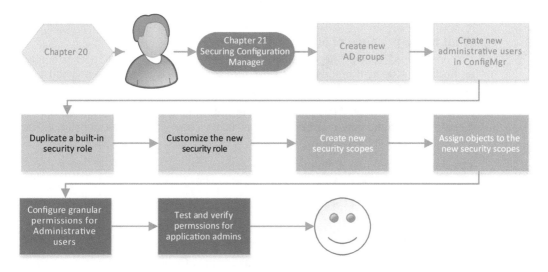

Figure 21.1 Admin permissions for all is the enemy, and security is the solution.

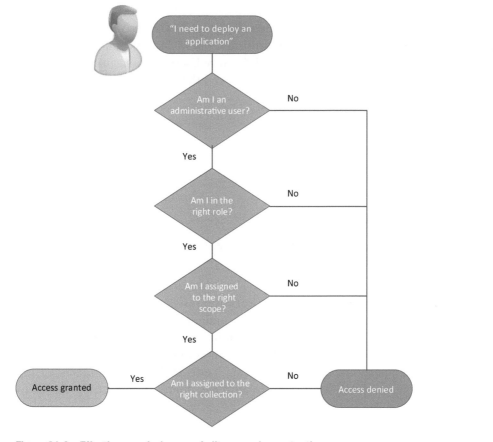

Figure 21.2 Effective permissions are built up one layer at a time,

What is the principle of least privilege?

The *principle of least privilege* requires that every securable module (for example, an account, a user, a process) has only sufficient access to run its assigned task legitimately.

In the context of ConfigMgr, an example is not making the client push account a member of Domain Admins, because this is an easy way for the account to be assigned local administrator rights.

You can read more about the principle here:
https://en.wikipedia.org/wiki/Principle_of_least_privilege

21.1   Administrative users

Administrative users are the entry point of access into ConfigMgr. The basic definition of a ConfigMgr administrative user is "any user or group member who can log into ConfigMgr to do something." That's a broad definition, but it fits. An administrative user can be anything from a help-desk officer with minimal access to a full ConfigMgr site admin. The level of access depends on other factors that we'll address shortly, *but if you're not listed as an administrative user, then you're not accessing ConfigMgr.* Full stop.

To see the current list of administrative users, in the ConfigMgr console navigate to Administration > Security > Administrative Users. As you can see in figure 21.3, only one user is listed (MOL\Administrator), and that user account is assigned to the Full Administrator security role.

Figure 21.3   Default site admin created during installation

This was set up during installation. There has to be at least one Full Administrator (the *god accounts* in the ConfigMgr world) to install and configure ConfigMgr for the first time, so the installer automatically configures the user account that's performing the installation as the default administrator.

Best practice is not to manually assign administrative access to individual users because it quickly becomes difficult to audit effectively. The recommended approach is to use security groups instead. To create a new administrative group, do the following:

1 On DC01, launch Active Directory Users and Computers.

2 Expand mol.sccmlab.net > MoL > Security Groups.

3 Right-click and select New > Group. Call the group `ConfigMgr Admins`.

4 Navigate to mol.sccmlab.net > MoL > Users.

5 Right-click the user account "Bob" and select "Add to a group."

6 In the object name field, enter `ConfigMgr Admins` and click "OK." The account should be added to the new group successfully.

7 In the ConfigMgr console under "Administrative Users," right-click and select "Add User or Group."

8 Click "Browse" and enter `ConfigMgr Admins`. Then click "OK."

9 For "Assigned Security Roles," click "Add" and then select the "Full Administrator" check box.

10 As shown in figure 21.4, select "All Instances of the objects that are related to the assigned security roles." Then click "OK."

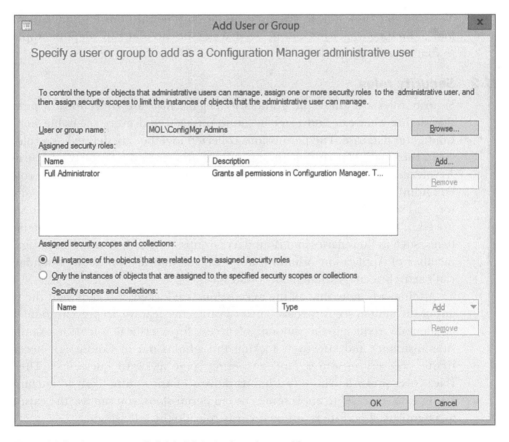

Figure 21.4   Create a new Full Administrator based on an AD group.

The new group is now listed as an administrative user. To test the functionality, perform the following steps:

1 Close the ConfigMgr console.

2 Go to Start, right-click the Configuration Manager Console icon, and select "Run as different user."

3 When prompted for credentials, enter the username Bob with the password P@ssw0rd.

4 The console launches with the same level of access as MOL\Administrator, even though MOL\Bob is only a standard user in the mol.sccmlab.net Active Directory hierarchy.

TIP   A ConfigMgr full admin also requires explicit permissions on each server in the hierarchy. Assigning a user/group as a Full Administrator in ConfigMgr doesn't make any changes to the underlying operating system, so you should use a mechanism such as Group Policy to assign appropriate permissions.

Now that you know how to give users and groups permissions to use ConfigMgr, let's look at limiting what can be done, so that no one "accidentally" deploys Apple iTunes to your domain controllers.

21.2 *Security roles*

Security roles are where the granularity begins. *Roles* are collections of permissions that define what can and can't be done on each and every securable item in the ConfigMgr database. The permissions collected together are defined as a role.

In the ConfigMgr console, navigate to Administration > Security > Security Roles. As you can see, 15 built-in roles cover a wide range of common ConfigMgr roles, from Full Administrator to Read-only Analyst. Right-click the role "Application Administrator" and select "Properties," and then go to the Permissions tab. As you can see in figure 21.5, the role defines permissions against all ConfigMgr securable items. Some items, such as Boundaries and Boundary Groups, have only Read access assigned, so a member of Application Administrators can see information about Boundaries, but can't actively manage them in any other way.

Additionally, note that all the permissions are locked; you can't edit the values of any of the built-in security roles. This is a protective feature, to prevent someone from accidentally reducing the amount of access for a critical role (for example, Full Administrator) and effectively locking the admins out of ConfigMgr, necessitating drastic recovery measures (and answering some awkward questions). The built-in roles cover pretty much every administrative scenario you're likely to encounter, but just in case you need to apply some custom permissions, you can use the existing roles as a template. To create a custom security role, do the following:

1 Right-click "Application Administrator" and select "Copy."

2 A window launches for you to create a new security role, prepopulated with all the permissions from the built-in Application Administrator role.

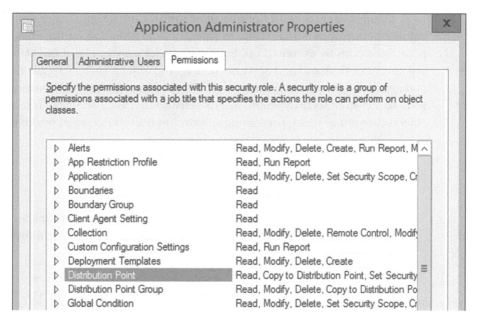

Figure 21.5 Create a custom security role based on an existing built-in role.

3 Call the new role MoL – Application Administrator.

4 Under "Permissions," expand "Configuration Item" and change "Read and Modify" to "Yes." Then click "OK."

TIP When creating new objects that are based on existing, built-in objects, it's a good idea to use a custom prefix (for example, MoL) so that it's instantly clear to anyone which are the custom objects.

You now have a new security role to work with. You can make further changes to the permissions (custom roles aren't locked), and you can also export the role definition to an XML file. This is useful when you want to create a backup of an existing role before making changes (basic version control), or when you want to re-create the role in a different ConfigMgr hierarchy, as you can import the XML file on a different ConfigMgr server without having to manually copy and customize a built-in role.

21.3 Security scopes

Security roles are perfect for restricting what people can do within ConfigMgr, but when someone has permissions to do something, that person can do it on *every* instance of that object. For example, if a user has the rights to delete an application, that user can delete *any* application. In a small environment this might be fine, but in a larger environment with dedicated teams, this isn't a great idea. To remedy this, security scopes come into play.

A *security scope* acts like a limiting filter within ConfigMgr. Scopes don't provide or enforce permissions—that's done by roles. Instead, they restrict the objects that those permissions can be exercised on. For example, let's say you have two IT teams in your organization: Desktops and Servers. By assigning objects such as applications, software updates, configuration baselines, and OS deployments that are particular to each team to a custom security scope, you can ensure that each team can interact only with objects relevant to them, preventing spillover to objects managed by the other team.

Creating a security scope is straightforward:

1   Navigate to Administration > Security > Security Scopes.
2   Right-click and select "Create Security Scope."
3   Call the new scope MoL – Desktops. Click "OK."
4   Repeat the process, creating a second new scope called MoL – Servers. As shown in figure 21.6, you now have two new scopes, in addition to the two default scopes.

Security Scopes 4 items			
Search			
Icon	Security Scope	In use	Description
🔒	All	Yes	A built-in security scope that contains all securable objects
🔒	Default	Yes	A built-in security scope with which securable objects can l
🔒	MoL - Desktops	No	
🔒	MoL - Servers	No	

Figure 21.6   Create new security scopes to protect ConfigMgr objects.

Easy, right? That's because a scope doesn't do much on its own. You need to assign scopes to securable items:

1   Navigate to Software Library > Application Management.
2   Right-click the application "Paint.NET" and select "Set Security Scopes."
3   Untick the "Default" scope and tick the "MoL – Desktops" scope.
4   Navigate back to Security Scopes, and you'll see that the MoL – Desktops scope is now flagged as "In Use."

TIP   All items that *can* belong to a security scope *must* belong to at least one scope. That's what the *default* scope is for, which is why you can't delete or modify it. The other built-in scope is the *all* scope. An administrative user assigned to the all scope has permissions over all securable items, effectively ignoring all other scopes. Use this one carefully!

So now you have users, roles, and scopes. Let's bring them all together.

21.4 *Granular permissions*

Effective granular permissions in ConfigMgr are a result of all the work you've done so far in this chapter. Granular permissions are most commonly used when an organization needs to protect the system from the people using it—not because they're incompetent or untrustworthy, but because enforced separation of roles is needed in order to ensure that one administrator doesn't accidentally derail another's efforts.

For example, you must have at least one Full Administrator who knows everything about the ConfigMgr environment and can make any necessary change, but it doesn't make sense to give the same level of access to the help-desk technician who needs to use only remote control tools. Assigning Full Administrator access might be easy, but it opens the organization up to potential nastiness. Additionally, if the help-desk technician isn't a ConfigMgr guru (and there's nothing that requires them to be), then it's also rather unfair to drop them into a massive system without providing administrative boundaries.

So to bring everything together, work through the following steps:

1. Repeat the steps in section 21.1 to create two new groups in Active Directory:
   a. ConfigMgr Application Admins – Desktops
   b. ConfigMgr Application Admins – Servers
2. Add user Frank to ConfigMgr Application Admins – Desktops.
3. Add user Johan to ConfigMgr Application Admins – Servers.
4. In the ConfigMgr console, create a new administrative user with the following settings (as shown in figure 21.7).
   a. User or group name: MOL\ConfigMgr Application Admins – Desktops
   b. Assigned security roles: MoL – Application Administrator
   c. Security scopes and collections:
      i. Remove all default instances
      ii. Add the security scope MoL – Desktops
      iii. Add the collection All Windows Workstation Clients
      iv. Add the collection All Users and User Groups
5. Create another administrative user with the following settings:
   a. User or group name: MOL\ConfigMgr Application Admins – Servers
   b. Assigned security roles: MoL – Application Administrator
   c. Security scopes and collections:
      i. Remove all default instances
      ii. Add the security scope MoL – Servers
      iii. Add the collection All Server Clients

Let's take a moment to dissect what you've just done. Each new administrative user is based on a different AD group, and each group has different membership—so far, that's normal. Each administrative user has the same permissions applied to it, since

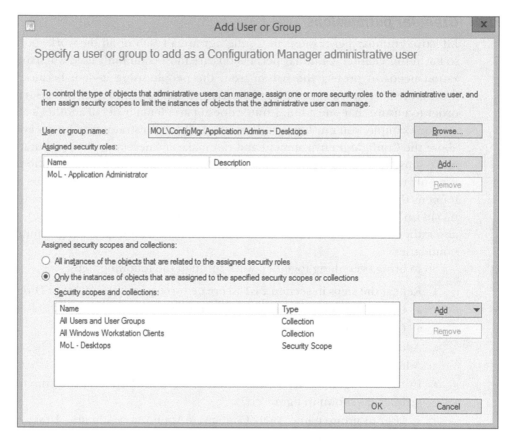

Figure 21.7 Create a new administrative user with the least permissions necessary.

each one has been assigned to the same security role. But each administrative user has been assigned to different security scopes *and* different user and device collections.

> **TIP** You didn't assign the All Users and User Groups collection to the ConfigMgr Application Admins – Servers group because when working with server clients, there's usually no need to target user accounts. When the ConfigMgr client is installed on a server, the purpose is to manage the machine, rather than the user who logs on to the machine (from a Config-Mgr perspective, at least).

Assigning collections?
You assign an administrative user to one or more user and/or device collections in order to limit the computer and user objects within the ConfigMgr database that those users can interact with. An administrative user can interact only with objects that appear in the collection(s) that have been assigned to them, as well as every other collection that is ultimately limited to that collection.

For example, ConfigMgr Application Admins - Desktops can work only with objects that appear in the All Windows Workstation Clients collection. This is good, because it means they can't interact with any nonworkstation (server) clients.

If an administrator then created another collection that was limited to All Windows Workstation Clients (for example, All Windows 10 Clients), the desktop admins could target those systems too.

But if someone accidentally (or even sneakily) created a collection that queried for server operating systems and limited it to the All Windows Workstation Clients collection, they would be out of luck. Why? Server operating systems don't show up in the All Windows Workstation Clients collection, so they won't show up in any other collection below it either.

It's an effective way of restricting what can and can't be done without preventing people from being able to do their jobs.

What now? Let's see what your new users will see:

6 Close the ConfigMgr console, and then open it again using "Run as a different user."

7 When prompted for credentials, use username Frank with password P@ssw0rd.

8 Navigate to Assets and Compliance > Device Collections. You'll see that user Frank can see only the All Windows Workstation Clients collection.

9 Navigate to the Software Library. You'll see that user Frank can see only items under Application Management. Everything to do with Software Updates and Operating System Deployment isn't visible.

10 Expand Application Management > Applications. User Frank can see the application Paint .NET, but no other applications.

11 Close the ConfigMgr console, and then relaunch it as user Johan with the password P@ssw0rd.

12 Navigate to Assets and Compliance > Device Collections. User Johan can't see All Windows Workstation Clients, but can see All Server Clients.

13 Navigate to the Software Library. Note that user Johan sees the same options under Application Management as user Frank (due to the same assigned security role).

14 Expand Application Management > Applications. User Johan can't see any applications because none have been assigned to the MoL – Servers scope.

And that's how it's done, people! What's happening here is that ConfigMgr is applying role-based administration (RBA). The idea is that you should be able to see only the things that you have access to. Everything else isn't there. This isn't just a security feature; it can be extremely irritating for administrative users to try to access something visible in their console, only to be told that they don't have sufficient permissions. RBA gives people access to what they need, without dangling everything else in front of them like forbidden fruit.

21.5 *Labs*

As Full Administrators, it's easy for us to get lazy when assigning securable objects to a security scope, and forget to assign something important. You know you've done this when the Software Update admins call you up to say that a Software Update Group has "been deleted!" It hasn't. You just forgot to assign the right scope, so they can't see everything that they should have access to.

The best remedy for this is to walk a mile in their shoes, and that's what you'll do in this lab:

1 Create two new security roles based on the built-in roles Operating System Deployment Manager and Software Update Manager.

2 Create two new groups in AD:
   a ConfigMgr OSD Managers – Desktops (assign user Marcus)
   b ConfigMgr Software Update Managers – Desktops (assign user Mathilda)

3 Create new administrative users in ConfigMgr for each group, limited as follows:
   a Scope: MoL – Desktops
   b Collection: All Windows Workstation Clients
   c Collection: All Users and User Groups

4 Go through Software Library > Software Updates and Software Library > Operating Systems and set the security scope for each securable item to MoL – Desktops.

5 Log on to the console as each user and *do* something; create a new Software Update Group and modify an existing one, try to edit existing OS task sequences, and try deploying something to a client. User Mathilda will be able to interact with software updates but nothing under operating systems, whereas user Marcus will have the opposite experience.

22

All engines
full steam ahead

You've come to the end of this book. You now know everything there is to know about Configuration Manager, and there's nothing anyone else can teach you.

Did you spot the glaring inaccuracies in the previous statement? Good! ConfigMgr is as big as you care to make it, and there's always more to learn. As you wrap up this phase of learning, this last chapter offers some direction on where you can go next to accelerate your progress toward becoming a ConfigMgr guru.

22.1 Advanced ConfigMgr projects

Many of the topics covered throughout this book have more-advanced applications that I'd have loved to have covered. But if I'd written everything I wanted to, the book would be twice as long and you'd get lower back strain from lugging it around.

The lab environment you've created has built the foundation for you to tackle more-advanced ConfigMgr functionality. Here's a list of projects to get you started—each of these is involved and requires a fair amount of research and learning, but all are worth your while.

22.1.1 More infrastructure

Your lab is a relatively simple one, with a single server servicing a single IP subnet. In more-complicated environments, you're likely to have many disparate subnets across geographical regions, and these often need dedicated ConfigMgr services. Try extending your lab environment by doing the following:

1   Provision another domain-joined Windows Server instance.

2   Use the ConfigMgr console to install the distribution point role on the remote server.

3   Distribute some content to the remote DP only, and make sure that your managed client can access it.

22.1.2   Use HTTPS

In your ConfigMgr lab, all the server roles (distribution point, management point, and so forth) communicate by using unencrypted HTTP. That's fine for labs and many small ConfigMgr environments, but at times you need to use HTTPS, which requires SSL certificates issued by an internal certificate authority. The certificate requirements for ConfigMgr are well documented, and ConfigMgr supports a mix of both HTTP- and HTTPS-based roles. Try enabling HTTPS in your ConfigMgr environment:

1   DC01 already has the necessary Active Directory Certificate Services roles installed, so you have a certificate authority ready to go.

2   Read the step-by-step TechNet article on creating the certificates necessary to support ConfigMgr (https://technet.microsoft.com/en-us/library/gg682023.aspx).

3   Add the correct certificates to the IIS server and distribution point roles on CM01, and use Sites > Site Configuration > Client Computer Communication to configure HTTPS communication.

4   Deploy a client certificate to a managed client (for example, CLIENT01), restart the ConfigMgr client, and then check the properties to make sure that the client is now using a PKI certificate (HTTPS).

22.1.3   Go to the cloud

If the idea of another distribution point in your environment doesn't appeal to you, put one in the cloud! ConfigMgr has the ability to talk with your Microsoft Azure subscription to provision DPs that your managed clients can talk to. Sign up for a trial Azure subscription and use the ConfigMgr console to deploy a new cloud DP:

1   Sign up at https://azure.microsoft.com.

2   Use Administration > Cloud Services > Cloud Distribution Point to create a cloud DP in your Azure trial.

3   Create an application with a small payload (for example, 7-Zip) and distribute the content to the cloud DP.

4   Enable client settings to allow clients to access content from cloud DPs.

5   Monitor the DataTransferService.log on the client to ensure that the content is being downloaded from Azure.

22.1.4   Take control of your database

The ConfigMgr database can be a sensitive beast, and if it's allowed to become unhealthy, you're in all sorts of trouble. Responsibility for the database may fall to a dedicated DBA team, but if not them, it's up to you to take control. The first stop is the latest

MaintenanceSolution.sql script by Ola Hallengren (https://ola.hallengren.com/); get this configured on your ConfigMgr database server and configure the IndexOptimize, DatabaseIntegrityCheck, and DatabaseBackup jobs. Then sign up for Brent Ozar's First Responder Kit (www.brentozar.com/first-aid/) and check out the contents—particularly sp_Blitz. These guys have done the hard work for you, and their expertise will kick-start your SQL learning.

22.1.5 *Advanced client configuration*

ConfigMgr enables fine-grained configuration of your managed clients, including deploying certificate profiles so that they have the right trusted certificates and Wi-Fi profiles so that they'll always be able to connect to the corporate network; and VPN profiles so that your users can always connect back to base. This is much better than having to push out Group Policy– or script-based configuration. If you're feeling brave, try setting up Network Device Enrollment Service (NDES) and a VPN in your lab and deploy the profiles with ConfigMgr (lots of reading about this on TechNet right here: https://technet.microsoft.com/en-au/library/dn261205.aspx).

22.2 *Learn from the community*

ConfigMgr admins are fortunate, in that the product has attracted many clever people who give of their time to publish what they learn. There are too many out there to list them all, but here are the core resources that I strongly recommend you keep a close eye on:

- www.jamesbannanit.com—Yes, yes, shameless plug for me. Any updates to content contained within the book, companion videos, blog posts about changes to scripts as well as links to Git will be here.
- http://deploymentresearch.com—Johan Arwidmark blogs here, and you've already used some of his content when setting up your lab environment. Lots of deep information on Windows deployment and MDT.
- www.windows-noob.com—Niall Brady blogs here, and he's written some of the best how-to guides on ConfigMgr I've ever read. Additionally, if there's something he doesn't know about deploying Windows, chances are it hasn't been invented yet.
- http://blog.configmgrftw.com—Jason Sandys blogs here and has a wealth of resources for supercharging your ConfigMgr environment.
- http://deploymentbunny.com—Mikael Nystrom blogs here, and it's an awesome resource for advanced deployment scenarios as well as some terrific PowerShell.
- http://blog.coretech.dk—Based in Denmark, Coretech employs more MVPs than you can shake a stick at, and most of them offer great blog content about ConfigMgr and PowerShell. Also, please don't shake sticks at MVPs—we don't like it.

Don't be reluctant to reach out to individuals within the ConfigMgr community. All of them are active on social media and are happy to give you some ideas or introduce you to someone who can. We're nice—really!

Well done for reaching the end of this book and for not turning up at my house to hit me over the head with it. Best of luck in your adventures in ConfigMgr.

index